Stolen Dreams
A Manchurian Legacy

Julie Kowalska Sormark

Copyright © 2019, Julie Sormark

ISBN: 978-0-9980098-5-8

Library of Congress Control Number: 2019938163

All Rights Reserved. No part of this book may be reproduced or transmitted in any form or by any means, electronic or mechanical, including photocopying, recording, or by any information storage and retrieval system without written permission from the author, except for the inclusion of brief quotations in a review.

Printed in the United States of America.

Acknowledgments

I WOULD LIKE TO GIVE RECOGNITION TO MY MOTHER FOR ALL THE ENDLESS hours she spent with me, telling me stories about our family, specifically about my grandfather. I was happy to have written down what my mother told me over the years and am privileged to pass this on to others. I am sorry she is not with us today to have witnessed the completion of this tribute to her father, Vladislav Kowalski.

I would like to thank my husband, Ulf Erik, who has supported me with the research and contributed and assisted me all the years that it has taken me to write this book. I am so lucky to have such a dedicated, patient, supportive and loving partner. I also would like to thank our three wonderful children, Jeanette, Kristina, and John for enthusiastically urging and inspiring me to document the history of our family. I am forever grateful to Kristina who, with incredible dedication and patience assisted with the editing, using up many of her precious vacation days, to John who read the manuscript over and over helping to find and correct the mistakes and for helping me with the publishing process and to Jeanette for valuable advice and guidance. The pride, respect, and devotion that our three children have for the history of our family has meant the world to me. I thank Ariana Dolgoff, my dear godmother, who herself has ties to the city of Harbin, for the positive encouragement that she has given me over the years.

I am indebted to Jerzy Czajewski, president of the Harbin Club in Szczecin, Poland, for encouraging me every step of the way. His dedication to Harbin and his generosity in sharing pictures, stories, articles, and information about my Polish grandfather has been invaluable. When we visited Szczecin, he took us around to visit former Harbin residents, universities, and libraries in search of material, and spent many hours discussing history, stories of Harbin, and of the Poles in Northeast China.

I have great appreciation for Tania Sherlaimoff, for all the guidance, support, and coaching that she offered me throughout this project. Her knowledge of the history and life in Vladivostok, Harbin, and China that were related to her by her father were invaluable. She played an integral part in this endeavor and I am so grateful to her for her participation, input, support, and supervision.

I would like to extend a special thanks to Patricia Polansky, Russian Bibliographer at Hamilton Library University of Hawaii, for the treasure of information and references that she so generously shared over the years, even when my mother was together with us. Academically, she has guided me, helping me with the bibliography and the valuable articles and books that are part of her amazing collection at the Russian Northeast Asian Collection.[1] Thank you to Amir Khisamutdinov, who teaches in Vladivostok at the Far Eastern Federal University and is a senior researcher at the Russian Academy of Sciences Library, for insisting that the true and accurate story of my grandfather needed to be documented and for sharing articles, information, and facts along the way.

I have used historical reference material from the Hoover Institution and the Green and Meyer Libraries at Stanford University, California, the University of Hawaii Hamilton Library, and the Japanese library at the International House in Tokyo, Japan, and am grateful for their efficient staff helping me to locate historic facts from many years ago.

I am so grateful to have had one of the great authorities on Harbin, Olga Bakich, retired Russian language and literature senior lecturer at the University in Toronto, to review the book and to offer her guidance. She was always willing to "come to the rescue" and I certainly would not have felt comfortable publishing my book without her input. Thank you to my friends Valentina Yarovaya and Alex Bykov for helping with translations; to the late Bud Ingoldsby for his guidance; Yves Franquien at the Museum of Russian Culture in San Francisco for his assistance; Ambassador Folke Lovgren and his wife Ragnhild for their advice and guidance; Swedish sinologist Britta Kinnemark, in her capacity as a Chinese language specialist, I thank her for visiting Harbin together with us and for reviewing the manuscript offering valuable advice; Sue Hornik for professional editing and advice; and Margaret Coberly for offering pointers. And finally, a special word of gratitude to Rodney Smith, journalist and broadcaster, for his professional comments and advice, and to his wife Sheri, whose parents John and Mary Besford helped us to leave China in 1951 by securing visas for us to move to Japan.

And finally, a special thanks to the management and staff of the Revolutionary Leaders Visiting Heilongjiang Memorial Museum and the members of the Harbin Foreign Affairs Office for their friendship and support, as well as to Mrs. Kang Yu in Harbin, a dear friend, a supporter, and a person who has helped our family keep the spirit of my grandfather alive in Harbin for all these years.

Table of Contents

Date	Unit	Subject	Page
	1	Vladislav Fyodorovich Kowalski, My Grandfather	1
1890s	2	The Beginning	4
1896	3	Vladivostok	11
1896	4	Siberian Wilderness	17
1894–1897	5	Chinese Eastern Railway	21
1898	6	Harbin	27
1900	7	Boxer Rebellion	31
early 1900s	8	A Growing City	35
1902–1903	9	Xing'an Tunnel	40
1902–1903	10	A Trip to Kozuchow	45
1903	11	Alexander Alexandrovich Arrives	49
1903	12	The Railway Opening	55
1904	13	Russo-Japanese War	60
1905	14	Helena Alexandrovna	65
1906	15	Making a Home	69
1907	16	A Growing Population	73
1908	17	Ariadna Vladislavna	77
1910	18	Back to Tsarskoe Selo	81
1911	19	Yablonia Concession	85
1911	20	Victoria Vladislavna	91
1912	21	A Chinese-Russian City	95
1914	22	World War I	99

1917	23	The Fall of the Tsarist Regime	103
1918	24	A Family Outing	108
1918	25	Summer Vacation	113
1918–1922	26	Polish Independence	122
1919	27	Lucia Mikhailovna Solovov	126
1919	28	On the Concession	130
1920	29	General Dimitrii Leonidovich Horvath	136
1920s	30	Acheng (Ashihe) Sugar Factory	141
1921–1922	31	1 Yi Yuan Street	146
1922	32	Mulin Concession	151
1924	33	Relatives	157
1924	34	The Gem of the East	161
1924	35	Lawless Behavior	168
1924	36	Secrets	174
1925–1927	37	Living the Good Life	178
1927–1929	38	Setting the Stage	182
1927–1929	39	A Dream Come True	187
1929	40	A Great Honor	195
1931	41	The Invasion of Manchuria	200
1931–1934	42	A New Country	208
1934–1936	43	Manchukuo	215
1935	44	Another Life	221
1930s	45	The Imperial Way	227
mid-1930s	46	Story After Story	232
1936	47	Annulment	237
1938–1939	48	Stolen Dreams	241
1940	49	The Legacy	246
		Epilogue	253
		Notes	265
		Bibliography	269
		Endnotes	279

Władysław Kowalski (Vladislav Fëdorovich Koval'skĭ—Russian spelling of his name); referred to as Vladislav Fyodorovich Kowalski in this story

THIS IS THE FASCINATING STORY OF MY GRANDFATHER, VLADISLAV Fyodorovich Kowalski, and his incredible journey arriving as an adventurer in Manchuria, China, in 1898. It tells the story of a unique city, Harbin, and how this city reflected the historical struggles that took place at the turn of the century. It centers on the development of the Chinese Eastern Railway through Manchuria and the thousands of Russians who settled in China. The city of Harbin and Manchuria capture a riveting part of this history where the countries of China, Russia, and Japan engaged in a power struggle for over fifty years.

Stories about life and events in this corner of China and how they affected the Chinese and foreign residents are seldom chronicled. The captivating stories of a fascinating time, of dynamic accomplishments and heartbreaking outcomes that took place in northeastern China, enlightens us about a time and place that cannot be compared to any other.

—Julie Kowalska Sormark

FAMILY TREE

Alexander and Tatiana Denisovna Zaharoff

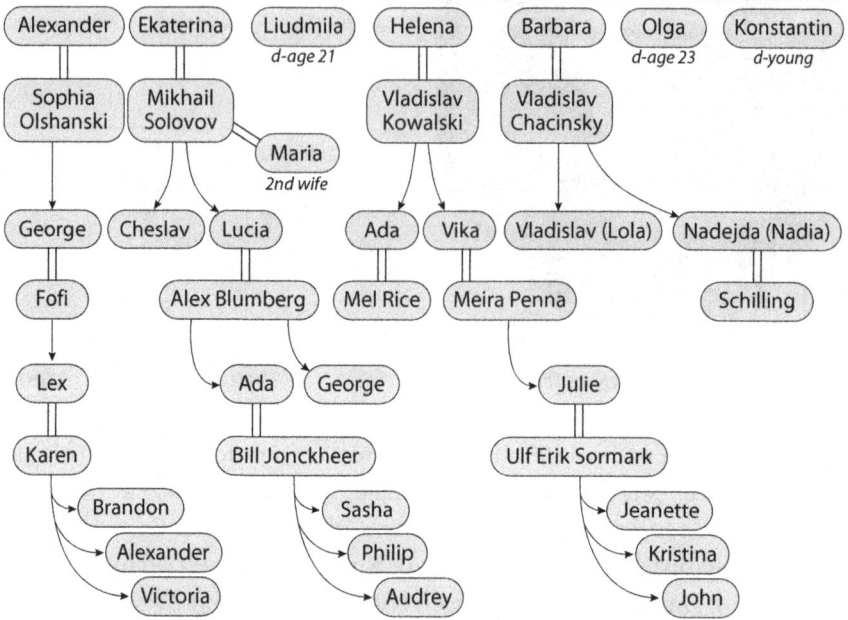

Feodor and Maria Apolonia Kowalski

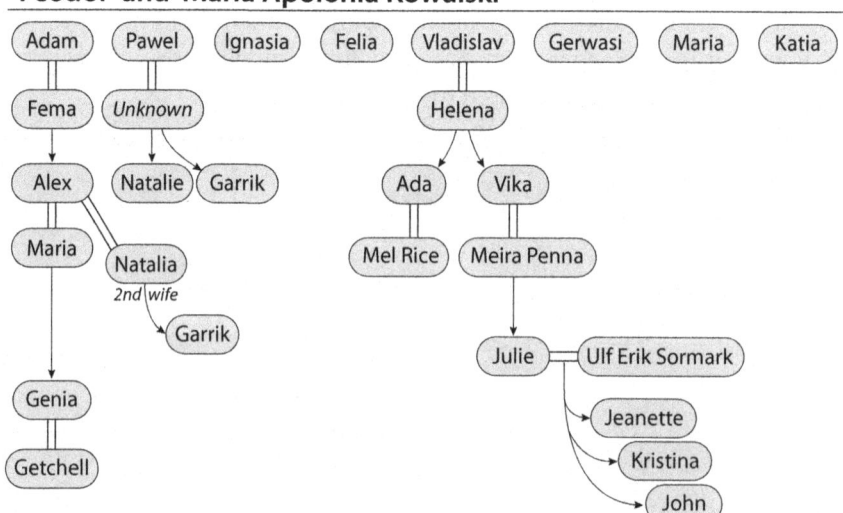

NORTHEAST ASIA

1 | Vladislav Fyodorovich Kowalski, My Grandfather

As I am sure is the case with many children, I grew up listening to the stories about my family, specifically, my grandfather, Vladislav Fyodorovich Kowalski, and what it was like for him to have lived in Harbin, a city in Manchuria,[1] China, over 100 years ago. Vladislav Kowalski, arrived there in 1898 from Podolia Gubernia[2] in what is today Ukraine. He was a proud Pole from the patriotic Polish gentry. When my grandfather arrived in China, Harbin was a small Chinese fishing village located on the banks of the Sungari River.

My mother told me about her childhood in Harbin and details about everyday life in this unusual setting. She told me about the Chinese Eastern Railway (CER)[3] that ran through northern China. Harbin was the center of her world. She would tell me about the forestry industry that her father developed, about their home and their daily life that included a very high level of culture, schooling, and quality of life.

I understood that Harbin was an unusual city with a very unique history. The complicated historical events that took place over the years cannot be compared to any other city in the world. The historical and political climate in Harbin was affected by western nations, the political happenings within China and certainly from the surrounding powers, specifically Russia and Japan. Wars, rebellions, and political upheavals were frequent and tainted the lives of so many who struggled to live in this environment. Throughout its development, Harbin experienced a unique social interaction with different cultures, mentalities, and circumstances coming together. The economic accomplishments brought about by modern railway transportation and by the incredible natural resources that existed there made Manchuria distinct.

Grandfather watched Harbin grow into a sophisticated, cultural, cosmopolitan city with sixteen consulates, international banks, and nationals from over thirty-three countries. He felt proud to be a part of this transformation.

My grandfather could see already in 1898 that this was a very special place, but he could not imagine that Harbin was going to become one of the most important cities in China and that this would change the course of history for the whole region. My grandfather loved Harbin, he loved China and the Chinese people. He was a modest person who gave credit to everyone but himself, and we know that he was an amazing, generous, and incredible human being. Many of Harbin's religious, scientific, and social institutions benefited from his financial support. He always worked for the common good and was a person who had vision and determination.

With the progress came the challenges—no, grandfather did not have an easy time as conflicts, wars, and revolutions affected his life and business. The local and international laws and rules and the interpretation of them created situations that were hard to deal with.

Vladislav Kowalski lived in Harbin until he died in 1940. His funeral was attended by hundreds of Chinese, Harbin Russians, Poles, and residents of all nationalities and religions. It was the last tribute to a man of integrity who was remembered for his good deeds for Harbin and its inhabitants. His original tombstone does not exist anymore, but a gravestone was erected in the new cemetery on the hill outside of town. For his descendants, the house at 1 Yi Yuan Street will always stand as a symbol of his legacy.

In 1985 my mother and I returned to Harbin for the first time since she left in 1940. We checked into a hotel located up the hill from the railroad station. When we entered the room and looked out the window, I saw for the first time the majestic house that grandfather had built. We changed, put on some comfortable shoes, and walked over to the house. We entered the garden and Mother started to tell me about the layout of the garden and how it used to be. Suddenly, a man came up to us with a lady who spoke some English to tell us that we were not allowed to be there. Mother told them that her father had built this house. The two disappeared and 10 minutes later an official group together with a translator appeared. When she told them her name, immediately there was a frenzy of excited people. They contacted Edward Stokalski, one of the last Poles who had stayed behind in Harbin, and he rushed over from his residence in another district of the city. When he arrived, he was so excited to see Kowalski's daughter, his hands were shaking. They invited us into the building. Then the questions started. Two hours later we were exchanging contact information. Since then we have returned to Harbin several times and have kept in touch with everyone.

Let me share with you the fascinating story of my grandfather by going back to the late 1800s and the beginning. This is a story about him, about his life through the eyes of my mother. Her memories are verified and enhanced by memoirs (published and unpublished) as well as through contemporary newspaper and journal articles. The many hours she spent telling me the stories and the experiences she shared need to be told and passed down to the next generation. It is the story of a man, a place, and a time like no other. It is the legacy of my Polish grandfather, Vladislav Fyodorovich Kowalski, and his life in the city of Harbin in Manchuria, China.

2 | The Beginning

1890s

I am going to start from the beginning. Grandfather came from a very modest background.

Vladislav Fyodorovich was the son of Feodor (Teodor) and Apolonia.[1] He was born in 1870 into a large Polish petty gentry family in Podol'sk Province in the village of Kozuchow. He was the fifth of eight children, four boys and four girls. His father took pride in owning the land that adjoined their farmhouse in Kozuchow, which consisted of 270 acres of land, half of which was cultivable, and always repeated to his children: "You must own your land and have pride in ownership. This will give you

Young Vladislav Fyodorovich Kowalski

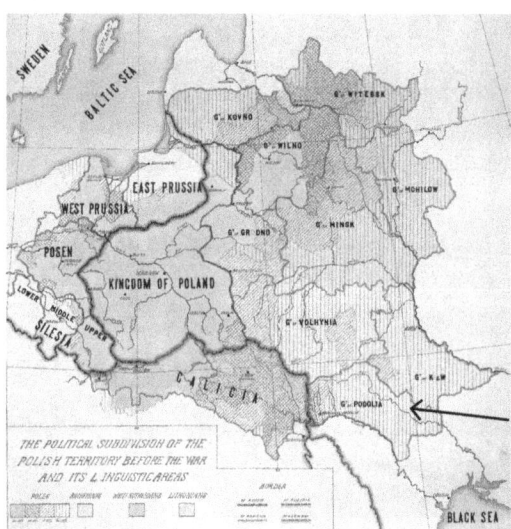

Map of political subdivisions of Polish territories before World War I[2]

Stolen Dreams

Apolonia and Feodor (Teodor) Kowalski, Vladislav's parents, with Gerwasi, their youngest son

Pawel, Vladislav's older brother

Sisters: Ignasia, Maria, Felia, and Katia

Oldest son Adam

dignity and self-respect among your peers. Life is about what you achieve, and you have so little time to fulfill your goals."[3] These words of respect for the environment, the importance of ownership and maintaining pride and dignity shaped Vladislav's destiny.

Over the centuries, the rich, black soil and the steppes of Podolsk Province had been occupied by a smorgasbord of people who included the Mongols, Lithuanians, Ukrainians, Poles, Prussians, Austrians, Jews, Turks, and Russians. Although the region was chiefly populated by Ukrainians when Vladislav was growing up, the Polish colonization that began in the fourteenth century increased significantly, and Poles became a sizable minority group in the region.

Throughout history the Podolsk Province held economic importance as a territory blessed with a moderate climate, rich black earth, and the navigable rivers of Dniester and Southern Bug. In the three partitions between 1772–1795, Poland was completely wiped off the map of Europe and was absorbed mainly by the Russian Empire. By the time Vladislav was born in 1870, the people of the region were referred to as "persons of Polish origin" rather than as Poles.[4]

Growing up, Vladislav absorbed the rich tradition of national uprisings and the cultural mix of the Polish Eastern borderland where Polish, Ukrainian, Jewish, and Gypsy cultures had coexisted for centuries. He was an heir to the romantic idea of Polish independence, and he supported a return to the former borders of Poland. Despite the loss of Polish statehood and the defeat of successive Polish uprisings, Vladislav and his family adhered to their Polish national identity, and tolerated their situation under the Russians. His grandfather Antoni (Anthony) had been exiled after the Polish uprising of 1863 for his opposition to Russian rule and oppression.[5]

The policy of the Russification of Poland began in 1863 when Russian became the official language and the Orthodox Church was encouraged at the expense of the Catholic Church. The children of the Kowalski family grew up under this suppression—they were not allowed to speak Polish at school or among friends and would be beaten if they were caught speaking the language. In classes, neither the history of Poland nor the Catholic religion were allowed to be taught. Polish university students were forced to study Polish authors by reading Russian translations. Everything Polish was hunted down and repressed, yet Vladislav's parents tried to nurture the Polish identity behind closed doors. Through their encouragement, Vladislav retained his Polish identity and love of his heritage throughout his life. He spoke both Russian and Polish, and though his Polish had a slight accent, Poland and the Polish language were in his heart wherever he went.[6]

In Podolia, farm life followed the agricultural seasons and the church calendar, a predictable timetable interrupted only by bad weather and political winds. Vladislav was frustrated by the inertia of Polish society and he wondered what lay beyond Podolsk Province and Kozuchow. Vladislav was young, strong, and broad-minded. He was confident of his good judgment and prided himself on his ability to make his own decisions. He felt he was the master of his destiny.

Vladislav and many of his Polish and Jewish friends chaffed under Russian discrimination and the Ukrainian intolerance, making life unpleasant. Poles welcomed emerging opportunities to participate in economic and technological developments and searched for a better life. They were prepared to emigrate even to "the end of the world," to the Russian Far East, to Vladivostok where the largest of all railway construction projects was taking place—the Russian Trans-Siberian Railway. Vladislav's imagination wandered even beyond the Far Eastern horizon with his desire to someday travel to America.[7]

Since 1892 the Russian government had encouraged those from European Russia to settle in the Amur and south Ussuri region (Primorsky Krai) located in the Far East. As an incentive, the government granted assisted passage to heads of families who possessed 66 rubles (worth a little under 100 USD at the time), which was deposited with a government official in Odessa. A portion was repaid to the emigrant on landing in Vladivostok.[8] In lieu of payment for the trip, some passengers would sign a contract with a five-year commitment to work in the emerging railroad industry in the Russian Far East.[9] Perhaps an even more important incentive for Vladislav was that by volunteering his services in the railroad project, he would not have to serve in the Russian military.

In 1896 at age 26, Vladislav left Kozuchow to seek adventure and change. His parents and seven brothers and sisters bid him farewell knowing that they would not see him for many years. He was the adventurous soul of the family, and they knew that for him the horizons always extended way beyond the boundaries of his village or motherland.

Because Vladislav was a Russian subject of Polish origin, he made sure to obtain a Russian passport before going down to the offices of the Volunteer Fleet Agency[10] in Odessa. He purchased his ticket outright, so that he would have no obligations to tie him down in Vladivostok.

The captain of the passenger freighter, the SS *Vladimir,* was on the bridge when Vladislav strode on board. A crusty veteran who wore his cap with a flair, he was a typical small-ship captain who did not stand on unnecessary ceremony.

Vladislav had little luggage, just a bag with a change of clothes, and a warm coat and blanket. He selected his bunk and was soon joined by some rough characters in the adjoining beds. As the SS *Vladimir* left the Odessa wharf, Vladislav thought of his family and felt sad, but as Odessa disappeared over the horizon, he became excited at the prospect of his future now being entirely in his own hands.

As the ship slid through the Dardanelles into the Mediterranean Sea, Vladislav was on deck to watch the coastal scenery, admiring the many minarets in Constantinople, the capital of the Ottoman Empire. He did not want to miss a moment. There was so much to see. Going through the Suez Canal and the Red Sea, green farmlands and villages with camels, date palms and Egyptians could be seen standing on the African side of the ship, and on the other side was the vast Sinai Desert. He and his fellow passengers exclaimed in wonder at the sight of such exotic scenery.

"Look at that, look what they're wearing!" someone yelled.

"Have you ever seen anything like that?" Vladislav pointed to the sailing craft plying the waters.

"These boats are sailing straight out of ancient history," he remarked.

The Volunteer Fleet— SS *Vladimir*[11]

"Yes, they may look unwieldy," said the captain, "but they have certainly proved their worth over time."

"How often do you make this trip to Vladivostok?" asked Vladislav.

"At present, we are making five roundtrips a year. This is the regular line between Odessa and Vladivostok, stopping at Nagasaki and Shanghai. We even go up to Sakhalin. The interest and demand is strong, and we have more and more passengers every trip, therefore, we will probably increase the number of trips in the future. Odessa is growing in importance as a free port for cargo, and our destination Vladivostok, as the main Far Eastern city, already has a population of almost 38,000 people."[12]

"It's quite amazing that you are connecting Odessa and Vladivostok in such a meaningful way," Vladislav said.

"I agree. We like to think we are contributing to making a better future for many."

"No doubt, you are," said Vladislav with a smile.

Vladislav stayed on the deck until late into the evening. So far, the voyage had been calm, but the Indian Ocean had other plans for the SS *Vladimir*.

The ship was long and narrow, capable of a top speed of 13 knots in calm waters. However, the sea was rough going through the open ocean past India toward Malaya. Vladislav's tough companions retreated to the cabin and did not emerge for days, leaving him alone in the ship's saloon to enjoy heaving waves and lashing rain. At times, he would go out on deck to breathe in the salt air. It was exhilarating. The wild weather was a novelty. Several mornings the violent waves would jar him awake, and he would jump out of his bunk and throw on his trousers in one quick swoop. Then it was off to breakfast. His cabinmates stayed put and just groaned with each heaving motion of the ship.

The ship sailed on through the steamy Malacca Strait and into the South China Sea, a long-standing haunt of pirates. The captain alerted all the passengers and posted armed guards at the approach to the bridge. If the pirates were sighted during the day, all the women were to go to their cabins and all the men would assemble on deck in a show of force. Vladislav had confidence in the captain and was glad to have a naval crew on board. Nevertheless, he armed himself with a knife and spent most of his time on deck helping to keep watch for pirates.

Finally, the ship entered the Sea of Japan and arrived at Vladivostok. It was exhausting for Vladislav and the other immigrants because of the difficult conditions and long voyage that had taken almost forty days.[13] It was well worth it, for sailing into the beautiful Golden Horn Bay was magical.

Vladivostok: The cathedral and Golden Horn Bay[14]

3 | Vladivostok

1896

Grandfather arrived in Vladivostok, a city on the other side of Russia, far from home. He was looking for adventure, but what attracted him more was the freedom that he felt living in the Russian Far East. Here, he was able to pursue the opportunities that were available in this part of the world.

VLADISLAV ARRIVED IN VLADIVOSTOK ON A HOT SUMMER DAY IN 1896. As the passengers disembarked, there was much confusion and he wished he had rushed to get off the ship. The queues were long and slow as officers checked each passenger against the arrival list and made certain that appropriate payments for the passage had been made in Odessa or that commitment contracts had been duly signed. Looking around, Vladislav could see that all the new arrivals were there for the same purpose and held the same dreams and goals. Vladislav felt uneasy, a rare feeling for him. Luckily, he had the company of two mates that he met on board.

"This looks organized and yet disorganized, wouldn't you say?" Vladislav complained to his friend, Dimitri.

"Yes, quite unsettling," his friend replied. "And it looks like it is going to take a very long time."

He was right, for it was three hectic hours later that they were finally registered. They decided to celebrate their new beginning with a drink. Spotting a tavern on the corner, they headed inside and found it densely crowded with many familiar faces, all from the ship.

"I can see we are not going to get away from our immigrant group," Dimitri grinned.

"Don't worry, Dimitri Ivanovich. Everything will be fine," Vladislav said, ordering the vodka. *Dve riumki vodki, pozhaluista,** he called out to the Russian server. The evening lasted into the early hours of the morning.

Vladislav and the others from the *Vladimir* were provided decent lodgings in barracks, and they could purchase, at cost, food and the required agricultural implements they needed from a government depot set up for the newly arriving population.

After a week in the barracks, Vladislav and five friends from the ship, among them Dimitri, were able to rent a room on Pologaia Street for two rubles a month. It was cramped and the living conditions were filthy, but it was near the center of town. The summer monsoon welcomed Vladislav to Vladivostok with torrential downpours for days on end. He explored his new urban environment with keen interest, wandering through the seedy Oriental Quarter known as Millionka and peering into the grand Kunst and Albers Department Store that was filled with European finery.

Quite a few Poles had already immigrated and were established in the city, and Vladislav happily accepted their help and counsel. As they were his countrymen, he felt he could trust them. Although Vladivostok was a vibrant and colorful gateway to Asia and the Pacific, it was also a raw naval outpost at the end of the Russian Empire. The town hummed with new arrivals from European Russia as well as foreign merchants; Chinese and Korean workers; opportunists from North and South America, Europe, and Australia; and bureaucrats and military personnel. Everyone was seeking a quick fortune. Prices were inexpensive even though everything in Vladivostok was imported, even the fruits, vegetables, and eggs were brought in from Japan, as Vladivostok was a free trade port.

This frontier town represented the beginning of something new and promising for Vladislav, and he was filled with hope and determination to build a good life. In the beginning, every evening he and his roommates wandered to one of the nearby taverns to meet friends. The conversations were the same and he soon tired of them. "Where can we make some quick money?" was the common question asked. While the local charlatans would offer "Have I got a deal for you" to the naive arrivals, Vladislav remained sober and warned his companions to steer clear of them.

Tired of carousing, Vladislav began, instead, to walk into the surrounding countryside of the Muravyov-Amursky Peninsula to take its measure.

---

* "Two shot glasses of vodka, please."

He could walk for miles and miles in the crisp autumn air, searching beyond Vladivostok; with his long legs and youthful energy, he was known to walk over 50 versts (53 kilometers) a day, marveling at the forests and the richness of the soil. Under his breath he would whisper, "This is a powerhouse—this land, this soil is incredible."[1] Along the way Vladislav would talk to people in the villages and learn how they lived in that special environment. He soon came to appreciate the enormous potential of the immense rich area of the Russian Far East. He was certain that he would find many opportunities beyond the town, along the railway advancing northward through the Ussuri forests toward Khabarovsk,[2] as labor was in short supply and all work hands were welcome.

As the endlessly depressing fog of winter descended on Vladivostok, Vladislav inspected his meager funds and decided to seek work on the construction of the South Ussuri Railway, which was in full swing. There were many contracts offered and Vladislav got one immediately. He was placed in charge of Chinese workers on a construction project and was provided with an interpreter.[3]

He lived in forest camps and discovered many new areas as the Ussuri Railway construction moved north and he moved along with it. Vladislav took every opportunity to develop his skills while he was working on the Ussuri project. The workers appreciated him greatly because they considered him a sympathetic person and a brave man. On one occasion when he was riding the train trolley with some workers, the trolley came to a sudden stop. A large snake rested on the rails. Vladislav grabbed the snake with his bare hands and lifted it up. The snake wrapped itself around his arm and he then proceeded to unwind it fearlessly and tossed it into the grassy area saying, "I will not kill you. Go and tell your relatives and friends that not all people are evil." The Chinese were astonished and amazed at his bravery. They approached him, and with reverence called him the "Tiger Man."[4]

It was at this early point in his career that Vladislav met the man who would play a pivotal role in the development of his future business. That man was Lieutenant Colonel Dimitrii Leonidovich Horvath (also spelled as Khorvat) from Russia who was appointed chief of the Ussuri Railway in 1895. He was a young lieutenant colonel, a seasoned military engineer and the great-great-grandson of Marshal Mikhail Kutuzov who had defeated Napoleon in 1812.[5]

In St. Petersburg, Horvath had worked with Count Sergei Witte who was the Russian director of railway affairs in the Ministry of Finance. Since both men had experience working with the railway, they had much in com-

Lieutenant General Dimitrii Leonidovich Horvath[6] (His name was also spelled as Khorvat.)

mon. Witte was the minister of finance for Russia from 1893 and had implemented many progressive ideas that had an enormous impact in the years that followed his appointment. In his position, he was able to play a dominant role in the strategic command and development of the railway expansion in Russia and in China.

Vladislav met Horvath in 1896 when Horvath turned up at the forward camp in midwinter to inspect progress. It was a bitterly cold morning when a sleigh emerged out of the forest and stopped at the camp. Out stepped a huge figure dressed in furs. He strode over the crisp snow toward the chief engineer of this section of the line. After a brief discussion, the chief engineer introduced Horvath to Vladislav. Horvath noticed that like him, Vladislav also towered over the Chinese crew. Here was a man whom Horvath could look at eye to eye.

Vladislav and Horvath developed a mutual respect that continued to grow over time. Years later Vladislav said of him, "When I saw him for the first time, I thought he was too young to be a lieutenant colonel. He had a beard that was totally black. All of us were drawn to him, he was a very likeable person, he was amicable, polite and sensitive which you could tell because of his courteousness. In business, he had experience and was a very clever man."[7]

Vladislav evolved quickly into an able building contractor for the Ussuri line and his interests turned to constructing railway stations. He was given a contract to clear the land to build the railroad station at Pogranichnaia in a rugged area of the Ussuri region on the Russian side of the border with China. An established engineer by the name of N. S. Sviiagin worked with him, and the two of them became close friends. They lived in simple wooden sheds at makeshift campsites and together created a congenial working environment for the entire camp. The employees at the camp got along well and even enjoyed evenings of music and theatrical events.[8]

The station in Pogranichnaia[9]

Agents of the depot at the Pogranichnaia station[10]

Vladislav built approaches to the station, using dynamite to blast through the rock and made the required excavations. He was diversifying his talents and proving to be a versatile operator. His reputation among the officials grew as each of his projects was accomplished with timeliness and skill. Unlike many other contractors, he treated his workers with respect and acknowledged their hard work. He looked after them and addressed their concerns about anything to do with the project, resolving issues and scrutinizing each detail. His workers admired and looked up to him. Vladislav understood early on that the rapport he developed with every worker, from senior to junior, was going to be the key to his success.

Already Vladislav had the reputation of being modest, simple, and frugal. He understood early on that this was an environment where you could earn money quickly and easily, but could also lose money just as fast. He was a levelheaded young entrepreneur. He would eat modestly at the local *zabigalovki* ("simple eateries") and did not frequent restaurants like the popular Pacific Ocean restaurant, to celebrate successful deals or conduct business gatherings as did other businessmen.[11] Even though he was frugal, he was generous to his employees. All his workers were well paid but, in return, he demanded hard work and loyalty.[12]

With each new challenge, Vladislav realized that it was possible to make money by supplying the lumber needed by the railway companies, not only to build stations, but to also construct the berths in the trains, secure the wood for the train track, and provide fuel for the railway cars. Many other contractors were unable to keep up with such a high demand for lumber, but Vladislav ran a tight and efficient operation. He gathered several different teams of dedicated workers who simultaneously worked on different aspects of the projects. He worked right along with them, felling trees, negotiating deals, suggesting improvements at the sawmills, and organizing the transport of lumber. With his determination and energetic spirit, he managed to accumulate enough money to tide him over to the next year.

Although the construction on the Ussuri Railway line suffered many setbacks, it was completed in six years using 17,000 laborers and provided travel between the cities of Vladivostok and Khabarovsk with six stations along the way.[13] After its completion in 1897, the entire journey took two days.

Ussuri Railway Line between Vladivostok and Khabarovsk[14]

4 | Siberian Wilderness

1896

Grandfather felt comfortable in his new environment. He loved the area, the nature, his work, and everything that came with the move. The opportunities inspired him to plan, work, progress, and achieve. There were opportunities everywhere, and his challenge was to choose the right direction.

Continuing his pursuits away from Vladivostok and the Ussuri basin, Vladislav heard stories about the rich land beyond the Russian border and the Amur River with the abundance of forests and fertile fields in Manchuria, the northern part of China. He was also warned about the savage bandits and robbers that roamed the area, the *Honghuzi* or "red beards," who populated the thick forests.[1] They would swoop down from their mountain hideaways, pillage villages and caravans, and prey on travelers, sometimes slaughtering people. After gathering their loot, they would swiftly disappear, occasionally with a few captured officials to be held for ransom. Local folklore was filled with stories about the Honghuzi and their ruthlessness.

Vladislav was not deterred. Despite all the warnings, he found a good horse and set out alone to find his "pot of gold." Whenever he could spare the time, he would ride or walk through dense untouched forests for days on end. Using his axe to hack away underbrush, he gradually climbed to higher ground where open fields revealed breathtaking views of endless virgin forests. There were no fences or markers, but he knew he was no longer in Russia and that he had reached Manchuria, China.

Riding along the side of a mountain, he suddenly came upon an area of mud huts in the woods. As he approached the clearing, Vladislav was suddenly surrounded by a group of the wildest-looking Chinese he had ever seen. They were Manchurians, taller and stockier than the Han Chinese. He knew immediately that they were the notorious Honghuzi. They circled

Vladislav and made menacing gestures. He held out his arms to show he had no weapons and then jumped off his horse. He walked toward one of the huts where a figure, dressed differently than the others, sat at the entrance on a straw mat. He was smoking a long-curved clay pipe.

The man stared calmly as Vladislav approached. When he came within a few feet, the leader made a sign to his men and they grabbed Vladislav and held him while others formed a tight semicircle around him, preventing his escape. The leader then made another gesture and they loosened their grips, but remained standing very close to him. Vladislav could smell their harsh breath. He felt uneasy, but made sure that they did not see this. He did not want to show weakness.

Vladislav spoke to them with authority and confidence in Russian, rather unsuccessfully, and finally resorted to sign language. One of the bandits spoke some broken Russian, which made things a little easier. He walked away from this "capture" with a handshake and a pat on the back. Vladislav's fearlessness, adaptability, and confidence would allow him to thrive as a pioneer in these isolated forests in this part of the world. He would cross paths with the Honghuzi many times in the future, for they played a large and menacing role in Manchuria. The lack of police power or a united military made for lawlessness, and these strong bandits were known to gather in large groups to support the Chinese military as mercenary soldiers.

Vladislav explored the area, hitching rides on riverboats and blazing his own trails through the forests of Manchuria. There were no paths or roads and the wilderness was full of challenges. Treacherous rivers and mountain terrain blocked the way. He was an inquisitive and audacious young man with calm gentle eyes and an intense energy that took him everywhere. He talked to everyone and listened carefully. He was often seen nodding his head, encouraging others, and gaining knowledge. When he questioned the Russian traders who ran the riverboats full of goods and people, they warned him that some of his business ideas were too risky. Vladislav listened to their advice but followed his own instincts.

During the winter months, darkness in the forest came early, and blizzards and

Honghuzi leader Tulisan (ca. 1904–1905)[2]

snowstorms were relentless. The calm before and after the storm characterized the unpredictable climate. The calm was so peaceful and the fury was deadly. Vladislav loved the forest and the wilderness, especially during winter. Sometimes the winter storms would obliterate everything in sight. After the storm and at the end of the day, the stillness he felt only in the heart of the forest on a cold autumn or winter night was something that would make him feel at peace.[3] Vladislav would stare up at the sky and marvel at the brightness of each star. He felt the stars were different here; they were bigger and brighter. The snow would sparkle with the reflection from the moon. On his scouting adventures, he would collect firewood and start a fire to brew a cup of tea and have it together with a container of kasha (porridge) and some pirozhki (meat pies), which he brought with him. He loved the calmness of nature and he felt the solitude exhilarating.

While walking in the wilderness, he occasionally met other adventurers. Most of them were hunters and collectors, some Chinese, some Russian. They often sat down to share a story or two. These men were ransacking the forests for ginseng or mushrooms. Trappers and hunters hunted for sable, tiger pelts, and other treasures. Vladislav sometimes heard the sound of an approaching tiger, nature's most feared and efficient predator, the man-eating killer, and his horse would stir nervously. When Vladislav sensed a tiger was near, he stayed very still and, fortunately, was always able to avoid confronting it. The last thing he wanted to do was to kill one of nature's beautiful animals.

On one of his "alone in the wilderness adventure hikes," as he called them, he came upon a young, abandoned boy. Even though it was summer the boy was trying to cover himself with an old burlap bag to ward off the cold. Vladislav could see he was sick, shivering, and very frightened. The swarms of mosquitos and flies were attacking him ruthlessly. The Manchurian mosquito bites produced incredible discomfort and itching, but the boy was already too ill to care, which worried Vladislav. He tried to talk to him, but his glassy eyes just stared back with desperate emotion. He sat down next to the boy and offered him a drink from his flask. He had slipped a little vodka into the flask but figured it could not bring any harm to this young child. With cautious reluctance, the boy reached for the flask and took a sip. His eyes squinted as he swallowed the strange-tasting water.

Vladislav could see that he had been alone for some time. He was full of sores and was covered with lice and fleas. It was apparent he had not eaten for days and was frightened, nor did he have the energy to run. Vladislav took off his coat and wrapped it around the child. He decided to sit there with him, spending quite a while talking to him knowing he did not understand a thing, but wanting to make him feel comfortable. He then took his hand to indicate that they should walk together; however, he was too weak. Vladislav picked up the trembling boy and carried him for an hour back to his campsite. The whole time they did not speak, but he could feel the boy's body shuddering.[4]

Vladislav arranged to have the boy looked after by the Chinese at the camp. They bathed him, shaved his head to get rid of the lice and fleas, and fed him a hot meal. After a few weeks of care, supervised by Vladislav, the child began to recover and to smile. They learned that his name was Toubin.

Toubin was a scrawny boy with inquisitive eyes and, although he didn't talk much, he was curious and eager to learn. He copied everything Vladislav did, which Vladislav thought was humorous and endearing. He could see that this young boy was quite special. As he grew, so did his attachment to Vladislav, and he became like a shadow following him everywhere. Vladislav developed a great empathy for Toubin and welcomed his company. In the beginning, he would use Toubin to run simple errands and have him help with menial tasks. Toubin took his responsibilities seriously and became a fantastic asset to Vladislav. He worked hard, never complained, and lived to serve him. Throughout his life, Toubin never left Vladislav's side and he even learned to speak Russian. Vladislav taught and guided Toubin, and, years later, they worked together, traveling the countryside, sleeping in Chinese peasant huts called *fanza*, assessing land, mapping territories, and going to meetings with the Honghuzi. Vladislav laughingly recounted a story about some unfriendly Honghuzi who approached them. Toubin cleverly told them that Vladislav was an official and that a battalion of Russian troops was right behind them. He suggested it would be wise if they left immediately, which they did.[5]

5 | Chinese Eastern Railway

1894–1897

Years later grandfather had admitted to his daughter, Vika, that when he arrived in the Far East, he did not know anything about the history of China, Korea, or Japan. Everything was new to him. He was eager to learn the dynamics as he could see that political, economic, and social situations played an important part in the history and the development of the region. It was evident to him that the dynamics of the east and west caused tension and friction that appeared in the strained relationships between the countries. Though he eventually came to understand China, the Great "Middle Kingdom," and the Chinese people, he always admitted that he had so much more to learn.

Vladislav began questioning Japan's ambitions in Korea and China. One friend from St. Petersburg was a professor at the university and a historian focusing on the Far East. Vladislav spent time with him during his visit, listening and learning about how Japan had gone through phases in its exposure to the outside world.

For many years, Japan had stood closed and isolated. It was attacked by Emperor Kublai Khan in an expedition from Korea in the 1280s and the invasion ended in a great defeat.[1] Three hundred years later, from 1592–1598, the Japanese ruler Toyotomi Hideyoshi landed troops in Korea to conquer lands but was unsuccessful and withdrew back to Japan. That was the first time Japan attempted to extend its territory on the Asian continent. It would be about another 300 years before Japan attempted to expand its territory again. With the Meiji Restoration in 1867, Japan transformed itself into a modern and military nation after the many years of isolation from the Western world.[2]

Vladislav learned that Western countries, with Britain as a leader, had aggressively developed their trade in China, and the United States had been forcing Japan to open for trade and foreign relations. The Meiji Restoration encouraged the idea of modernizing Japan, and even managed to get the backing of the samurai class to develop Japan into a rich country with a strong military. The Japanese believed that it was important to strengthen the emperor's rule and did so by gathering knowledge from all over the world. Ito Hirobumi, who later became the first prime minister of Japan, went to England and Germany with a group of friends to gather knowledge about writing a new constitution, studying rules and policies to benefit Japan, and learning how to adopt Western ways to become a leading military and imperial nation.

In its ambitions for a military buildup, much effort was put into developing the Japanese naval power. On July 25, 1894, a naval battle between a Chinese convoy carrying troops to Korea and Japanese warships ended with the sinking of the Chinese convoy. Japan had become increasingly aggressive toward Korea and China, and this led to the Sino-Japanese War of 1894–1895. The outbreak and progress of the war came as a shock to many as a war between China and Japan was something few had foreseen. Most people thought Japan had no chance against China, and yet the Japanese sank the Chinese fleet at the Yalu River, took Pyongyang, chased the Chinese troops out of Korea, and eventually won a battle at the Chinese naval base at Port Arthur. The Manchu government of the Qing Dynasty in China was weak and powerless under the rule of Empress Dowager Cixi. This made the way for Japan to expand and challenge China and strengthen its influence over Korea.[3]

Japan emerged as the victor from the first Sino-Japanese War of 1894–1895 with important territorial gains. It was here that Japan seriously began paving the way to building up its empire, with a victory that was sealed by the Treaty of Shimonoseki in April 1895. China lost claim to Korea (its former tributary state), the Pescadores Islands, Formosa (Taiwan), and the Liaodong Peninsula. With the defeat, China also had to pay Japan a war indemnity of 360 million yen or three times the amount of the national budget of Japan in 1894.[4] Moreover, Japan demanded the indemnity be paid in gold because the price of silver had depreciated, but the Qing Court only had silver on hand.

The Russian government offered to help China with the payment of the indemnity. The Chinese Imperial Commissioner, Li Hongzhang,[5] had travelled to Russia to attend the coronation of Tsar Nicholas II in November 1894. He stayed in touch with Russia and at the end of the Sino-Japanese War in April 1895, he took the opportunity to discuss financial arrangements with Count Witte for the war indemnity to Japan. Russia was prepared to assist China with its substantial debt in exchange for the possibility of building a railway corridor through Manchuria, northern China, to Vladivostok.

Stolen Dreams

Chinese Eastern Railway Line[6]

Chief engineer of the CER, Aleksandr Iosifovich Iugovich[7]

Discussions for the construction of a railroad line from one end of Manchuria to the other through the city of Harbin along the way had begun. Under the direction of Count Witte, the Russo-Chinese Bank, later renamed the Russo-Asian Bank, was created on December 10, 1895, in St. Petersburg. The bank, in turn, established the Chinese Eastern Railway Company to manage the railway. Engineer Aleksandr Iosifovich Iugovich (1842–1925) was hired as the first military and civil engineer of the Chinese Eastern Railway and would be in charge of the construction; he spoke several languages having been educated in London and already had experience in railway projects.[8] It would be August 1896, shortly after Vladislav's arrival in Vladivostok, when the Chinese government partnered with the bank and invested five million silver tael* for a minimal share of interest in the railway.[9]

The Li-Lobanov Treaty was signed between China and the Russian Empire for the construction of the Chinese Eastern Railway through Manchuria. The treaty required the railway to be completed within a six-year period. The project was principally brokered by Count Witte who stated that the railroad was intended for peaceful and commercial purposes.[10] The treaty placed all Chinese Eastern Railway activities in China under the control of the Ministry of Finance of Russia through the Chinese Eastern Railway Company. Aspects

---

* Tael is a unit of weight used in China. One tael was worth 1.3 ounces of silver.

of the Li-Lobanov Treaty were kept secret, specifically the agreement that if China should ever be threatened by Japan, Russia would come to its defense.[11]

The Japanese gains after the Sino-Japanese War alarmed Russia, France, and Germany, and this led to the organization of the Triple Intervention of these three countries to reclaim the Liaodong Peninsula for China. In exchange for the return, Japan would be awarded a further indemnity of 30 million tael from China.[12] This agreement allowed Russia to later gain a 25-year lease from China to construct a 600-mile railway line south from Harbin to Port Arthur and Dalian.[13] (See the map on the previous page.) The Chinese Eastern Railway (CER) would provide a direct route across the Chinese territory of Manchuria to the Russian seaport of Vladivostok and would be an almost 340-mile shorter route than the originally planned Trans-Siberian line through the Russian Siberian territory.[14] The railway would allow for an alternative solution as problems were being encountered with the construction of the Trans-Siberian Railway through Siberia due to the extreme weather conditions, the wetlands, and the mountainous terrain. For Russia, this was a perfect solution. In the agreement, Russia would manage funds, construct railways, post railway guards along the route to protect the rail line, establish telegraph lines, and have legal jurisdiction and policing authority for the CER corridor along its entire route.[15]

There were many administrative and organizational issues that would have to be set up and settled due to the scope of this massive undertaking. This Russian project would develop the area, generate business and, increase the population of Harbin and all the Manchurian towns along the rail line, which would bring its own challenges along with it. How suddenly things had changed. The future of the whole region would be affected.

Chinese Eastern Railway[16]

It became evident that the Sino-Japanese War and the outcome of it would play an important role in the future of this region. These conflicts would engage Russia and shape the political, social, and geographic map of the area and cause security issues, tension, and conflicts of global importance.

Businessmen and adventurers arriving in the Far East had little comprehension of the dynamics that existed or those that would soon develop among the major powers. They had little occasion to dwell on anxieties about the changing political environment and how it would set the stage for their future. Vladislav tried to distance himself from the reality and concentrate on business as he could see the potential in this part of the world was immense. He continued to work tirelessly to set attainable goals, which would give him the contracts that he needed, one after another. Vladislav never needed much sleep. He would sleep three hours a night and would be ready to go the next day. A productive day for him was a twenty-hour work day. He often said, "sleep is a waste of time."[17]

Vladislav sat on a stump of a sawed-off tree, taking a rest and thinking about the developments. He had already put in a ten-hour workday and it was still early afternoon. The summer sun was shining brightly through the forest and offered a peaceful and calming atmosphere. His thoughts drifted to the historical events that seemed to be consuming everyone's lives.

"Interesting," he caught himself saying aloud. The Japanese had won the war and demanded a tremendous war indemnity that China would not be able to pay. "What was China to do with such demands?" he asked himself. China brought in Russia to solve the problem. Russia had an agenda and wanted a railway line through Manchuria to allow for the convenience of a shorter and alternate route for the Trans-Siberian to the Russian Far East. China needed the indemnity to be paid off. A win-win situation for both sides—Russia would pay and invest to have a railway corridor through China and China would thereby clear itself of its debt to Japan. The Russians also managed to tie into the deal the lease of the Liaodong Peninsula's railway zone and the possibility to expand the rail line from Harbin south to Port Arthur, an ice-free port and an excellent location for a Russian naval base. If the Japanese had not made such a huge monetary demand, he wondered if developments with the CER would have been different. There were so many circumstances that brought Russia and Japan into China, thought Vladislav. He would share these thoughts with his family many times over the years.

Vladislav was energized by the news of Russia's plans to build the railway. This was truly an enormous endeavor and the fact that he was there, already seasoned and ready to take on this new challenge, was to his advantage. For Vladislav the timing was excellent. He found new friends, mainly among the Polish and Russian arrivals like himself who had drifted into this part of the world looking for opportunities, and they spent hours talking about these new railway projects. The news and the excitement spread fast and plans began to materialize overnight. He was among the first entrepreneurs who had moved to Manchuria and was prepared to participate in the planning, the work, and the construction of the railway line.

6 | Harbin

1898

One of grandfather's favorite stories was about the first time he arrived in Harbin. To him it was important that he was there in the beginning. He was a pioneer and was proud of it. When he started his lumber business, he used the natural resources to his advantage. He managed to secure one contract after another, cleverly negotiating so that he could continue to build his base. Although his work was centered on lumber, he was open to explore every opportunity that came his way.

THE SURVEYING OF THE CER ROUTE WAS COMPLETED IN JANUARY 1898 and soon after in April the first group of Russian builders and engineers arrived in a caravan of carts to what became the future city of Harbin. The influx of the Russian population between May and June is believed to be the start of the Russian presence and settlement in Harbin.[1] In this massive new project all talents were recruited—laborers, engineers, clerks, guards, and others. The first teams that arrived purchased and repaired an abandoned distillery in Harbin to service the workers and engineers arriving by ship on the Sungari.

Groups of engineers and workers from Russia, Poland, and China began pouring into Manchuria for the railway project. Construction work on the CER started in July 1897 and went along the Siberian city of Chita, across northern inner Manchuria via Harbin, Ussuriski, and would continue to the Russian port of Vladivostok.[2] The railway line from Harbin to Dalian was started at the same time. (See map on page ix.)

Vladislav, having arrived in Harbin around the same time that the CER was started along its projected route, saw his new home as a small fishing village on the banks of the Sungari (Songhua) River. The name Harbin was a Manchu word meaning "a place for drying fishing nets." This was one of the many early interpretations of the word *Harbin*.[3] Harbin, at that time, had only a few houses, which lined the banks of the river. This land that was sparsely populated would soon change as the potential of the resource rich area and the possibilities that the CER line would bring was becoming evident.

It was in the spring of 1898 that Vladislav moved his business to Harbin, together with a group of future Polish and Russian railway workers. In 1898, he opened his first office and lumber warehouse quite a distance away from the Sungari River in an area known as Starei Harbin, "Old Harbin," where some other businesses were already established. Vladislav's office grew with a warehouse for the lumber business and, soon after, he proudly made his company official with a sign over the door: *V.F. Kowalski's Lumber and Timber Company*. Looking to further expand, he began advertising his company in different local publications.

Harbin very quickly embraced the responsibility that was expected of a town playing an important role in a strategically located Russian-Chinese transportation center. Harbin would soon become the hub of the CER route with its railway line extending west to east as well as south from Harbin to Dalian. A major part of the city was dedicated to Russian railway areas, with many CER buildings and facilities. The early pioneers immediately started to set up their businesses. The population of Harbin consisted mainly of the Chinese and Russian workers employed on the railroad. Chinese migration from neighboring provinces increased and all became a part of this new beginning. Offices, small factories, and businesses sprouted everywhere and, at the same time, small eateries and tea shops began appearing. Enterprises like Vladislav's providing wood for the CER received access to large tracts of land in the railway zone to facilitate the building of the railroad.

Early picture of Harbin, around 1898.[4]

Along the eastern section of the CER was the small village of Qilidi. Early on, Vladislav established a timber plantation there in hopes of providing lumber for the railway construction. This soon became the largest lumberyard in the Mudanjiang region surrounding Qilidi, a city located to the east of Harbin about halfway to the Russian border. (See map on page ix.) Vladislav secured the first lumber license issued to fell timber and registered the rights to access this property with the Chinese authorities. He became one of the major suppliers of timber for the CER construction, as well as for the construction of stations and housing. Before long, he was one of the largest employers in the region.[5]

To access areas along the CER route, Vladislav built and laid special railway tracks between the tracks and the forests where lumber was plentiful, and set up an efficient system of transportation as well as lumberyards. According to the treaty, the CER line would accommodate a corridor with six li (Chinese mile) on either side of the railway where lumber could be felled; this right of way was often referred to as the CER zone.[6] Vladislav learned fast, knew his business, and took advantage of this, making certain that the timber processing was done efficiently by his team. He was a hands-on operator and his business model quickly started to pay dividends.

In the city of Harbin the Sungari River which served to facilitate the lumber business was over a kilometer wide with seasonal variations. During the summer the Sungari offered residents fishing, swimming, and boating access. As the seasons changed, so did the use of the river. The winters in Harbin were known to be one of the severest in the world, as temperatures dropped down to −40°C. The Siberian winds would sweep down from the north and would freeze everything. The ice on the Sungari River got so thick that a locomotive could travel on it without the ice cracking. During spring the breaking up of the ice was a spectacle as huge slabs dramatically snapped away and swept downstream. The treacherous currents threw the huge pieces of ice against each other as the fury of seasonal change made its mark. During the winter months, small sleds would zip back and forth on the frozen ice.

A heavily dressed Chinese man stood at the back of the sleds clutching long wooden pole with a spike at the end. The passenger sat in front with a thick blanket to cover his legs. This form of transportation was called *tolkai-tolkai,* a word that was a form of Sino-Russian pidgin coming from the Russian verb *tolkat*—"to push."

Vladislav decided to try out this new mode of transportation. He waved to one of the tolkai-tolkai operators and asked him to take him to the other side of the river and back. He sat down comfortably on the sled and made sure he was securely seated. The operator covered his legs with the thick blanket and the ride started. The wind was blowing in the opposite direction of the sled as it raced across the ice on the river. He could feel the biting cold wind numb the exposed parts of his face and his eyelashes seemed to freeze instantly with the tears that had welled up in his eyes fighting the cold. As they flew over the ice, he understood that the winters in Harbin would be nothing like he had ever experienced. Vladislav tugged at his hat and tried to pull it down farther just below his brows. He put his gloves up to his face to shield it from the wind, but by this time his face and lips were completely numb. The trip back, now gliding with the wind, was a little faster and not as painful. The speed at which the sled traveled over the ice was amazing, and made this a memorable experience.

Talkai sled on the Sungari[7]

7 | Boxer Rebellion

1900

Vika remembered the stories that her father told her about the Boxers, who were groups of Chinese opponents to foreign presence and exploitation in China. He told about the Boxer Rebellion and the precarious situation that foreigners found themselves in. The mass hysteria that overtook a portion of the population was alarming. All foreigners and foreign interests were vulnerable. When her father told her about the Boxer Rebellion, his descriptions were so vivid and detailed, it was almost as if it had just happened the day before. In telling the story it was the first time Vika sensed that her father was worried that his business projects could have been affected negatively in a permanent way.

THE CONSTRUCTION OF THE CER WAS A MASSIVE CHALLENGE AS VAST areas of forest had to be cleared and temporary roads and settlements had to be developed to accommodate the work and the workers. The construction was in territories without population, settlements, or roads. The forest work became the most important activity for Vladislav and his team. When the tracks had to be laid, contractors like Vladislav began to take it upon themselves to invest in and take the financial risks with the logging operations, including transporting timber material and firewood to Harbin.

In 1900 the branch line from Harbin to Port Arthur was almost finished, whereas the east-west corridor of the CER would take longer.[1] With all the foreign exploitation, the political winds of discontent blew across China, Manchuria, and the CER. The Boxer Rebellion started in Peking and Shanghai and did not, in the beginning, threaten Manchuria. As the Boxers received official support from the ruler of the Qing Dynasty, Empress Dowager Cixi, the protest movement spread and intensified. The rebellion was an anti-foreign movement rejecting the presence of foreigners in China, their technologies, and the newly constructed railways. The Chinese Boxers captured and destroyed large portions of the railway during the summer of 1900.

The caricatures include Queen Victoria of the United Kingdom, William II of Germany, Nicholas II of Russia, French Marianne, and a samurai representing Japan.[2]

A French political cartoon illustration that appeared in *Le Petit Journal* on January 16, 1898, captures the sentiment—Chinese upset by the reality of foreign powers with their imperialistic tendencies to divide up China for themselves.

In Peking and other cities, Boxers ran through the streets in a frenzy—missionaries were killed, foreign legations were destroyed, and anything to do with a foreign influence was targeted. As the foreigners continued to be attacked, shock waves reverberated among those living in Harbin. Rumors, some true and some fabrications, were rampant and panic set in. The Boxers terrorized foreigners with the motto "Kill the foreign devils! Kill, kill, kill."[3]

When the rebellion reached Manchuria, all the stations south of Mukden (Shenyang) were savagely assailed by the rebels. Although the Russian railroad guards and employees heroically defended building sites, they were quickly overpowered. The military governor of Heilongjiang warned the public that the Boxers would be attacking Russian women and children, and they were evacuated to Khabarovsk. Many Russians fled leaving Harbin.

On July 26, the Harbin railway station and businesses in the Staryi Gorod (Old Harbin), were attacked. Along the railway line, rebels burned station buildings and staff dwellings, plundered warehouses, destroyed rolling stocks and coal mines, and demolished telegraph lines. Only one third of the laid railway track remained unscathed.[4] Most of the businesses in the area of Old Harbin were wiped out, Vladislav's among them. He told of the rebels who wore red turbans and red bands around their wrists and ankles, and how they terrorized the city.

Count Witte informed the Chinese that Russia, to defend its interests against the Boxers, planned to increase railway guards[5] stationed along the CER route to 25,000 men, and would withdraw the troops only when the disturbances subsided.[6] Ignoring Witte's advice, Russian Minister of War Aleksei Nikolaevich Kuropatkin (1848–1925) mobilized many more troops to counter the Boxer attacks. Russian forces poured into Manchuria from the Trans-Baikal Region, Blagoveschensk, Khabarovsk, and Port

Arthur in July 1901.[7] During the rebellion, several hundred Russian soldiers were wounded or killed.[8] As the railroad lines came under attack, many Russian engineers and workers left, abandoning everything—their work, their materials, and their property. In outbreaks throughout northern China, over 200 missionaries and their families were murdered at the hands of the Boxers, as well as more than 20,000 "secondary devils" who were Chinese converts.[9]

On August 2, more Russian troops from Khabarovsk arrived just in time to save the besieged defenders of Harbin. After the Boxer fighting ended in September, there were many Russian troops that stayed behind in Manchuria. Count Witte was worried about the massive cost for Russia to have its troops in Manchuria and wanted the soldiers to be withdrawn; however, the tsar and Ministers Aleksandr Mikhailovich Bezobrazov and Aleksey Nikolaevich Kuropatkin preferred to keep the troops in China for possible further expansion of Russian interests in the Far East.

After the Boxer Rebellion, the presence of Russian and Japanese troops, who had also come to "defend their citizens," created further political problems. The Japanese wanted the Russians to withdraw their troops from Manchuria, and refused to discuss the neutralization of Korea until the troops were evacuated. The large presence of the Russian troops was one of the causes of the conflict that developed between Russia and Japan in the years to come.

The Boxer Rebellion was quelled, and the repairs of the damages and the construction of the railroad resumed apace, with logging operations back on track for Vladislav. The destruction brought about a strong demand for wood, exclusively for the railway. It was estimated that the Boxer Rebellion had created repair costs amounting to US$35,872,939.[10]

Amid all the developments, Vladislav was surprised and puzzled to hear that Count Sergei Witte had been dismissed by the tsar. To him, Witte was a hero. Over a glass of tea together with his friends at the tavern, Vladislav voiced his opinion.

"Count Witte has done so much for the railway. It was he who pushed everything forward. He certainly had to fight to get the message across when many were against the prospect of a Russian railway line through northern China. It was an epochal and progressive move that he implemented. I am sure that negative forces had influenced the tsar who had other preoccupations, one of them being the possible acquisition of land and lumber in the Korean border region. I heard that Minister Bezobrazov was influential and had succeeded in persuading the Tsar," said Vladislav.

"That is exactly what I heard as well," replied Misha, his devoted friend. "Bezobrazov had perhaps great aspirations of having Russia one day control Korea and Manchuria, politically and economically, but he seems to be driven by possible personal and commercial gains. He must have come up with quite a plan and story to counter the efforts of our dedicated and ingenious Count Witte."

"I heard that Minister Bezobrazov wants to develop and take over Brynner's[11] large Russian lumber concessions along the Korean border,"[12] said Vladislav. "That is not going to sit well with the Japanese."

"I can see the situation over Korea could possibly spark a political conflict between Russia and Japan," Misha said as he reached for a glass of vodka, preferring that to the tea.

"Russia is definitely creating its share of problems."

"Hopefully not. We've just gone through the Boxer Rebellion. It would be nice to live in peace and harmony for a change," continued Misha. "*Na zdorov'e* [a toast—for health], Vladislav Fyodorovich, "

"*Na zdorov'e*, Mikhail Alexandrovich," replied Vladislav.

8 | A Growing City

early 1900s

People were very resilient in this part of the world. Nothing appeared to stand in the way of progress, not wars, not rebellions, not climate, and not language. Harbin was growing fast, developing almost overnight. This was a development throughout Manchuria.

AFTER THE BOXER REBELLION ENDED IN 1901, THE DEVASTATING destruction was assessed. The Railway Headquarters, previously located in the Staryi Gorod part of Harbin, was moved to Novyi Gorod. Pristan and Fujiadian were two of the fastest developing and growing parts of the city. Pristan, where many railway workers lived, became the commercial and social center of the city, and Fujiadian along the Sungari River was where many of the Chinese lived.

Businesses were established and grew at a fast pace. Harbin's first flour mill, a liquor factory, a private machinery business, the Harbin Brewery, and the Churin Department Store chain opened for business. The influx of population increased the need for housing, stores, and offices. In 1904–1905 a new CER headquarters was completed, as well as an assembly hall. The first theater, the first library, and schools were opened, all financed by the CER. An official Russian newspaper was established and several other newspapers in different languages appeared. Despite interruptions with the Boxer Rebellion, the St. Nicholas Cathedral was completed in Novyi Gorod in 1899–1901. Buildings destroyed by the Boxer Rebellion were replaced. Nothing was stagnant. Harbin was a frontier town on the steep ascent to modernization with the railway construction as its engine.

By May 1903 the population of Harbin had grown to about 44,576 residents (compared to 13,000 in 1900), of which 15,579 were Russian and 28,338 Chinese, 462 Japanese and less than 200 citizens of other

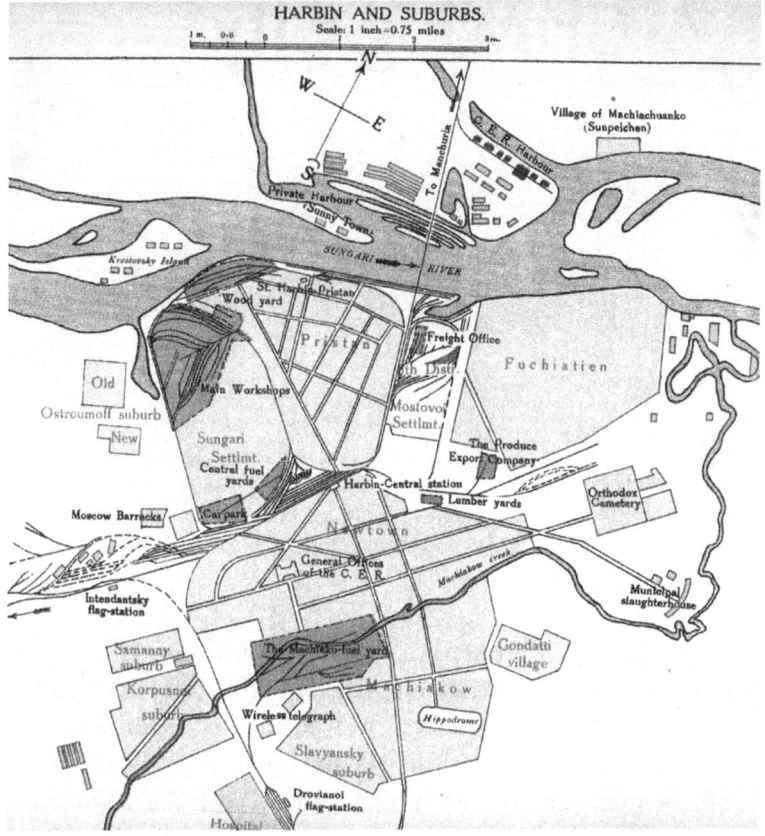

Harbin city[1]

nationalities.[2] In the same year the ratio of women to men was 14 women to every 100 men.[3] Though the population of the city was mainly growing due to the influx of Chinese labor for the railway construction, it was also attracting business entrepreneurs, traders, and families from other parts of the world. The Japanese began moving to Harbin for commercial reasons, opening schools and establishing newspapers to accommodate their citizens. They enhanced security "to protect Japanese interests" even though the rebellion was over.

In the cities, social stratification existed and each group in the society would mingle with their own class. This was even visible in the restaurants and at social venues. The segregation was more evident between the Russians and the Chinese. Established Chinese who could afford investments could lease land lots from the CER under financial terms based on the area in the railway zone.[4] The Chinese were often tolerant of many situations as the Russian presence in the city meant more business.

The timber and mineral wealth of the land earned many fortunes, which were reflected in the new houses and gardens that were constructed. Harbin's dominant Russian and foreign population began to collect donations to finance an opera house and a theater for ballet performances. Construction of a yacht club commenced on the banks of the Sungari River, a project to which Vladislav contributed the lumber.

Ignacy Cytowicz, a Pole, designed the Harbin Railway Station building, which was built in 1904–1905 and became one of the biggest and most important landmarks in the city. The large, majestic, art nouveau style building stood as a symbol of classic design, bringing people together from the east and the west. In the railway station, a Russian Orthodox icon of St. Nicholas was displayed protecting its many travelers. Harbin Station became the gateway to the city for people from all over China, Europe, Asia, and the world. This was the final stop for many travelers who came to start a new life and to live and flourish in this part of the world. The building itself was a welcoming symbol.

Vladislav preferred the energy of Harbin to that of Vladivostok and the Ussuri basin, and was inspired by the pace of development. The ingenious Russian railway corridor running through China would bring the world as well as business to Harbin.

Returning home from the office, Vladislav ran into his friend Andrzej who had arrived in Harbin one year after Vladislav. They met at the tavern by chance and discovered in conversation that they came from the same province of Podolia. Vladislav was always happy to see him and felt their friendship comforting.

Harbin Station,[5] built in 1904–1905. Before that in 1899 the station was housed in a lengthy barrack, according to Olga Bakich.

Andrzej had left behind a tragic past in Poland. His father had been arrested by the Russians for a trivial matter, sadly a common occurrence emphasized by the fear that the victim would be imprisoned for years or never return home at all. His mother was distraught with the arrest and lived for the day her husband would return. She tried every avenue possible to have him freed, but her efforts were in vain. After years of waiting, word came that her husband had mysteriously died in prison. She was grief-stricken, not wanting to live, eat, or talk. Shortly after the news, she suffered a stroke and passed away. Andrzej was the only surviving child as his two sisters died at a young age.

Vladislav admired Andrzej for his character. Despite past tragedies, he was a positive, strong-minded, and personable man. The two of them seldom made plans to meet, but whenever they bumped into each other, they would make time for a meal.

"Andrzej, I am struggling with the latest investment I made. It was not a good decision." confided Vladislav.

"And which one was that, Vladislav?"

"Remember, I once mentioned to you about a sawmill that I bought? Well, the sawmill was fine, but the deal came together with the purchase of eight rather large boats. I thought I could use the boats for my business, to pull the logs down the river. They were sturdy and had previously been used for military transportation," explained Vladislav.

"Well, that sounds like a good plan," assured Andrzej. "Who did you buy them from?

"I am so glad you agree, Andrzej, it doesn't make me feel so foolish," said Vladislav. "A friend of mine, Ikner, introduced me to a contact at the Russo-Chinese Bank, which had acquired the boats as compensation for a shipowner's financial debt."

"So what was the problem my friend?" Andrzej questioned.

"The river was not good for floating timber. As you know during the spring the winter ice melts, and during the summer months at the height of the rainy season, the currents go wild. The problem was the flow of water from the mountains resulted in tumultuous torrents that would throw the logs in every direction. The rivers are too shallow, the currents too strong, and the boats too big. The boats couldn't be maneuvered." Vladislav continued, "It was a disaster. The logs were floating everywhere and the boats started capsizing."

"What are you going to do with the eight boats?" asked Andrzej.

"I am in the process now of selling them. The only offer I could get was pathetic. Unfortunately, I'm going to have to take a 200,000 gold rubles[6] (about US$140,000) loss," lamented Vladislav.

"How devastating, but you seem to be handling the loss quite well, Vladislav."

"Actually, not at all. This is a substantial amount, especially now when I am trying to expand. Well Andrzej, all I can say is that this is a good lesson for me, though an expensive learning experience."

Despite the setback, Vladislav quickly moved on, refusing to dwell on failure. He continually involved himself with other ventures, but he had learned from this experience to be more cautious. People who were close to Vladislav agreed that he was never afraid of failure and that is why he was able to comfortably take on new challenges.

In 1902, Vladislav invested in a flour mill, an industry which was expanding rapidly. He, together with his Polish partner Eugeniusz Dynowski developed the first steam-driven mills.[7] The flour mill was built in Sijiazi, located in Fujiadian, an industrial area in Harbin. The millers in Harbin formed an organization called the Society of United Manchurian Mills. They exported flour to the Maritime Province of Siberia, and later also via the South Manchurian Railway (SMR) to Dalian and on to Japan.[8]

Despite the diversions, Vladislav never lost focus of his main business in lumber. He took advantage of the arrangement of the corridor, the 6 li (Chinese mile) cushion on either side, which allowed lumber merchants like him to fell trees, cut logs, and conduct business in these railway corridors. They paid a tax on each tree that was felled.

Vladislav had his eye on a piece of property along the Sungari River where he decided to build a modest house to live and use as an office. He designed the house with a large room in the front, so that he could conduct business comfortably, and a room in the back that would serve as his bedroom. Years later he turned the property and house into a sawmill, being an ideal location for business and transportation.[9]

"Come Andrzej, let me show you my new office and home. It's along the Sungari River. I figured it would be convenient to have the office and accommodations under the same roof."

"You are certainly a work addict, my dear friend. I don't think I have ever met anyone like you. Do you ever get tired?" questioned Andrzej.

"Seldom. The only thing I find frustrating and tiring is dealing with misjudgments. I can't afford to make any more foolish mistakes, but that is over and done with. I must move forward. That's life, my friend, right?"

9 | Xing'an Tunnel

1902–1903

There were opportunities that presented themselves, that catapulted grandfather into prominence. The scope of the challenges was daunting, yet grandfather never hesitated to take them on. Where did he get that kind of courage?

BESIDES THE LUMBER BUSINESS, VLADISLAV WAS RESPONSIBLE FOR several excavation projects, which helped to establish him as an authority on excavation engineering, a skill he had learned over the years. He had the opportunity to work together with talented engineers and a seasoned crew in different fields of business. N. S. Sviiagin, with whom he had worked on the Ussuri line some years earlier, was a good teacher. Sviiagin taught him, not only about the technicalities of engineering and construction, but also about business ethics. He was a brilliant and talented person and Vladislav was grateful for their friendship.

Sviiagin was impressed with Vladislav and respected him, both as an excellent contractor and a friend. As was written in one of the interviews that Vladislav had given, at the end of one of the projects, Sviiagin gave Tikhon Mikhailovich Tikhomirov, the head of all the excavation projects, a recommendation letter full of praise for Vladislav. He highly recommended him for future projects. Tikhomirov was a man who liked to make his own judgments. He

N. S. Sviagin: Assistant to the chief engineer for the construction of the CER, constructor of the eastern section of the railway, and chief of the accounting department[1]

did not know Vladislav well and hence did not take much stock in the recommendation. Sviiagin knew this and arranged a meeting. The first encounter started off awkwardly, but Sviiagin smoothed the way, and quickly the conversation and drinks began to flow. By the time the meeting was over, Tikhomirov offered Vladislav a contract for a railway excavation project between Daimagou and Mulin, which Vladislav readily accepted.

Sometime later while Vladislav was working at one of the sawmills, he was invited to dinner by Sviiagin who wanted to offer him the possibility of working on a unique contract. They dined at Sviiagin's office like old comrades from the Ussuri railway days. After the first course, Sviiagin presented Vladislav with the proposition.

"Vladislav Fyodorovich, there is a section of the Chinese Eastern Railroad construction between Gaolinzi and Shitouhezi that needs special attention. The part requiring this attention is in connection with the Xing'an [Khingan/Ghingan] Tunnel construction, which cuts through a mountain range. Construction of the tunnel is underway, but is taking longer than expected as the rock is so solid that they are having difficulty blasting through and this is delaying the construction.

He continued, "We can see that this is going to take a year or two to complete, if not longer. The entire CER will be delayed. What we need to do is to build a *petlia* [a Russian word meaning "a loop"]. This construction requires an ingenious plan and you are the man for the job," he intently said to Vladislav. "This would be a railroad track laid on the side of a mountain, basically traveling over the mountain. Not only is the construction of this 'miracle project' challenging, but the laying of tracks would require

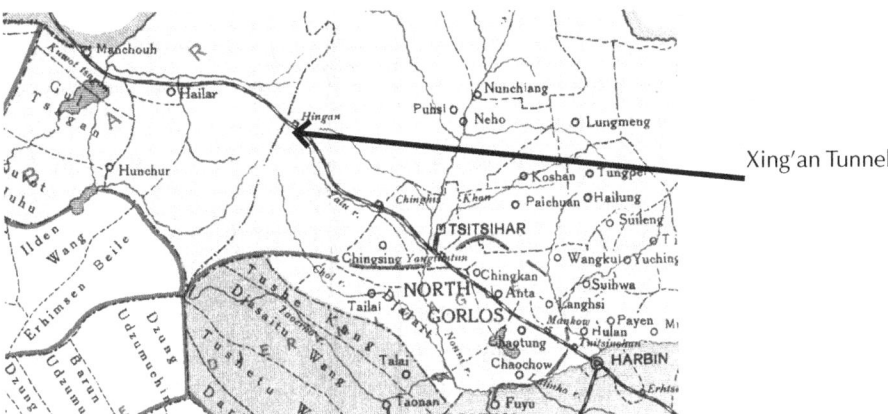

The Xing'an Tunnel cut through the mountain, between the station of Irekte and Bukhedu, with stops at Xing'an Station and Petlia Siding Stop no. 26.[2]

massive dynamite blasts. The rock is like solid steel and that poses the biggest problem."

"Are you suggesting laying the entire line in the mountains?" Vladislav replied, a little stunned.

"Yes, my friend."

"But you're aware that I've only dealt with construction on relatively flat ground?"

"I know that, Vladislav Fyodorovich. But I see in you the potential for greater things, and so I am offering you this chance. It is perhaps the biggest opportunity of your life. You will have Chief Engineer Aleksandr Iosifovich Iugovich, whom you already know, to help with the details. However, you will be responsible for all the excavation and the dynamite blasting as well as for the railway construction. I might add," Sviiagin encouraged Vladislav, "should you complete this feat, it would help you in this line of business, and you will become well known for the accomplishment."

Without a pause he continued, "I don't want you to think it is going to be easy. No," Sviiagin shook his head slowly, "It will be far from it. Furthermore, the conditions of the contract are severe. The construction must be completed during a four-month period, not a day later, as the railway has to open. If completed on time, Vladislav Fyodorovich, you will earn a very comfortable sum; however, if not, you will be fined a huge sum of money for every day over the commissioned period. Not meeting the deadline may bankrupt you. I don't expect you to take the decision lightly."

Vladislav was silent for a few minutes. Sviiagin allowed him time to digest the proposal. Vladislav picked up his glass of vodka, swirling it around as he thought. After what seemed like forever to Sviiagin, Vladislav looked him straight in the eyes.

"You know, my friend, I have never been afraid of confronting even the biggest challenge. I can see that you are putting me to the test." He took a deep breath and said, "I accept the offer."

"Do you need time to think it over? You can give me your answer tomorrow," Sviiagin added.

"I am a man of my word, my dear friend, I accept this challenge." And with that they toasted.

"*Nazdarovia*," as they downed their glasses of vodka.

A few minutes later, Vladislav stood up, finished off a final glass of vodka, shook Sviiagin's hand, and walked to the front door. When he opened the door, a sobering splash of cold night air hit him. "What an unexpected turn of events," he thought as he disappeared into the darkness.

Vladislav went home that evening and sat up all night planning the construction. *Sviiagin will certainly help supply the dynamite for the blasting. I will need to hire a few key workers and make available Chinese laborers who, with their endless energy, will be important for completing the project within the tight deadline. Iugovich was known to be relentless and demanding and will certainly put pressure on me,* thought Vladislav. *It will be a good thing. It will be what I need,* Vladislav convinced himself.

The first candle burned out and without hesitation Vladislav lit the next one, writing, drawing, and scribbling. The excitement was exhilarating. He didn't even notice that the light of day and the glow of the sun already filled the room and the area around the flickering candle. According to Sviiagin's plan, Vladislav would have two months to set everything up and four months to complete the job.

"How difficult can this really be?" he asked himself out loud. He thought for a moment, with apprehension, about his hasty decision, and wondered if he was truly in his right mind to have committed to taking on the challenge. Thinking back on this question years later, he was glad he didn't dwell on the trepidation, as this would certainly have stopped the project before it even started.

Vladislav had a large group of professionals and workers to draw on when needed. There were cutters, engineers, blasters, builders, and hardworking Chinese laborers who he could depend on. Vladislav stepped up the pace by scheduling men to work twenty-four-hour shifts to work full speed on the petlia.[3] It was here that Vladislav felt the true loyalty of the workers.

Picture of the Petlia and Xing'an Tunnel in 1903[4]

With the endless hours, the grueling job, and the incredible challenges, the workers never wavered. His bond with the Chinese became even stronger, and with this project he came to admire and respect the Chinese character even more. It was a mutual respect that remained throughout his life.[6]

Eastern mouth of the Xing'an Tunnel[5]

Vladislav was working hard and rarely ate. He lost much weight and became a skeleton, but he was determined to finish what he set out to do. With his fortitude, he not only earned respect but gained tremendous experience. He hardly slept during the project and was present every minute of the day and night to make sure things moved along. As for the Chinese, Polish, and Russian teams under him, their attitude and demeanor also changed as successes and milestones were reached, for through their "never quit" mind-set they had gained total confidence in themselves. They were achieving what many said was impossible and they knew it. So did Vladislav.

The job as a contractor for the petlia was the first big, single project that Vladislav took on in Manchuria. The loop-like railroad project would be a temporary solution for the CER line. The railroad would be constructed around the perimeter of the mountain, sometimes having to meander up the side of the mountain in a back and forth movement. The tracks would be laid along the side of the mountain, built at a slightly slanting angle. After the completion of the petlia, the CER line could be opened for operation and the Xing'an Tunnel located under the petlia could continue to be constructed without any urgency.

With great difficulty, the petlia was completed in the allotted four months, to the day. The jubilation was well deserved. Dignitaries came to celebrate the crowning moment and everyone hugged incessantly and gave each other the traditional three kisses on either cheek. Vladislav modestly gave the credit to his Chinese workers and team. The completion of the project was due to a magical mixture of fear, determination, and the ability to listen.

The Trans-Siberian, along the CER route, was almost completed except for the Xing'an Tunnel, but the petlia solved that problem. The construction of the Xing'an Tunnel under the petlia was started in 1899 under the guidance of engineer Nikolai Nikolaevich Bocharov and was a feat that involved Russian and Polish engineers and an Italian drilling team.[7] The tunnel itself was two miles long. The project was led by a team of engineers among them Leon Skidelsky, a Polish-Jewish engineer who soon became one of Vladislav's best friends.[8]

Vladislav received a lot of credit for this epochal feat and the achievement is documented in the history of the construction of the CER.

Xing'an Tunnel during construction[9]

10 | A Trip to Kozuchow

1902–1903

It was when grandfather began reaching out to others for help in his business that his life became complicated. He was a trusting man. He had an honest work ethic and he expected that of others. He was a little naive and was not always a good judge of character, or perhaps it was just the circumstances that changed those around him.

EVEN THOUGH HIS BUSINESS WAS GOING WELL, VLADISLAV UNDERSTOOD that it would be necessary to hire an engineer for his company in order to expand his business. He needed someone skilled he could trust implicitly in all aspects of his work and decided to start interviewing candidates immediately. A good salary would be offered for the job, allowing him to look for applicants with an engineering background and a proven track record of success. Vladislav set off in his search.

Before the CER officially opened, Vladislav traveled on the completed railway to make a trip back to his hometown of Kozuchow. The journey gave him the opportunity to experience the ride on the CER from Harbin along the petlia route and onto the Trans-Siberian Railway. It was an exhilarating experience. The trip over the mountain was the most memorable portion, made even more meaningful as he looked out the window recalling every inch of hardship that was endured. What an incredible accomplishment. He had a hard time imagining that this all started for him over a dinner of chicken cutlets and kasha.

Vladislav planned a visit to his family in Kozuchow to see if they could reach out to any of their contacts to suggest someone suitable as an engineer for his company. He took this opportunity because it gave him a chance to see his family again and to tell them about his adventures. He knew that they were worried about his life so far away; hearing the stories about conflicts and the Boxer Rebellion had no doubt been unsettling.

Returning to his village was emotional for Vladislav. He missed his parents, his brothers, and his sisters and talking to them every day. They were a close-knit family and it seemed so natural to be together once again. Life was different in the Far East and he longed to be part of the family again and enjoyed the Polish way of life. It was hard to believe that things had changed so much for him in such a short period of time. It was wonderful to be home.

The women of the house prepared the usual feast.

"You remembered all my favorite dishes, I have missed your cooking so much," Vladislav said as he gave his mother a big hug.

"I have to find a way into your heart. Perhaps you will come home more often to have a good home-cooked meal. Here is your favorite *baranina* [grilled mutton], just the way you like it. *Golabki* [cabbage rolls with meat, mushrooms, and rice], *kapusta zasmazana* [sauerkraut], it's all here my dear son, and you must leave room for your favorite dessert."

"Please tell me you made *sernik* [cheesecake]," Vladislav clasped his hands together anticipating the acknowledgment.

"Of course! I miss cooking for you. I notice that you have lost considerable weight, and I worry about you, Vladislav. You must take care of yourself."

"Dear mother, I am fine, you always worry too much. I am as strong as a horse. Remember, I am a Kowalski."

"You certainly are, my son."

After dinner the men gathered around to talk about the business and hear all the incredible stories of life in the Far East and the progress he had made. The two days that he spent at home went by so quickly. He wanted to stay longer, but knew he had to continue to St. Petersburg to finish his search.

Family and friends gathered to hear about his Far East adventures. Vladislav is at the back left of the picture on the left.

He traveled to St. Petersburg the next morning and spent some time scouting companies looking for a responsible and talented engineer. He finally found the man he was looking for after many interviews and introductions. His top choice was a brilliant Russian engineer named Alexander Alexandrovich Zaharoff. Vladislav met his friend, Dimitri Leonidovich (Horvath), who was planning to leave St. Petersburg in April 1903 for his new post in Manchuria as head of the CER. He asked him about Zaharoff. Horvath didn't know him personally but had heard that he was highly thought of, not only by his bosses but also by the Russian government.

Alexander was an outstanding construction engineer, who graduated top of his class with a gold medal (*s zolotoi meadaliou*) from a university in Russia. Immediately after he had graduated he had been offered a position at the prestigious Trans-Siberian Railroad Headquarters in St. Petersburg. Since the Trans-Siberian Railroad project was now almost complete, he knew that talented people like Zaharoff would be looking for new positions.

Vladislav met with Zaharoff and his wife, Sophie. After a few dinners, he offered the engineer the number two position in his company at a salary three times that of his current salary at the Trans-Siberian administration office.

Instead of accepting immediately, as Vladislav expected, Zaharoff sat quietly looking at his drink. "I've lived in St. Petersburg for some time and like it here. All our friends and family live in Russia." He raised his eyes to meet his wife's. While Vladislav wasn't looking, she winked quickly at him and lowered hers.

Vladislav asked, "Alexander Alexandrovich, tell me frankly, is there a problem with my offer?"

"No, I thank you for your offer, it has nothing to do with you or your company. Friends in the tsar's intelligence service tell me you are very successful and that your company is expanding and growing rapidly," assured Alexander.

"I have a very secure job in St Petersburg," he continued. "Sophie and I are content with our lives here, and the thought of going off to the Far East, where we don't speak the language and don't understand the people or the culture, makes this a difficult decision. I don't know how you did it, and I am reluctant to make the same choice," Alexander explained.

"I understand your hesitation, but you will be quite surprised when you come to Harbin. It is a combination of Chinese and different nationalities, each respecting one another and helping each other. It is a very unusual setting," reassured Vladislav.

"I am worried about Sophie; how will she adjust? She has no friends or family there. How will she manage during the day when I am away at work?"

"I assure you as a Russian-speaking resident she will adjust without any difficulty," interjected Vladislav.

"What about the politics? Isn't it an unsettling situation?" asked Alexander.

"Alexander Alexandrovich, I do not concern myself with the politics. Frankly, I am so busy with the business that it consumes every minute of my day," explained Vladislav. "I need a commitment from whoever takes this position to be devoted to the business and to all the circumstance that come with it."

Alexander then surprised Vladislav again.

"I can accept on one condition, Vladislav Fyodorovich," Alexander said.

"Name it."

"That Sophie and I will be allowed to travel for three months first class by boat, stopping at choice locations on our way to Harbin, all expenses paid."

Vladislav thought for a moment. He'd hoped that Alexander could start immediately but three months was not that long a delay. "All right, Alexander Alexandrovich. I accept."

"Oh, and one more thing. My salary will begin the first day of my trip and an advance against my salary for expenses will be paid immediately."

Vladislav considered that a step too far. This man had a bit of rug merchant in him he thought, and said, "I can agree to half pay for the time you are away and should you exceed the three months for any reason, no pay at all. I think this is fair."

Sophie was nodding her head and Alexander agreed. They shook hands and the agreement was confirmed.

That night, Vladislav arranged for money to be sent and later made the preparations for Alexander and Sophie's trip. Vladislav was sure he would work out well.

His new employee's political concerns about Manchuria were perhaps not entirely unfounded, he had to admit. After all, Manchuria had been subjected to a substantial Russian military presence since 1901. Russia, though, was never in a situation to formally annex the area. The strong Russian influence in the area met opposition, from the Chinese and especially from the Japanese who had their own ambitions. The CER project would add to their concern. Clouds of tension, political shifts, and looming conflicts were already forming as Japan became more assertive.

11 | Alexander Alexandrovich Arrives

1903

Years later the question was, how differently would life have been for grandfather if Zaharoff had refused to move to the Far East, and instead he had picked someone else for the job. It is interesting how one decision can have such a large impact on the direction life takes.

Alexander and his wife Sophie arrived in Harbin on a sunny, somewhat cool day in May 1903 from Vladivostok, where their ship had docked on arrival from Japan. Tokyo had been their last stop on the tour from St. Petersburg to the Far East. Their arrival had been delayed, so instead of the planned three months of travel, four months had passed since Vladislav had agreed to Alexander's terms in St. Petersburg. He'd also paid an advance salary while the Russian engineer and his wife toured in luxury, but he decided not to make this an issue because he was eager to use Alexander's talents in his rapidly expanding business.

Alexander came from a large family of four sisters and one brother. Two of his sisters and his brother died at a young age. His two sisters, Helena Alexandrovna and Barbara Alexandrovna, lived in Tsarskoe Selo together with their mother, Tatiana Denisovna.

Both Alexander and Sophie were very cheerful on their way from the train station and regaled Vladislav with stories of their adventures in Cairo at the pyramids, a safari in Africa, the rich cities of India, and the wonderful temples of Bangkok. Surprisingly, Japan had impressed them the most.

"The people in Japan were so polite and well organized," Sophie said. "Tokyo was different and exotic."

"Yes, it had truly been a wonderful trip," Alexander agreed. "Japan was the highlight of our trip."

Alexander Efrimovich Zaharoff (Father)

Tatiana Denisovna Zaharoff (Mother)

Top, left to right: Liudmila, Ekaterina, Alexander, and Helena; bottom, left to right: Konstantine (died as a child) and Barbara

Stolen Dreams

Helena

Barbara

Liudmila (died young)

Ekaterina (died young)

Alexander

Alexander's wife Sophie

Despite their enthusiasm about their travels, as they toured the city of Harbin their demeanor suddenly turned critical.

"It's so dark here," Sophie exclaimed.

"We're a work in progress," Vladislav replied. "We're going to make this into a spectacular place all will admire."

"I'm sure," Alexander chimed in without great enthusiasm. Surveying the darkened primitive houses and dirty streets, he added, "It's going to take some effort."

During his first weeks, Alexander complained about the rough conditions in which he was forced to work, but he gradually adapted. His wife also began to meet and socialize with others in the foreign community in Harbin. To Vladislav it appeared they were settling in nicely.

He invited them to dinner often and continued to get to know them better. At one of these dinners Sophie turned to him and said frankly, "You look much younger than your age, Vladislav Fyodorovich. Alexander tells me that you're thirty-four years old. Could that really be true?"

"Yes," Vladislav said laughing. "Middle-aged and I sometimes feel much older."

"But haven't you ever thought of a wife and of starting a family?"

"I've been much too busy with my business. Besides, there are very few single women of marriageable age here in Harbin."

"Well, now that Alexander is here, you'll have more free time, don't you think?"

"I certainly hope so, but—"

"You know," Sophie interrupted, "Alexander's mother, Tatiana Denisovna, was a great beauty in her day. It is said she had over thirteen proposals of marriage. After the marriage, they had six children, three died."

"I see," said Vladislav, wondering where this conversation was going.

"After all the children were born, Tatiana's husband disappeared. He left, saying he was going to Kronshtadt and never came back. They never heard from him again."

"It was rumored," Alexander coughed, "that robbers attacked his coach on the way and that he was killed."

"There was never any proof," Sophie countered. "I think the man was irresponsible."

"So, what did she do?" Vladislav asked.

"Tatiana raised all those children alone without any help. She never married again even though she could have," Sophie said firmly.

"Quite a woman," Vladislav offered.

"She certainly is," Sophie agreed. "Her daughters are very beautiful, though somewhat independent of mind since they were raised to be so."

Vladislav said, "I've always thought an independent woman has more integrity."

"Yes, and would make a better partner," Alexander suggested.

"It turns out," Sophie continued, "that two of Alexander's younger sisters are, as yet, unmarried and live in Tsarskoe Selo."

"And how old are they?" Vladislav asked carefully so not to show his growing interest.

"Helena Alexandrovna is almost twenty-one years old. She's an extremely attractive woman and very pure if I may say so."

Alexander nodded.

"Her sister Barbara Alexandrovna is a few years younger."

"You know," Alexander said scratching his chin, "it occurred to me that we should invite them here once we've settled in. The change would do them good, don't you think, Sophie?"

"An excellent idea, darling. Travel is educational, particularly for the young."

"And I'd welcome them," Vladislav said.

"It's settled then," Alexander lifted his glass. "A toast to the future."

They all touched glasses and drank. Then Vladislav said, "You will decide the timing and give me advance notice so that we can prepare an appropriate reception party."

"That would be wonderful." Sophie glowed. "I'm sure they'll love to come. At first glance Harbin seems rather…underdeveloped, but there is much building going on and people here are ambitious. It really is a 'boom town' like the Wild West you hear about in America."

"Yes," Vladislav said. "Our own Wild West is right here."

Several days later Alexander and Vladislav were having lunch at one of the new restaurants in town, Alexander leaned over his plate and said, "I hope you don't think Sophie was too forward in suggesting matters of a personal nature the other night."

"Not at all," Vladislav replied. "To be honest, I haven't given marriage much thought. Perhaps it's time I should."

"Most certainly," Alexander agreed. "There's a growing foreign community here, and I notice Sophie is making many connections with some of the businessmen's wives. A wife can be very helpful socially and indirectly in business connections."

"You're probably right, Alexander Alexandrovich, but I've been so busy with my work that I have not had time for such matters."

"Listen," Alexander lowered his voice. "Marriage doesn't have to be thought about too seriously. It's the appearance that's important. I am sure that married life would be a very positive step for you at this time in your life."

"But shouldn't marriage be based on love?"

Alexander chuckled, "Rarely, my friend. Rarely. In our social circles back in Moscow, many marriages are arranged, and in Japan I've discovered it's much the same. Marriages are arranged by parents, not participants. It makes a great deal of sense, don't you think, and works very well too."

"How about you and Sophie? How did your marriage come about?"

"Our story is quite the exception. I will be very honest with you, and I hope you don't judge us for this. Sophie was married by arrangement to Dr. Olshansky before we met in Moscow. She was a Russian Jew and her husband was a very successful doctor. While she was married, Sophie and I met and eventually had an affair, which we didn't take too seriously at first, but gradually we came to appreciate one another's character. Finally, she decided to divorce her husband and enter the Russian Orthodox Church where we were married. It's been a very happy marriage, I must say. But, this probably is the exception, not the rule, Vladislav Fyodorovich. To find true love is as difficult as finding the rarest jewel. One could waste one's whole life waiting for the perfect mate. And you're nearly thirty-five years old."

"True, I promise I will give it some thought," Vladislav said with a smile.

12 | The Railway Opening

1903

Grandfather remembered well that summer day when the CER was finally completed and the opening was scheduled. It was, in a way, highlighting his personal accomplishment as he was there and had contributed and participated in his own small way. Because of the delays and other circumstances, it was not celebrated on a grand scale, and the full operation just officially began.

THE CER WAS ALREADY OPERATIONAL IN NOVEMBER 1901, BUT ONLY partially as the Xing'an Tunnel was still under construction. The official opening of the completed CER for traffic was on July 24, 1903. The opening ceremony was not festive and was a low-key event. In attendance was General Dimitri Horvath, now the head of the CER and the Russian Railway Zone, who played a major part in overseeing the entire CER construction. The CER line, which ran through the northern territory of China was an important transport artery that would change the lives of millions of people. Russia had financed almost the whole amount and finished the project with few delays, despite the costly Boxer Rebellion disruptions.

Together with many friends who had been involved, Vladislav was proud that the years of toil, sweat, challenges, and dedication paid off. It had taken close to five years to construct the CER as well as provide equipment for its use. The length of the CER was 1,600 miles spanning from Manzhouli to Pogranichnaia and from Harbin to Port Arthur.[1] It had been an enormous endeavor in every aspect, further complicated by the fact that this area did not have available topographical maps. There were 624 bridges that had to be secured and built and four tunnels.[2] The Xing'an Tunnel alone was two miles long. It was estimated that between 60,000 to 200,000 Chinese laborers were employed for the construction.[3] In the end, the cost to build the CER was around US$300 million, which included the amount paid for the damages resulting from the Boxer Rebellion.[4]

An inauguration ceremony in August 1897 in the city of Sanchakou on the Sino-Russian border
Image by Eric Yang Soong.[5]

Manual labor for the construction of the railway was secured mainly from China and Russia. Laborers traveled and walked for miles to reach these remote areas of construction. When the CER project was at its peak, it employed around 130,000 laborers.[6] Because the CER line did not traverse any large cities, but cut through unpopulated lands, everything needed to be transported into the area. Much of the material and equipment, railway wagons, passenger and freight wagons, food, and products were brought in from Russia, and many of the locomotives were brought in from the United States.

The project was not limited to building the railway tracks but also extended to building towns along the tracks. This construction included houses for the workers and their families, in which Vladislav was sometimes involved, banks, shops, schools, hospitals, and telephone and telegraph lines. It was a massive undertaking.

With the completion of the CER, the travel times to and from the Far East were greatly improved. For example, between Vladivostok and Chita via Harbin would now take only 67 hours or close to three days.[7] An International Sleeping Car Company was formed that would now be in charge of the sales of the assigned seats and sleepers.[8] There were four classes to accommodate everyone.

The super luxurious class was reserved for use by special dignitaries. The next class was the VIP first-class car, offering great comfort, of which there was usually only one or two wagons. This class was designed to make the customers feel like they were in their own living rooms. The sleepers were cushioned with lovely down blankets and pillows, and the attendants made sure that all the comforts were offered and that everything was taken care of. The train ride was a memorable experience and a time to relax, read, and enjoy. The restaurant wagon offered full-course meals and proper seating. It was a place to socialize and indulge in the luxuries of the trip. The second-class wagons offered no luxuries. The third-class wagons were very basic with bench-style seats, with no comforts at all. These wagons were not heated and often made the long-distance travel quite challenging. There were usually five or six third-class wagons.

The cost advantage of traveling by rail was significant, especially for the lower- and middle-class wagons. The Harbin to Moscow route cost $118 for first class, $93 for second class, and $52 for third class, and the Harbin to Paris route cost $175 for first class, $142 for second class and $90 for third class.[9] In contrast, a London to Shanghai first-class ticket by sea cost between $567–$599 traveling through the Suez and taking thirty-six to forty-two days.[10] This difference in cost meant that more people from Europe could travel easily to the Far East.

The trains would stop at stations for 15 or 20 minutes along the way to allow the passengers to walk around the platform and enjoy some fresh air. At the stations, Russian ladies would sell tea, *pirozhki* (meat pies), and other Russian delicacies.

The new railway's freight possibilities, which opened with the CER, were especially important for Vladislav's business. The CER connected freight transport to Vladivostok in Russia along the northern route and to Dalian along the southern route, suitable for transporting goods to and from China and Japan. The railway assured faster and safer transportation of products, allowing for easy export and import to and from other countries. Vladislav suddenly had the opportunity to buy and import from all over the world modern equipment and machinery for his company and had access to many new buyers. Harbin, a previously isolated city in Northern China, had become accessible. Even Paris fashion reached Harbin sooner than it did Shanghai.

The atmosphere in the city of Harbin was electrifying the day the CER was officially opened.

The streets were filled with excited families and children. There were celebrations everywhere, and almost everyone participated in the festivities. This endeavor was something that all the citizens had contributed to, whether in the actual construction or in the restaurants and stores that provided food and products. The occasion brought people together and everyone deserved to celebrate the accomplishment. It was the end of one chapter in the story of achievements for the region and the beginning of a new one.

Vladislav enjoyed the celebration together with his coworkers, arranging for food and drink to be delivered to his office. Although Alexander and Sophie had arrived only three months earlier, Vladislav ensured that they participated and helped. Alexander not only joined the festivities but was tasked with reaching out to the employees to encourage them to come. Vladislav asked Sophie to help with the arrangement of food and to play the role as a "hostess" to the office staff. He was happy to see that she was feeling more comfortable, and her outgoing personality was certainly an asset. Alexander, on the other hand, had a typical engineer's personality, very strict, rigid, and dry, and the event put his social skills to the test. Although both Sophie and Alexander were not witnesses to the development of the railway line, they appreciated the great milestone that had been reached. There were many functions that Vladislav was obliged to attend that day, but he made sure that his employees understood his gratitude for their hard work and contribution. It was a miraculous day to be enjoyed by everyone.

Dining car[12]

By 1903, 536 locomotives and 11,509 passenger wagons were made available for the railway.[11] The cargo volume increased in coming years, making the railway a vital supplier of goods and materials.

Drawing room[13]

The building of the CER railway through Manchuria was a remarkable feat that opened endless possibilities. The enormous investment did not reap profits immediately, and during the first three and a half years the CER suffered substantial losses for Russia. As stated in the contract, Russia was locked in to administer and

Stolen Dreams

run the railway line and only after thirty-six years would China be allowed to purchase the CER.[15] One thing was for sure, the CER now made Harbin one of the most desirable locations not only for the Chinese, but for everyone, with a more convenient access between countries and continents.

The luxury wagon pictured from the outside.[14]

13 | Russo-Japanese War

> 1904
>
> *It was hard to imagine that since grandfather had arrived in the Far East in 1896, he had and would experience the effects of several wars and disturbances, at least indirectly—the Sino-Japanese War, the Boxer Rebellion, and now in 1904, the Russo-Japanese War. With each conflict, the dynamics in the region changed.*

JAPAN HAD NEVER OVERCOME ITS LOSS IN 1895 OF THE LIAODONG Peninsula, causing it to condemn Russian expansion and influence in northern China. During the 1903 diplomatic discussions between Russia and Japan, Japan required Russia's recognition of its authority in Korea, and in return would approve Russia's influence in Manchuria. The Japanese considered Russia an obstacle in their ambition to expand their dominance in China, and would focus its imperialism on Korea.

At the end of 1903, a tense atmosphere reigned in Harbin and the population feared that war could be imminent. In January 1904, the civilian Japanese residents started to leave the city in great numbers, after Russia rejected the Japanese plan to divide Manchuria and Korea into spheres of influence. The Japanese broke off the discussions with Russia, eventually leading to the start of the Russo-Japanese War. This war was about the control of Manchuria and Korea. Both countries eyed this region for its economic wealth and strategic location. Even though the war was fought on Korean and Chinese territory, China declared neutrality in the conflict.

The Russo-Japanese War started when Japan launched a surprise attack against the Russian naval base at Port Arthur on February 8, 1904. Since establishing a Russian naval presence in Port Arthur in 1898, the Russians had made a great effort in building and strengthening their fleet. Yet when the main armada of Japan's warships launched their attack, the Russians were completely unprepared, and by no means ready for war. The Japanese were notorious for employing a strategy of surprise attacks and never declared war until after the siege was over. They used this strategy at Port Arthur, immediately disabling two of the best Russian battleships and five cruisers.[1] Using mines they also sank the battleship *Petroparlovsk*, killing the much loved and respected commander, Admiral Makarov, who went down with the ship.[2]

Initially the Russo-Japanese War, 1904–1905, was popular and the subject of much conversation at gatherings in the Harbin foreign community. However, once the Japanese started to gradually take over the hills surrounding Port Arthur, attitudes changed. For the Harbin Russians, the unthinkable was happening; Russia was losing ground. The Japanese soldiers had better artillery and discipline and were overpowering the Russians. The heroic devotion of the nationalistic Japanese soldiers, who were fighting for the honor of the Japanese emperor, became legendary.

During the war, the Russian military reinforcements from Europe and the almost 5,900-mile (9,000-kilometer) journey on the Trans-Siberian Railway and CER became an important lifeline to reach the areas of military conflict and engagement. Unfinished railway work around Lake Baikal made the journey challenging because soldiers had to take a ferry across the lake in limited capacity. The real burden fell on General Horvath's shoulders as he, in his position as manager of the CER line and administrator of its territory, was responsible for the movement and protection of troops and military supplies.[3] The CER became one of the chief arteries for the transportation of military supplies and soldiers to the front.

After the attack on Port Arthur, Japan brought more troops to the Liaodong Peninsula and pushed northward. The Japanese overpowered the Russians in every battle, with staggering losses on both sides. On the Russian side, 6,000 soldiers died at Port Arthur and 89,000 died in the Mukden Battle, and the Japanese lost a total of 71,000 soldiers in the conflicts.[4] At the naval Battle of Tsushima, the Russian navy was completely wiped out. As the Russians retreated, the CER's southern branch fell into the hands of the Japanese, including the splendidly equipped Port Arthur and Dalian. All the Russian construction on the southern rail line was lost to the Japanese.

The outbreak of the Russo-Japanese War saw a dramatic surge in the economy in Harbin. Food for the Russian soldiers was manufactured in Harbin, restaurants catered to the growing population, and soldiers had to be looked after and accommodated. The Russian population increased from 100,000 to 250,000.[5] Businessmen arrived from Russia to cash in on the opportunities that became available, and more Chinese businessmen appeared. Hotel and restaurant prices rose steeply and a room in a Harbin hotel cost an unprecedented five rubles a day.[6]

One of the most popular restaurants in town was called Mars, located in Pristan. It was a coffee shop/restaurant with a very friendly social feel to it. It was constructed on different levels to accommodate many customers, and the tiered seating made it possible to enjoy meals in a pleasant atmosphere. The menu included borsch (beet soup) and pirozhki, a favorite of all the Russians and Poles. Before or after every function, Mars was the place to gather for a hot bowl of *pelmeni* (meat dumplings in hot soup) or for a cup of tea with a delicious pastry. At Mars there was a table that became a regular meeting place for a small group of Russian and Polish businessmen, which included Vladislav, who gathered every Monday at seven in the evening to discuss politics, local events, and updated news from their homelands.

"Good evening Vladislav Fyodorovich, have a seat. I just ordered some pirozhki, *zakuski*, *seledka* [herring], and *kartoshka* [potatoes]," offered Misha.

"Sounds wonderful, and the vodka?" Vladislav reminded him.

"Of course, it's on its way. Dimitri Ivanovich and Ignacy will be joining us. They said they would be a little late."

"How's your tobacco business, Mikhail Sergevich?" asked Vladislav.

"It's not a pleasant thing to say, but the war has really helped business. I have never seen so many soldiers here in Harbin." Misha was a part owner in a large tobacco company. "What about you?" Misha asked Vladislav.

"It is just so painful to hear of the Russian losses. It's hard to imagine that the Russian Baltic fleet that traveled halfway around the world was almost completely destroyed by the Japanese in the Tsushima Strait in just two days. Two thirds of the fleet was sunk and six ships were captured by the Japanese. Of the thirty-eight ships that entered the Strait only four made it through; thirty-four were sunk, immobilized, or captured; and the Russian casualties numbered 4,830 dead and 5,917 captured, which is shocking compared to Japanese casualties of only 110 dead in that particular battle,"[7] explained Vladislav.

"I didn't know all the details, but I understood that the Japanese army and navy overpowered the Russians. It is all very sad to see so many officers and young soldiers killed," said Misha as he took a big swig of the cold, strong vodka. "How could this be happening?"

"At least with this last battle, the war is over. It will be difficult for Russia to recover. The Japanese strength, dominance and influence in the region will be devastating for the Russians and for our situation in Manchuria," Vladislav added solemnly.

"I definitely agree with you Vladislav Fyodorovich. Why don't we start eating, Dimitri Ivanovich and Ignacy should be here soon."

Three months after the fighting ceased the Treaty of Portsmouth was signed, officially ending the nineteen-month Russo-Japanese War. As a result of the treaty, Japan advanced on the Chinese Liaodong Peninsula, received the southern railway line and all its branches between Changchun and Port Arthur, which they named the South Manchurian Railway (SMR). They gained influence and control of the Liaodong Railway Zone including Port Arthur and Dalian and strengthened their grip on Korea. The Japanese also acquired the southern part of Sakhalin Island. (See map on page ix.) It was further decided that like the Russians, the Japanese could now post fifteen guards at every kilometer mark along the railroads they controlled.[8] The treaty was signed carving up Chinese territories, yet China was not a participant in the war or in the peace conference. Japan did not win any indemnity with the Portsmouth Treaty, although they argued they needed it to rebuild their military. The Japanese victories in China impressed the United States and Europe and, in the worldview, had established Japan as a major military power.

After the war the Chinese government regained much of its authority in the "Three Northeast Provinces," that is, Manchuria. The Russian sphere of influence in the Russian Railway Zone in Manchuria—from Manzhouli via Harbin to Pogranichnaia and the railway on to Vladivostok, would remain like before under the management of the CER with Horvath as its general manager. This was a relief to Vladislav and the business community in Harbin. For Vladislav it meant that it would be possible to continue "business as usual" with his developments in Harbin and along the CER, in spite of the upsetting Russian losses and outcome in the war.

For the Russians, the mounting defeats were devastating. The demoralized troops were returning from the front lines and the Russian soldiers became unruly, causing crime to increase and street brawls to be a common thing. Dissatisfaction spread among the Russian people, and the effects of the cost and suffering created by the war was evident. Tsar Nicholas II was criticized for the bad outcome. As a consequence, in Russia the Russian Revolution of 1905 began on January 9 with a peaceful protest of 150,000 people led by a Russian Orthodox priest, Father Gapon.[9] They were protesting the terrible living conditions, the rise in food prices, and difficulties in their daily lives, and they demanded political and democratic reforms. The peaceful protest was organized to get the attention of Tsar Nicholas II, but turned ugly when troops opened fire on the unarmed demonstrators, killing about two hundred people and wounding many more.[10] This tragedy was called "Bloody Sunday," and it quickly changed people's attitude toward the tsar, who was rapidly losing respect and support from his subjects. As the news spread all over Russia, violence broke out, assassinations occurred, strikes took place, and the country was paralyzed. In the years between 1906 and 1910, 3,741 Russians were executed and thousands were sent into exile for political crimes.[11]

The tsar managed to restore some law and order with the help of the Russian troops that returned from the Russo-Japanese War and by promising a constitutional experiment with a democratically elected parliament, which helped to quell the growing unrest.[12] For the moment, everything seemed to be under control, but this would prove to be the beginning of the end for the monarchy in Russia. Manchuria and Harbin were affected by the events as waves of new Russian settlers descended on the region, trying to escape the turmoil back home.

Alexander and Sophie had arrived in Harbin the year before the outbreak of war, and were horrified to be so close to the crossfire.

"I knew this is what would happen. How could I have been so stupid to have been talked into coming here," complained Alexander to Sophie, implying that Vladislav was to blame.

Sophie answered in defense of Vladislav, "Alexander, have you heard what is going on in our country? I cannot understand everything, but there are killings, violent opposition to the tsar, strikes, and murders. Troops have been stationed everywhere in St. Petersburg and Moscow. A revolution seems to be brewing. It's a total mess."

"Perhaps you are right, but we should keep these feelings to ourselves. It is better if Vladislav Fyodorovich continues to feel I have done him a great favor by taking this position," explained Alexander.

"Don't worry, of course I won't say a word," Sophie assured him. "Do you think it is safe for Helena Alexandrovna and Barbara Alexandrovna to come to Harbin?" asked Sophie, clearly concerned.

"I am sure if it was dangerous, Vladislav Fyodorovich would have mentioned something, don't you think? The CER is running at full speed and there are many soldiers that are being transported back and forth. It will be safe," reassured Alexander.

The Russian defeat in the Russo-Japanese War received worldwide attention as a European nation had never before lost a war to an Asian country. The Japanese gained much notice with this important military victory. The Japanese were delirious with pride, gained great self-confidence and a sense of superiority, and their military victory boosted their morale and catapulted them into an era of ruthless expansionism.

14 | Helena Alexandrovna

1905

Alexander's two sisters were brave to make the journey during the Russo-Japanese War. It was an adventurous trip, especially for two young women.

HELENA ALEXANDROVNA AND BARBARA ALEXANDROVNA ARRIVED IN early March 1905, during the height of fighting in the Russo-Japanese War. The effects of the turmoil were evident in both Russia and in Harbin, with the transportation of soldiers along the CER and the devastating number of Russian casualties. The developments were troubling and the enormous troop presence in Harbin affected the lives of everyone living there. Despite the turmoil, instability, chaos, and confusion, Barbara and Helena still made the trip to visit their brother in Harbin.

It was a nice sunny day when Alexander's sisters arrived in Harbin. The cold north wind from Siberia was tempered by a clear sky and bright sun. Vladislav felt it was a good omen as he and Sophie went to meet them at the train station and brought them by horse-drawn carriage to the Zaharoff's comfortable house. The sisters were a long way from the civilized world of Tsarskoe Selo (the tsar's village), where they had grown up within sight of the royal family's holiday home on the outskirts of St. Petersburg.

Vladislav was immediately taken by Helena's porcelain skin and deep dark eyes. There was something mysterious about her, a characteristic of being distant. The few words she spoke to him seemed to hold a challenge, and he was intrigued. Barbara was attractive as well, but did not possess the same depth, Vladislav decided. That evening they had planned to welcome the sisters with a special dinner. Barbara was not feeling well from the trip and decided not to join them, and Alexander was working late, so it was just Vladislav, Sophie, and Helena.

Barbara Alexandrovna and Helena Alexandrovna arriving in Harbin

"So, you have been here in China for some years, Vladislav Fyodorovich." Her voice was husky but not from the trip. It had the indelible effect of wanting to hear more.

"I have lived in the region for over twelve years," Vladislav replied. *What a pleasant surprise*, he thought to himself. He could make time for this woman. There certainly wasn't another like her in this part of the world.

"And you plan to stay here?" she asked.

"Forever," Vladislav said, since that was the truth and the sooner she knew it, the better. Anyone he chose to wed must agree that their home would be here in Harbin. That was not negotiable.

"The people here are quite kind, Sophie tells me."

"Most certainly," Vladislav agreed. "Many have come from Russia and Poland to escape the turmoil and to benefit from the opportunities."

"I am sure you have heard about the events of Bloody Sunday that took place a short time ago," interjected Helena. "It was very frightening, and the situation has deteriorated quite rapidly since then."

"I did and was happy to hear that you and your family were far from the trouble," Vladislav replied.

"On a better note, I understand that there is a lively social life here in Harbin." Helena changed the subject. "Of which you usually don't partake, as I have heard your work keeps you very busy." Her laughter had a crystalline quality.

"Alexander Alexandrovich is helping to solve my scheduling problems," Vladislav countered. "I will admit, I do enjoy a good party."

"I'm very glad to hear that," Helena replied.

"How long do you plan to stay?" Vladislav asked.

"That will depend," she replied evasively, her husky voice full of innuendos.

That night Vladislav didn't sleep well. His mind kept thinking about Helena's dark, mysterious gaze. What secrets were behind those eyes, he wondered. There was something about her that drew him in, and he found this very alluring, yet could he live with such a complex woman? The question still perplexed him as dawn approached. That afternoon he called Alexander to his office and told him he found Helena most attractive and charming. Perhaps he should call Sophie and arrange a date.

"I wouldn't rush her, Vladislav Fyodorovich," Alexander said. "Take your time, and give her time to get to know you. She is one who does not love easily. I'm sure everything will work out."

"Are you saying she's not attracted to me?"

"No, no, not at all. It's just that she's been on a long trip and needs to get herself together. In fact, she told Sophie she finds you quite interesting."

"Well that is certainly encouraging," said Vladislav and he left it at that.

Vladislav and Helena were engaged within two months of that first meeting. The entire city was talking about her. She was a mysterious woman with an elegant style and makeup that fit in better with the fashions of Paris than

Helena Alexandrovna

Vladislav Fyodorovich

those of Harbin. Vladislav was enthralled, and still had not been able to decipher the messages in her dark eyes.

"One day I'll build a beautiful house for you, Helena Alexandrovna," he told her after the engagement party. "Better than anything else in Harbin."

For the first time he saw a flicker of warmth in her eyes. As if a door had been opened, then quickly shut.

The women made all the arrangements for the wedding and the celebration. The reception was held in a social hall often used for such occasions, and the wedding was held in 1906* in the Russian Orthodox Church. There had been lengthy discussions about where the wedding ceremony would be held. Vladislav belonged to the Polish Catholic faith while Helena was Russian Orthodox, but Vladislav gave in to her demand to get married in the Russian Orthodox Church and settled for receiving a quick blessing from the priest at the Catholic Church with whom he had close contact. The first conflict was settled. Helena got her way, a foreboding omen.

---

* Unfortunately, we have no records with the exact day of the marriage in 1906.

15 | Making a Home

1906

Before the wedding day, grandfather had started to scour the city for a suitable place to live. He was excited about the prospect of creating a home for him and his new wife.

Shortly after their marriage, Helena and Vladislav moved into an eleven-room house on the corner of Artilleriiskaia and Aptekarskaia Streets. The house was roomy and pleasant and had a huge garden in the back of the house, which was kept perfectly manicured by the Chinese staff. Vladislav also moved his office to his new home.

Everyone was delighted at how well the union had succeeded. They were happy that Vladislav had found a suitable wife.

Helena and Vladislav's first house.

Vladislav in his study

Even Alexander took Vladislav aside one day to remark, "I can see that the marriage is going well, Vladislav Fyodorovich. All your concerns were unnecessary."

"I'm also amazed how this has worked out," Vladislav said.

"You know, Vladislav, I have been thinking. It occurred to me that Helena might need someone to take care of her besides the servants, as you are often away from Harbin at the lumberyards. If I were you, I wouldn't want to leave my wife, your precious jewel, home alone, nor would I want her to get homesick. As you know, our mother Tatiana Denisovna came for the wedding and has stayed on with us until now," said Alexander as he took a seat. "I think it would be a good idea if our dear mother came to live with you. She would be a great comfort for your wife when you are away. After all, Helena Alexandrovna is the oldest daughter, and is very close to her mother. I am sure my mother would love to stay, and we do not want her to return to St. Petersburg because the current political situation is troubling."

"I think you are right Alexander Alexandrovich. She is most welcome to stay with us," agreed Vladislav.

After a brief silence, Alexander said,

"Barbara Alexandrovna has stayed on as well, and I do believe she's taken an interest in one of your employees."

"Which one?"

"A Polish manager of one of your mills, I think. But she won't tell me his name."

"Then it's Wladyslaw Chacinsky, an engineer at the mills. I've heard rumors but discounted them. He's a rather easygoing fellow but doesn't have much character. He has difficulty staying focused, and honestly I don't know if he has much of a future. Do you want it stopped?"

"No. On the contrary, I think it would be good for Barbara Alexandrovna to settle here, near her sister, rather than return to Russia. There's growing unrest with the tsar, and there have been several disturbing assassinations. The Marx Manifesto is being revived and this is troubling. I doubt it will come to anything, but one never knows."

"I'll see that Chacinsky is well looked after," Vladislav said. "Perhaps we shall have another wedding soon." It was decided that Tatiana and Barbara would stay and live together with Vladislav and Helena.

Tatiana was a beautiful person, both inside and outside. She held no resentment despite the difficult life she had of being abandoned by her husband and needing to raise all her children on her own.

Tatiana was very religious, and when she arrived in Harbin for the wedding of Vladislav and Helena, she was delighted to see so many churches being built. She attended church every day, and often stopped to speak with the Russian beggars near the church, sometimes bringing them food and drink. Frequently she would sit with them and read excerpts from the Bible. She even brought beggars to the back of the house to give them a hot meal. When Vladislav and Helena went out for an evening with friends, she made sure the staff prepared extra food to feed the beggars who came to the back door to receive their only meal of the day.

Unlike his mother, Alexander was calculating and manipulative. He had a way of making others feel that he was helping them, but he was primarily interested in his own welfare. He was selfish and self-centered. Alexander and Sophie were very compatible. They suited each other and supported one another. They had the same goals and would achieve them together. Alexander understood that his future lay in Harbin. Here, he would have many opportunities not available in Russia, especially now that the

Tatiana Denisovna Zaharoff

St. Nicholas Cathedral[1]

economic and political situation was deteriorating. Unfortunately for Vladislav, Alexander was always looking for the easy way out. For someone like Vladislav who was meticulous about everything, especially business matters, Alexander's attitude was often troubling.

At work, the following morning, Alexander announced that Sophie was pregnant. They had planned to share the news simultaneously, so Sophie showed up at Helena's home to regale Barbara and Helena with news of their good fortune. Helena was very excited and immediately made plans for lunch so the three of them could celebrate.

Early the following year Sophie gave birth to George, or Lola as they preferred to call him. Alexander and Sophie would now bring up their son in their home in Harbin.

16 | A Growing Population

1907

Grandfather was skilled at establishing relationships and was known for his generosity. He had difficulty refusing anyone. Russians, Jews, Chinese, and, of course, Poles would come to him with every concern, and he always tried to advise and help in any way he could in his own quiet way. He felt that there was enough work for everyone and championed efforts for the common good, such as schools, churches, and hospitals. He was involved in every aspect of the community, and to many individuals, he was an important pillar of the society.

WITH JAPAN'S VICTORY IN THE RUSSO-JAPANESE WAR, IT STRENGTHENED its presence and role in Manchuria significantly, increasing its population and business interests as well. With the Russian defeat, its military influence and presence in Manchuria declined. However, Russia's extraterritorial rights in the CER railway zone remained, and private companies that worked under the Russian umbrella, such as Vladislav's, continued to develop. Many opportunities existed for jobs, especially those associated with the ongoing maintenance of the railroad and infrastructure projects surrounding the stations along its lines. The prospect and the potential for riches in this rapidly developing part of the world drew many Chinese settlers from other provinces as well as those of other nationalities. Of these foreign emigrants, the Russian contingent to Harbin was the largest and continued to grow as they fled to escape deteriorating conditions back home.

In 1906, the Tsarist Russian Consulate was accredited in Harbin and the CER related parts were no longer deemed as "part of the Russian Empire."[1] During the war Harbin became a military hub, but after 1908 it turned into a civilian center where the city had assumed an atmosphere of normalcy. Intellectual life became a focus. The libraries opened their doors, newspaper companies were

Harbin, Novogorodniaia Street.[2]

established, and business interests grew with the backing of a Chamber of Commerce. The Yacht Club had started operations and catered to its members and the community, creating a stimulating social and cultural environment.

In 1906 the population in Novyi Gorod and Pristan was 95,000, comprised of about 62,000 Russians and 33,000 Chinese (about 50,000 more Chinese were living in the Fujiadian district).[3] Houses, offices, and industries were built. When a family arrived, everyone helped to erect a makeshift house with materials from established entrepreneurs like Vladislav, who provided lumber at a reasonable cost. Once a home was built, a policeman would come and hammer a house number on the front entrance, making it an "official" residence of Harbin.

Harbin fell into an economic slump that lasted from 1907 to 1908. Funds available from Russia for the economic development in Manchuria dried up, as Russia was in the midst of its own economic crisis where Harbin became a treaty port rather than a "Russian colony."[4] Russian businessmen from Harbin who had vigorously invested in the wartime economic growth were suffering with the downturn causing many bankruptcies. Three and a half years after its opening, the CER itself was running at a tremendous loss and was on the verge of bankruptcy.[5]

By 1908 the economy began to improve when soybean became the principle export crop in Manchuria and an important industry, mainly in the hands of Chinese industrialists.[6]

The high demand for soybeans from European buyers helped to put the economy on a fast track forward. Always on the pulse of opportunity, Vladislav also invested in this sector.

It was rare to find Vladislav relaxing at the Yacht Club together with his friends on a Saturday afternoon. It was a particularly beautiful summer day and the temperature was high, as it usually was during the summers in Harbin.

"Interesting how intense the seasons are here in Harbin. The winters are the coldest ever, the summers hot and balmy, autumn beautiful with the changing colors of nature, and spring with the blossoming of flowers. We are lucky to be able to enjoy four distinct seasons," commented Leonid.

"Yes, and with each year we see so many changes in Harbin. All of these changes have been within the last decade and before our own eyes," stated Ivan.

"Did you know that in 1905 there were an estimated 7,000 Poles living in Manchuria.[7] The Poles are ambitious. They built theaters, meeting halls, libraries, churches and concert halls.[8] So many key structures in Harbin were designed by Polish nationals.[9] Look around us, the Polish contributions include the bridge over the Sungari River, Harbin Railway Station, and the planning of the city of Harbin," boasted Vladislav.

"Now Vladislav Fyodorovich, you are clearly showing off," added Ivan.

"No really, I could continue but I won't. I truly feel that many Poles have unleashed their talents here in Harbin and have had a chance to express their creativeness and engineering skills without any restraint. I am sure that the ambitious and productive spirit of the Poles who moved to Harbin was enhanced by the freedom and the liberal climate that many of them felt in Manchuria," stated Vladislav.

Bridge over Sungari in Harbin[10]

"Poles built breweries, tobacco factories, developed the spirit and mining industries. Yes, I guess I am feeling a sense of pride," smiled Vladislav.

During and after the Russo-Japanese War there was a high demand for flour as bread became a sought-after commodity, especially among the Russian population. The flour mill business continued to grow and by 1910 there were eight flour mills established in Harbin and seven along the railway zone.[11] Vladislav had already invested in the flour business in 1902 and was a part owner of the Russian Flour Mills Company as well as several other smaller flour mills.[12] The Russian Flour Mills Company had three locations and was the largest of all the flour mills with a combined estimated output of 36,700 tons (short ton = 2,000 lbs.) of flour in 1911.[13] This business turned out to be a lucrative investment as well as a valuable export commodity and one that he maintained for many years.

Early on, Polish organizations became established and more continued to form: the Roman Catholic Charitable Society (1903); the organization the Polish Inn (*Gospoda Polska*)*; social, cultural, and educational groups; the Polish Youth Association; the St. Vincent de Paul Society Primary School;

---

* The organization the Polish Inn (*Gospoda Polska*) encompassed the Citizens Jury and the Court of Honor as legal institutions that were composed of members of the society to give legal advice in trivial cases.

and other organizations that helped to integrate the Polish residents into Harbin society.

To everyone's joy, Barbara and Wladyslaw Chacinsky became engaged. Sophie and Helena met often with Barbara to plan the wedding, as the women wanted to make sure it was the social event of the season. The wedding turned out to be a great success. Barbara and Wladyslaw Chacinsky moved into a small house nearby, and shortly after their marriage, Barbara became pregnant with Nadezhda (Nadia).

Helena, Barbara, and Sophie met several times a week at coffee shops or restaurants. They shopped often at the fashionable and accommodating Churin Department Store and enjoyed walking along the promenade, discovering shops that had just opened their doors. A new fashionable dress, a modish hat, a chic pair of shoes from Paris, or a stylish scarf to complement their outfit was always welcomed. Life for them was comfortable, frivolous, and lighthearted.

Barbara started a sewing club where a group of ladies would meet once a week to sew and gossip. This was their "wireless" connection to what was happening in society. Helena did not enjoy sewing—she was never inclined to frivolous feminine tasks, but she enjoyed the social aspect and pretended to like the needlework. With Vladislav's business attaining greater prominence, Helena received more and more attention from the other ladies. She was often guilty of showing off, and glowed in the attention unlike her sister. Barbara was on the shy side and allowed Helena to take the spotlight. Her marriage to an engineer gave her the sense of security and all the social standing that she needed.

Churin Department Store[14]

17 | Ariadna Vladislavna

1908

Family life agreed with grandfather. Though he could see that his wife's strong and stubborn character brought on new challenges, her opinionated nature gave him the opportunity to leave domestic matters to her. His even-keeled, level-headed character served as a good balance.

WHEN HELENA ANNOUNCED THAT SHE WAS PREGNANT IN SEPTEMBER 1908, Vladislav and the relatives were excited with the news. Although Vladislav was frequently away on business during the pregnancy, he kept in touch with his wife through the office staff. Fortunately, Helena's mother, Tatiana, was a great help during these long absences, offering her company, council, and advice at each stage of the pregnancy.

Their first daughter was born in April 1909. They named her Ariadna, or Ada for short, and she was the spitting image of her mother. Helena adored Ada. Vladislav was equally delighted with the miracle of becoming a parent. He never imagined such a strong feeling of responsibility. Fatherhood brought his life more meaning and was now a major family priority for him. Though he tried to put aside time with the baby each day, his business was growing rapidly and he needed to spend more and more time away at the lumber sites supervising and meeting with customers.

One month after Ada's birth, she was baptized into the Russian Orthodox Church. The occasion was celebrated with devoted attention to detail. Helena and Tatiana made all the church arrangements, choosing the godparents and ordering the special baptismal outfit and traditional

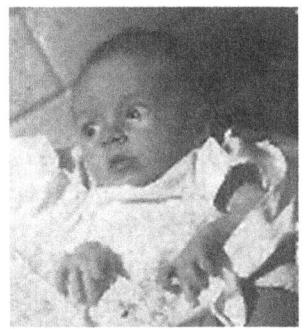

Ariadna, 2 weeks old

Ada, around 18 months old

gold cross. The paperwork was arranged by Vladislav. The baptism was beautiful, attended by all the Zaharoff relatives and some special friends. Tatiana was excited beyond words. Being a deeply religious woman, she knew the importance of this day. After the ceremony in the church, the family celebrated the joyous affair with a grand reception in their home. The cooks had been preparing delicacies for days and the festivities lasted late into the night.

As time passed, Vladislav recognized that he needed more help to run the business efficiently. He began to realize that Alexander was not dependable, nor someone to whom he could turn for advice on key operational matters. Alexander was taking things easy and setting his own priorities. He enjoyed life in Harbin and, together with Sophie, Vladislav felt he was entertaining and socializing more than necessary. Helena enjoyed socializing with them, and made it known to Vladislav that she disapproved of his dedication, as there was more to life than work. She demanded the luxuries and spoils from his hard work, but was not sympathetic to the dedication to his business it required. Helena, Alexander, Sophie, Barbara, and her husband spent more time together reveling, pressuring Vladislav to leave work to join them.

Vladislav became more frustrated with Alexander's attitude as the company's activities grew and his workload increased. He felt that Alexander's loyalties were not focused on the business. When he complained to Helena, she became difficult, always defending her brother. One day during a heated discussion between them, she stood up and angrily accused him of "not allowing her side of the family to make money and become rich."[1] Her statement marked the beginning of Vladislav's suspicion of his brother-in-law's aim and purpose. He started to question Alexander's devotion to the company and to him, for it became clear that he was concentrating on furthering only himself.

Vladislav could see that Helena's loyalty strongly lay with her family. While they were good company for his wife, he felt they were a bad influence on her relationship with him. Moreover, the age difference between Helena and Vladislav started to create problems. At 38, Vladislav was more grounded and focused on his responsibilities to his family, his employees, and his work.

His serious nature conflicted with that of his young 25-year-old wife. He had expected her to settle down to her motherly duties after the birth of Ada, but that was not the case. Instead, with time, she became more demanding and used her position in the household to order others around, leaving Tatiana and the servants to take care of Ada.

Socially, Helena enjoyed showing off her daughter and being a mother. She and Barbara spent time with their young children, Ada and Nadia, taking them shopping to dress them in the latest outfits, and parading them around town. Barbara was already pregnant with her second child and life revolved around the children.

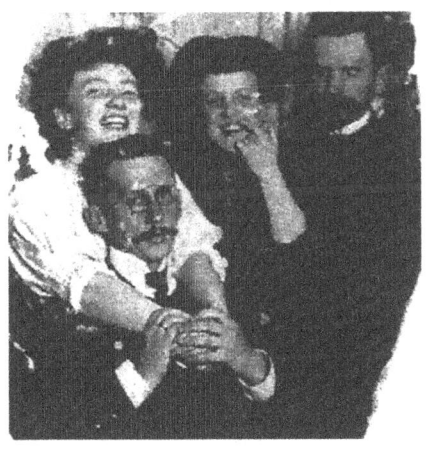

Barbara and Wladyslaw, Helena and Vladislav enjoying happy times in 1909

Barbara and Helena

Helena led a relaxed life. She left the details of taking care of baby Ada's needs to Tatiana, who bathed, fed, and looked after her. The summer of 1910 was one of the most relaxing, as the two mothers enjoyed their newfound happiness.

The outbreak of pneumonic plague in October 1910 brought change and havoc to the region. The plague started along the railway and was traced back to the marmot[2] fur traders. Chinese fur traders discovered that by dying the fur of the marmot it could be made to look like ermine, an expensive white fur that comes from stoats. To save costs, the safety and cleanliness standards were compromised when dyeing the furs, which resulted in the outbreak of the plague in the whole area. Medication was scarce, and in some places nonexistent. The epidemic reached Harbin in October, killing 5,149 people.[3] Everyone knew someone who was sick and Vladislav and Helena were very worried about the safety of the family. When the epidemic was at its worst, over 130 people died in Harbin every day, affecting both the foreigners and the Chinese.[4]

The local government tried to control the situation by imposing a quarantine and making door-to-door searches to weed out the sick patients. The only deterrent was quarantine and isolation. Panic spread among the residents in Harbin. They conducted mass cremations because it was impossible to bury all the dead in the middle of the winter, despite it being against the traditional Confucian protocol. Vladislav, when necessary, provided wooden coffins for the dead. Within a short period of time, the number of deaths jumped to the thousands. Functions were cancelled and many stayed indoors, taking great care not to come into contact with others. Skilled and ambitious Chinese and Russian doctors managed to finally control the epidemic; however, by the time the plague, which lasted six months, ended, 60,000 people in Manchuria had died.[6]

Pneumonic plague—bodies of victims together with a health officer[5]

18 | Back to Tsarskoe Selo

1910

This is where Vika, my mother, comes into the picture. It would have been natural for her mother to have the baby in Harbin, but that is not the way it eventuated. Various circumstances prompted my grandmother's decision to travel back to Russia for the birth of her second child.

IN 1910, HELENA BECAME PREGNANT WITH THEIR SECOND CHILD AND SHE insisted on traveling to Russia for the delivery. Vladislav protested, especially as the news of the political unrest in Russia was growing. Turmoil had continued after the 1905 revolution, with Russia now operating under a constitutional monarchy and a succession of weak governments. The influence of Rasputin over Tsarina Alexandra Feodorovna, with regard to the health challenges of their son, further destroyed support for the unqualified Tsar Nicholas II.

Despite these circumstances, Helena was adamant about going to Russia. Vladislav had not previously seen this level of insistence from his wife and could do little to dissuade her. She gave one explanation after another for wanting to go, but her concern regarding the plague outbreak in Harbin was most justifiable and, because of that, Vladislav finally gave in. It was arranged for her to travel to her hometown, Tsarskoe Selo, where he was sure she would have access to the best doctors. He made reservations on the luxurious first-class wagon on the CER/Trans-Siberian Railway for her to travel in comfort on the long journey to the other end of Russia. Helena left in the fourth month of her pregnancy, taking Ada and Tatiana with her. It would be more than a year before she would return to Harbin.

Tsarskoe Selo, located a short distance from St. Petersburg, was a special place, being the location of the summer home of the imperial family.

The Catherine Palace at Tsarskoe Selo[1]

The city was famous for the many parks and beautiful gardens that surrounded the area. It was only the Alexander Palace garden that was off limits to the public as it was the private garden where the royal family could take a stroll and enjoy the outdoors undisturbed. It was reputed to be one of the most beautiful gardens displaying the magnificence of the exquisitely manicured flowers and vegetation. It was said that 500 gardeners tended the garden.[2]

It was during her stay in Russia that Chacinsky, Barbara's husband, visited Vladislav.

"Vladislav Fyodorovich, I come to you as a friend, actually, as a relative, as you are my brother-in-law. You are a good man and deserve the best, and if I offend you with what I am about to say, I ask forgiveness, but I feel I cannot keep this to myself any longer. Barbara has told me some things about her sister in confidence, which I feel I should pass on to you because I consider you as family and as a true friend. Frankly, I do not know why you let Helena Alexandrovna go to Tsarskoe Selo."

"She insisted on going to Russia to have the baby."

"For God's sake Vladislav Fyodorovich, you shouldn't have let her go."

"I tried to persuade her not to, but I've never seen her so fiercely inclined or stubborn about anything. I spoke of the turmoil there. When she insisted that the plague here in Harbin was a concern, I relented."

"To have a baby in all that madness?"

"She seemed almost on the point of insanity if I did not let her go. I had no choice."

"Her excuse to go to Russia to have the baby was not the only reason, I suspect. There is something else I think you should know."

"What?"

"I'm reluctant to tell you this, Vladislav Fyodorovich."

"Then you confuse me."

"It's about Helena Alexandrovna."

"Well then, what?"

"Did you know that Helena Alexandrovna was very much in love with the husband of Ekaterina Alexandrovna, Helena's sister? Her husband,

Mikhail Alexandrovich Solovov, comes from nobility and was an officer on the tsar's royal yacht, the *Standart*. To be an officer on the royal yacht was very prestigious, where he often danced with the daughters of the tsar and tsarina. The officers were promised that when they baptized their children, the tsarina would become the godmother and presented each child with a Fabergé egg. Mikhail Alexandrovich's children each received a small Fabergé egg from the tsarina."

He continued, "According to Barbara Alexandrovna, Mikhail Alexandrovich was a very charming man and a handsome figure in uniform. He married Helena's sister who was a sweet, lovely, feminine, and beautiful person. They were so much in love and enjoyed a beautiful and loving marriage. However, Helena Alexandrovna was also very much in love with him and was embittered that he chose Ekaterina Alexandrovna to be his wife. Even after they married, Helena Alexandrovna persisted in flirting with him and continued to have affection for him."

"But that is all over now, is it not?" Vladislav asked.

"Well, the story continues. Tragically, just before Helena Alexandrovna came here to Harbin, Ekaterina Alexandrovna died of TB. In her last moments before dying, she took her sister's hand and asked her to look after Mikhail Alexandrovich. Apparently Ekaterina Alexandrovna always knew that her sister was in love with her husband. Even in her final moments, she was concerned about her sister and her husband, who would be left to care for two children. Helena Alexandrovna saw the opportunity with this last request and took it very seriously. She would now be able to marry the man she had been in love with for years."

Vladislav sat motionless, listening to every word. "Why hasn't Helena Alexandrovna said anything to me about her past? I suppose this is behind her and obviously nothing has come of it."

"That is why I am telling you this. Mikhail Alexandrovich was devastated by the death of his wife. He had absolutely no thought of pursuing anything with Helena Alexandrovna. In fact, he had to be very rude and blunt with her and let her know that he had no intention of ever being together with her. She was grief-stricken."

"Why are you telling me all this?"

Ekaterina and Mikhail Solovov

Officers on the royal yacht, the *Standart;* Mikhail Solovov in the middle

"From what I understand from Barbara Alexandrovna, your wife still has feelings for Mikhail Alexandrovich."

"What do you mean?"

"It is said that your wife never got over him, and that she still loves him very much even to this day. She continues to send him letters even after marrying you."

Vladislav stared at his friend for a long time, trying to contain the hurt. Finally, with a sigh, he let go. He felt the pain coursing through his body, throbbing in his heart, making him weak and helpless. He took several deep breaths. Chacinsky had found some vodka and poured both of them shots.

"Truly, I'm sorry to be the one who tells you this, but as a friend—"

"You did right. Do not feel badly. Still, the shock is great. Yet, it allows me to understand some things, so many things about Helena Alexandrovna that I could not make sense of." He took the shot glass Chacinsky handed him and let the vodka make its way through his body. He slowly shook his head. "I would like to deny your words, but somehow I know they're true."

"What will you do?"

"Nothing, of course. I will greet her with great joy when she returns with the new baby. Isn't that what a gentleman does?"

"Yes, it is."

That evening Vladislav sat alone drinking and thinking of his situation with his young wife. The family dynamics would change, how could it not? It would now enable Vladislav to comfortably devote more time and energy to his work and develop more interaction with his friends. He was fine with this, life would go on.

19 | Yablonia Concession

1911

From the moment grandfather stepped off the ship in Vladivostok fifteen years earlier, he knew that this new home offered many opportunities to succeed. But, to do so, he needed to learn everything he could about the area and its surroundings. Grandfather's unlimited thirst for knowledge and his endless energy had him walking everywhere, talking to everyone, and constantly asking questions, helping him to understand and appreciate his new environment.

OUTSIDE OF THE CER ZONE, THE CHINESE FORESTRY AUTHORITIES IN 1911 were preparing to lease out large expanses of forestland to private timber merchants for the development of forestry concessions. Vladislav had always dreamed of one day owning his own tract of land to run a lumber business. He could see the potential in the opportunity and wanted to be one of the first to engage the offer. To make sure he understood the scope of this, he traveled for days, exploring the countryside and the area that was being offered. By now Toubin was older and became very helpful to Vladislav, accompanying him everywhere. With Alexander and Toubin, he investigated, inspected, calculated, and negotiated the potential. Of the concessions being made available, Yablonia, located east of Harbin and north of the CER, interested him the most. It was one of the largest concessions offered by the Chinese authorities.

"What do you think, Alexander Alexandrovich? Are we taking on too much?" asked Vladislav. "We are, after all, very familiar with the area as we have worked felling trees in these woods along the rail line. The pines are the most valuable timber species and I can see a lot of beautiful Manchurian pine here in the Yablonia forest."

"It certainly helps that we aren't walking into this blindfolded. We know that this is an area with incredibly rich forests and a variety of trees," reassured Alexander. "But, we also know that the forests and vegetation in these parts are incredibly dense and not easy to penetrate. Do you think we will have problems transporting the logs?"

"I have thought about that. This piece of land is close to the rail line, which is advantageous. I can build smaller lines within the concession that link to the main railway, making movement of the logs easier. It is a fantastic investment made even more valuable by its access to several rivers, which would be very good for transporting timber. Personally, it would be a dream come true for me to lease Yablonia," said Vladislav, having difficulty containing his enthusiasm.

"I fully agree, Vladislav Fyodorovich. From what you have shown me, it is a big, new step for the company. It offers exciting prospects for the future. Even if some consider this too adventurous, it is an opportunity that has substance. My only concern is that you are making this decision without consulting Helena Alexandrovna who is away in Russia. Are you all right with that?" Alexander felt that he needed to throw that into the conversation.

"I make my decisions based on what is best for all. It is not an emotional decision, and besides, she does not interfere in business matters," Vladislav said emphatically. Especially now, he thought.

It was the first lumber forestry concession he acquired, and one he could lay claim to for a thirty-year period. The anticipation lasted for a final two days while he waited for the approval. While waiting for a positive outcome, Sophie and Barbara helped in planning and coordinating arrangements with the servants to prepare the celebratory feast for family and friends. Vladislav sensed that this was the beginning of something very big and important. He would now devote all his energy into developing his own project, and already had plans about how he would tackle this challenge. This was a special day for Vladislav, and years later he often would tell the family, many times, about when he signed the first lease document and about that memorable event.

Friends dropped in to extend congratulations. This lease was viewed as an accomplishment for the whole community, not only for Vladislav. The celebration included his friends and colleagues and also his competitors in the lumber business. That was what life in Harbin was like. Everyone was happy for the achievements that were made, offering their best wishes and support.

"Vladislav Fyodorovich, I hear you are leasing half the territory of Manchuria," Ivan Ivanovich shouted out across the room.

"No, not half the area, Ivan Ivanovich," laughed Vladislav. "Just a small tract of land."

"You are certainly an ambitious man. You know, we can't keep up with you," assured Ivan.

Stolen Dreams

"I didn't know we were in a race. It's good you tell me these things, otherwise I may have started to take things easy," joked Vladislav.

"That will never happen, Vladislav Fyodorovich, we know you too well. I congratulate you on your new venture and know that you will turn this into a fruitful undertaking. I offer a toast to you for success and happiness."

"I thank you, Ivan Ivanovich, and thank you all, *za schastie*."* And with that, Vladislav downed the vodka, which tasted potent, exhilarating, and invigorating.

The Provincial Board of Finance in Jilin, together with the Harbin Tax Office, sanctioned and registered the contract for Yablonia West in 1911.[1] In 1913, Vladislav signed and added another concession contract for Yablonia East; the two concessions of Yablonia East and West were a combined area

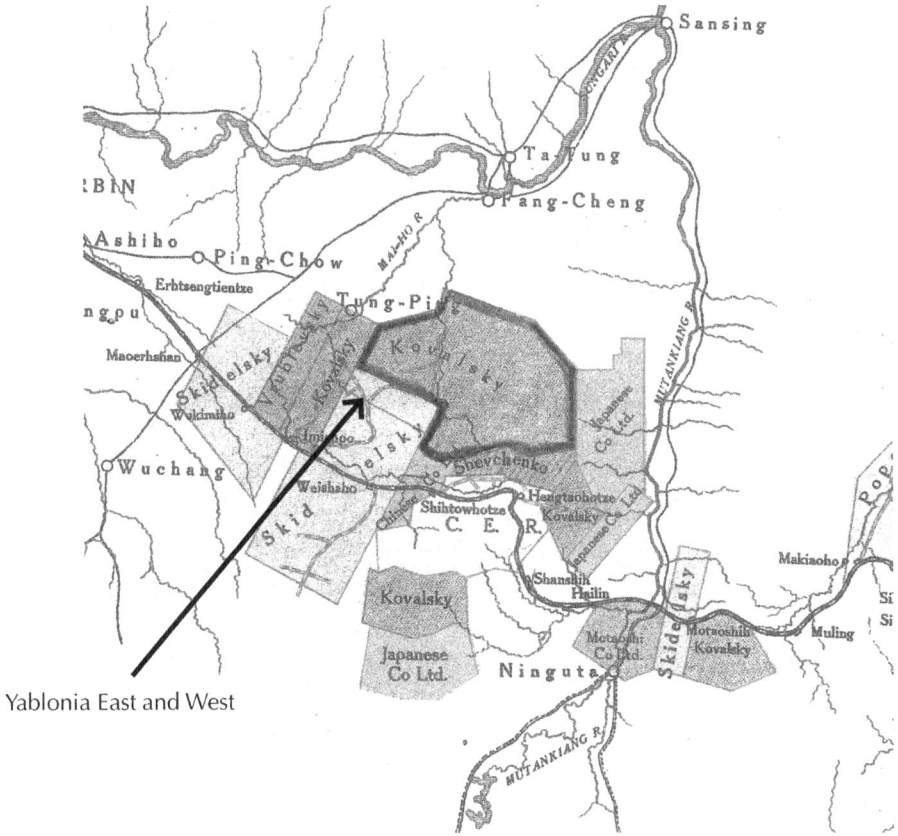

Kowalski's Concessions—Yablonia East and West: The other Kowalski concessions were acquired in later years.[4]

---

* A toast for good luck.

Pulley to move the logs

Cut logs floating on the river

of 2,430 square Russian miles (1 Russian mile = 1.067 kilometers).[2] This contract was also properly registered by the Forest and Mine Tax Office in Harbin and the Commissionaire of Foreign Affairs where Vladislav was deemed as the sole owner of the leased land for a period of thirty years.[3]

This was a great opportunity for Vladislav to further develop the industry and to supply wood not only for the railroad, but for the growing city of Harbin. In the following years, the lumber industry of Manchuria grew to be one of the most successful business ventures in China.

After the contracts were signed, Vladislav and Toubin would make exploratory expeditions into the area to assess the territory. The two of them slept in the small *fanza* huts in the woods and spent days exploring. They always carried with them "Persian Powder" and cologne to try to deter the tremendous number of fleas in the fanza. It was amazing how the two of them would communicate in an abbreviated Chinese-Russian pidgin, which was a combination of Russian and Chinese words. This form of pidgin was prevalent in Harbin.

Having laid the groundwork, Vladislav immediately began to mobilize his workforce, mostly of Russians, Poles, and Chinese migrants, who quickly settled in and around the areas that had been cleared on the concessions. Vladislav set to work building a massive railway transportation system within the concession, understanding the importance of needing to have access to the forest and to transport the logs because of the tremendous distances. Over time he constructed 106 kilometers of a railway system within the concessions, as well as cable cars to transport material over the mountains, and used his own railway wagons and cars for transportation.[5] This made his operation very efficient.

Vladislav was at the forefront of this development and was one of the few entrepreneurs who had chosen timber and wood processing as a trading business. He had already established networks and had gained valuable experience in organizing and running the lumber business. Of the almost 800,000 tons of firewood produced in 1913, a little over 700,000 tons went to the CER.[6] The lumber and wood industry was the most lucrative business in Manchuria, and Vladislav became one of the most established lumber businessmen in Manchuria and one of the richest in the North Manchurian region. He hired Poles, Russians, and Chinese to work in his lumber business. It was estimated that one third of the 13,000 workers employed in the business in Manchuria were Russians.[7] Vladislav was determined to create the most efficient and productive concession, and within a few years the most important supplies of lumber originated in Yablonia and from the concessions of Kowalski.[8]

Vladislav taking a rest at a riverbank

On the concessions, Vladislav set up social halls, schools, small banks, and medical clinics to accommodate the resident employees. It was important to him to create a warm and friendly social surrounding for the families, and he made it a point to pay the employees an extra month, which ensured their loyalty.[9] The number of employees hired varied depending on the seasons. The administrative staff was made up of full-time Russian, Pole, and Chinese employees.

The Kowalski factory[10]

Vladislav spent less time at home and more time on the concession. He loved this project and was determined to make it a success. He was a no-nonsense man and he needed to prove to himself that he could manage this undertaking.

With the lumber business so closely connected to the CER, Vladislav was in constant contact with Horvath, who became a well-respected and appreciated Russian leader. He was instrumental in contributing to the atmosphere and realization of positive economic and commercial development. He was an open-minded person without any national prejudices. Vladislav valued him as a close friend, Harbin associate, and very important customer, with the CER now being his largest buyer.

20 | Victoria Vladislavna

1911

My mother, Wiktoria (Vika for short), was born on June 27, 1911. She had red hair and green eyes. When her mother returned to Harbin together with Tatiana, Ada, and her newborn baby, her husband was delighted to see that Vika looked so much like his side of the family. He felt so proud to be a father and vowed to give the girls a good and comfortable life. It was rare that he would take several days off from work to spend time at home with the family, now with their return he made sure to spend a couple of days enjoying his fatherly duties.

AFTER THE BIRTH OF THEIR SECOND DAUGHTER, LIFE SETTLED BACK to normal, Vladislav concentrated his attention on the new concessions that were under development and expansion. Helena did not seem to mind. He stayed away longer on trips, staying in the houses on his concessions, and when he was home in Harbin he often met with friends for a drink or a game of bridge, comfortably making arrangements to enjoy his own social interests. The relationship between Vladislav and Helena continued to deteriorate. In public they acted as a couple, but as soon as they were alone, the conversation assumed an overly polite tone and one of indifference. In some way, he felt more comfortable with this arrangement. He had his work and no longer dealt with the everyday drudgeries of married life. He could lead his own life. The one thing that they both agreed to keep sacred when he was in Harbin was to have meals together with the children. This he always enjoyed, and it was his special time to interact with the children.

Home life became strained due to Helena's extreme behavior and litany of demands. The staff was unable to

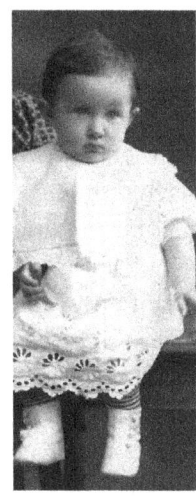

Vika

keep up with the endless requests. Helena soon found a 35-year-old Russian woman, Akulina Semenova (Lenochka), and employed her as her personal maid. The day Lenochka arrived to work for Helena was a godsend for everyone in the household. Lenochka was like an angel who descended on the family. She was patient, gentle, and kind, an all-round amazing person. She looked after Helena twenty-four hours a day until the day Helena passed away. She never voiced her opinion and did everything with a smile. She was a very religious woman, and it was evident that she found solace in her faith.

Lenochka   Lenochka's family (Lenochka in the back)

As the girls grew, it became clear to everyone that Ada was her mother's favorite. Helena doted on every word, every action, and made her preference for her older daughter obvious. With each passing year, Ada's resemblance to her mother became more apparent. The hair color, eyes, features, and personality were a duplicate. Vika, on the other hand, exhibited all the Kowalski characteristics, even her giggly and delightful personality. She was a lovable child, who was easy to please and charming in every way. But sadly, her resemblance to Vladislav was not a positive in the eyes of her mother. The marital discord and the way Helena felt toward her husband started to reflect in her attitude toward Vika. She became indifferent to her second daughter.

Ada was delighted with her favored position and reveled in her mother's attention. As the girls grew, Ada openly expressed her dissatisfaction at having a sister and repeated many times that the worst day of her life was when Vika was born and wished she was an only child. She hated her sister with a passion and used every opportunity to demonstrate it. Ada was consumed with a daily challenge of finding ways to manipulate situations to prod Vika. The animosity that she felt for Vika was an extreme case of sibling rivalry, and as the girls grew, this attitude became ingrained.

Vika already took for granted the daily torment by her sister. Even at a young age, she was tuned in to this unfair treatment. She started to find ways to avoid conflict and interaction. On the few occasions she went to her mother to complain, Helena would just smile, often praising Ada for her clever schemes. Vika could not understand her mother's favoritism. She always endeavored to please her mother, working extra hard to extract the slightest praise. But no matter how hard she tried, she was unable to break through.

Arrangements were made to have a nursemaid, for both children—one for Ada and another for Vika. A nanny would take care of each child, bathe them, dress them, and bring them to the table for meals. The girls were entertained during the day to make sure they did not cry or fret. Often, Helena would ask for Ada to be brought in to her room to play on the carpet so she could dote. The girls were seldom taken out of the house, unless the weather was warm and comfortable. Helena was not motherly and lacked sensitivity, and the girls were subjected to discipline through Helena's constant commands. It was her way of taking care of the children.

Left to right: back row—a friend and Lola, Barbara's son; front row—Vika and Ada

Helena's primary dedication was to the Orthodox Church. She never missed a Sunday service and would make a big production in preparing for church. She marked all the special days for the saints, and always placed a candle for the saint to whom she paid reverence to. As soon as the girls were old enough to attend church, she arranged for Lenochka and the nursemaids to bring them with her to the services. She felt no compunction to support her husband at his Catholic Church.

Though status conscious, Helena was not a social person. She could be charming when she wanted, but was extremely selfish, demanding, and manipulative. These characteristics were accentuated after she had the children. She felt comfortable being with Barbara and

Ada and Vika

Ada and Vika

Barbara (upper left) with her daughter; Helena with Ada and Vika

her husband and Alexander and Sophie, but she did not fit in with other ladies or couples in the Harbin society. Daily activities were planned together with Barbara, sometimes including the four children. The two mothers regularly shopped at Churin Department Store and Helena did not deny herself anything. She believed that her standing in society demanded and entitled her to have the best.

Helena had a strange inherent bitterness. Vladislav refused to talk to anyone about his observations, but did confide in his sister Fema, to whom he was closest. They wrote letters to each other, and he greatly valued and trusted the empathy and advice he received from her. In his letters to his sister he questioned, "Why was Helena like this? Why was she so difficult and so negative?" It was hard for him to understand Helena's inclinations, as her sister and her mother were so different. Perhaps it was because Helena's father had abandoned the family, and being the oldest surviving daughter this could have made her resentful. One could only speculate the reasons. Vladislav wondered if it was because she felt abandoned. She did have a strong bond with her brother Alexander and, perhaps, his negative views also influenced her. Many questions were left unanswered, but her attitude definitely affected the family and the way she brought up the children.

21 | A Chinese-Russian City

1912

After Empress Dowager Cixi's death in 1908 politics in China became even more complicated and continued to be influenced by foreign powers and Chinese warlords. The ruling Qing Dynasty was weak and struggling, and the surrounding countries continued to interfere and play a decisive role, not only in its politics but also its economics and life in general.

CHINA WENT THROUGH A CHALLENGING TIME, AFTER THE BOXER upheaval and the Russo-Japanese War, due to the weakness and failures of the Qing Dynasty. The Qing government had unsuccessfully attempted to strengthen its influence over the foreign powers in China: the British, French, German, Russian, and Japanese.[1] The suggested reforms during 1901 had failed and the Qing government continued to decline. The aging ruler Empress Dowager Cixi fought to normalize the political and economic climate and thwart the foreign powers, especially the Japanese, from exercising their presence in China.

Empress Dowager Cixi was mindful that her adopted son and expected successor, Emperor Guangxu, was incompetent and weak, and she worried that under his reign the empire could fall to the Japanese. In a well-prepared attempt to prevent his ascension to the throne, the empress poisoned Emperor Guangxu the day before she died.[2] Pu Yi, Cixi's nephew and the legitimate successor to the throne, was still too young to rule, though he was officially crowned emperor; Pu Yi's father Zaifeng, whom Cixi had been preparing to lead and resist all Japanese advances, was designated as the regent to rule in the interest of his two-year-old son Pu Yi. For three years after the new regime took control, the country limped along.

The Qing government was further weakened when the leader of the Chinese Republican movement, Sun Yat-sen, declared the southern provinces independent, thus dividing the country. He threatened to overthrow the government and its weak leadership and promoted the establishment of the Republic. Sun Yat-sen was politically astute and had international support for his ambitions. He communicated with the Japanese and was even privy to their plans and ambitions in Manchuria.

The final collapse of the Qing Dynasty occurred in 1912 when Zaifeng, Empress Longyu, and five-year-old Pu Yi abdicated and transferred the right to rule the country to the Chinese people, creating a constitutional republic.[3] The dynasty had been in power for 268 years.[4]

The instability in China had created the opportunity for local, revolutionary, and military leaders to enhance their influence and power in this chaotic time referred to as the Warlord Era. Four leaders who asserted their strength were Republican leader Sun Yat-sen (the founder of the Nationalist Party KMT), General and warlord Yuan Shi-kai (a member of Cixi's Grand Council), the KMT military leader Jiang Kai-Shek, and the Manchurian warlord Zhang Zuolin.

General Yuan Shi-kai took over as ruler. As the country, China adjusted to its new status as a republic, the lack of unity and strong leadership resulted in continued turmoil and political unrest. Yet, despite the turbulent climate, and even with the transition between the Qing Dynasty and the new republic, Harbin was firmly established as the commercial center of northern Manchuria. This brought in more light industry, banking, and other services. Educational institutions of the highest standard were founded, helped by the generous contributions of the residents. Churches, cathedrals, synagogues, and mosques continued to be built, offering spiritual solidarity to the community. The residents of Harbin depended on each other and often met to keep themselves informed with the fast pace of development.

"Good evening, Leon Alexandrovich, Boris Ivanovich, I'm glad you could both make it tonight. I'm happy when we can all attend our Monday night get-together. It starts the week on the right footing. You look happy Boris Ivanovich. Do you have some news for us?" inquired Vladislav.

"No, nothing in particular, but I am happy to see that things are moving forward here in Harbin. I recently became a member of the newly formed Chamber of Commerce where I know that you, Vladislav Fyodorovich, are a member. I attended its meeting last Friday night and it was exhilarating. The Chamber is represented by all kinds of companies, big and small. Not only is every businessman there, but it is a place where we can all have dinners to sit and discuss the problems that we are experiencing and get advice on rules and regulations. Before, we were all on our own, relying on information and counsel from only a few friends, not to say that I have not appreciated all your good advice," quipped Boris.

"No offense taken," smiled Vladislav. "I agree with you. This organization is going to make a big difference for all of us. The Chamber has members who are lawyers and administrators who can offer professional advice. This is exactly what we need. Did you know that today in Harbin, there are 1,151 registered companies and, of these, 78 percent are Russian?[5] It is incredible; I guess Poles are again in the minority. On the other hand, we Poles are doing quite well. You know we make up only 3.7 percent of the population, today there are only 2,556 of us in Harbin, yet we seem to be quite established."[6]

"By the way, Vladislav Fyodorovich, they mentioned your name on Friday recognizing all the donations you made—the lumber for the Yacht Club, the churches, the generous donation to the Polytechnic Institute, and all the individuals that you have helped to get established. They spoke highly of you," Boris informed proudly.

"We do what we can, right?" said Vladislav, and then added, "We all do."

"I am glad you are being acknowledged. You are always so modest, my friend."

"No need for credit, I'm glad I missed the meeting." Vladislav nodded.

"I heard that a Chinese commercial association was also formed. There are more and more Chinese companies that are being formed. Many of them are the smaller sized businesses, but some of them are modern industrial companies. It is important that we all work together for the common good," added Viktor, who just joined the group. "Has anyone ordered food? I haven't had time to eat today, I'm starving."

That Monday their social/business get-together lasted later than usual. Vladislav always enjoyed the discussions and felt that the meetings allowed him to unwind and speak frankly about business affairs and world events, both good and bad. He found the meetings to be stimulating, and often through the discussions everyone could learn from the mistakes and poor decisions of others. The takeaway from the meeting tonight, thought Vladislav, was that yes, things were happening in Harbin in a very positive way.

The Harbin Stock Exchange that had already opened in 1907 represented largely foreign and some Chinese business in Manchuria, where the membership was made up of all Russians and one Chinese businessman.[7] One very positive factor that existed was the favorable trade and tax rules on goods imported and exported between Russia and Manchuria.[8] This was structured to increase trade between Russia and Manchuria and to prevent using the resources of Russian businesses in the railway zone.[9] Furthermore, "no tax areas" were established along the Sino-Russian border and around Harbin Station (a 10-mile radius), as well as around sixteen stations along the CER.[10]

Between 1907 and 1914 trade figures doubled in Harbin with a turnover of 54 million rubles (about US$38 million).[11] Trade and business in Manchuria attracted people from different countries, especially Japan. In 1913 the census showed that in Harbin, China there were fifty-two nationalities represented.[12] Japanese business in south Manchuria greatly increased during this period with investments from large Japanese conglomerates linked with the South Manchurian Railway Company entering the market.

The international presence and the city continued to grow, and this was reflected in the architecture of the buildings and homes in and around Harbin, as well as gardens that were designed with a distinctly European look. Roads were being paved, many of them cobblestone, and shops lined the sidewalks. Street signs and billboards were often written in Chinese, as well as in Russian and Japanese, and even sometimes in English. Cafés and restaurants opened and created a lively social ambiance. On the streets of the city, you could see many nationalities and hear different languages being spoken. Harbin was becoming a true melting pot, an interesting combination of East and West.

Vladislav was grateful for the camaraderie he had with his Russian, Polish, and Chinese friends and treasured their friendship. He felt energized by the onslaught of new challenges that he was faced with every day, and all of this fed into his personality and character. He would often think about how interesting and inspiring life turned out for him. He loved the business and all his friends and was fueled by the new possibilities of expanding and growing, learning and experiencing amid political, social, and economic uncertainties. He felt lucky to be able to live and thrive in such an environment.

22 | World War I

1914

The Yuan Shi-kai Government, which ruled China after the fall of the Qing Dynasty, was weak and faced many financial and political problems. Sun Yat-sen, the founder of the new Republic of China, opposed Yuan's warlord-style rule as he did not adhere to the constitution of the republic nor the democratic principles formulated by Sun Yat-sen. China was dealing with its internal problems, and Europe was on the brink of war.

The seasons in Harbin changed rapidly, almost overnight. The dark, cold days of winter were long and everyone yearned for spring, which always came suddenly, announced by the glorious blossoming of flowers and vegetation. The Harbin summers that followed were short and intense, just as it was on August 1, 1914, when World War I was declared. The declaration of war produced a most painful recollection in both Harbin and across Russia. The Russian military circles were especially disheartened, since the devastating effects of the Russo-Japanese War still remained vivid in their minds. Russia was reluctant to join the fight and when it did, it was believed in Harbin that the war had been forced upon it by German imperialism.

When the war broke out, many European investors left China, opening up opportunities for Chinese businessmen to take over. The Japanese saw the war in Europe and Yuan Shi-kai's weak leadership position as a chance to secure a stronger presence in China. Japan had its eye on the Shandong Territory, which Germany had leased from China since 1898 and where many Germans were living. The Japanese first pledged support to Yuan Shi-kai by sending troops to the Shandong Province. (See map on the next page). Then, under the guise of supporting Britain's war efforts against Germany and Austria, the Japanese Army attacked German and Austrian troops, in China easily

Shandong Province[1]

seizing and occupying the German Shandong area in China. They continued the war in the Pacific where Japan occupied German islands.

In 1915 Japan took further advantage of the situation by issuing the Twenty-One Demands to the Chinese, intended to solidify and expand its influence in China. The demands were presented in distinct points. First, Japan would officially assume the German rights in China's Shandong area; second, it would take over the mineral pits and mines (coal, iron ore, and gold); third, leases on Port Arthur, Dalian, the South Manchurian Railway, and other railways would be extended; and finally, it declared exclusive development rights in Manchuria and other critical areas of China. The Twenty-One Demands, most of which were accepted by Yuan Shi-kai under Japanese pressure, also included extraterritorial rights for Japanese residents and businesses, and exclusive rights for Japan to lease or cede coastal territories. Japan became the primary menace to China.[2]

These demands angered the Chinese and created widespread opposition throughout the country. Young activist leaders like Mao Zedong and Zhou Enlai appeared on the horizon opposing the Japanese requisitions. The anger also fueled the communist movement in China.³ Unprecedented riots, boycotts, and anti-Japanese rallies took place all over the nation, and an anti-Japanese sentiment swept over China that lasted for years. The May Fourth Movement, a strong national, intellectual, and political reform movement, was launched, spurred by student demonstrators. The opposition by the Chinese public forced Yuan Shi-kai to retract the Twenty-One Demands. Yuan Shi-kai died shortly after in 1916, in total disgrace. Because of continued Japanese insistence, the demands were, however, not officially canceled until the Washington Conference in 1920.

As so many Russians lived in Harbin, war in Europe and the political upheaval in Russia were subjects of concern. The stories of fighting in Europe and in Asia became a constant topic of conversation. Every religious, geographic, and ethnic group had its own troubles and stories to tell. Hearing all the depressing news from back home, Vladislav was worried about his family in Kozuchow. He wanted them away from the war front and was trying to talk them into coming to Harbin, where he felt the situation was safer. He did not hear much from the family as mail communication was slow and replies to letters were sporadic. The residents in Harbin became anxious and worried with news of the enormous casualty counts being reported as the war continued to escalate.

From 1914 to 1917 the railway transported military supplies from the Far East to the war zones in Europe. Dimitrii Horvath was busy making sure that the transportation and the supply chain was effective along the CER. He hoped it would be enough to support the Russian offensive to crush the enemies and victoriously end the war. However, Russia was bogged down by the decisions of Tsar Nicholas II in the costly war that led to devastating defeats with tremendous losses. There was deep and widespread discontent in Russia, and the situation worsened when food became scarce. The tsar's ineffectual leadership and numerous failures in the war took its toll.

World War I was devastating for all the countries involved, the Russians having suffered the most casualties. The number of Russian lives lost during World War I varies, but is estimated to be around 1.7 million dead with almost 5 million wounded.[4] The Japanese, in comparison, lost 300 lives in the war with around 900 wounded.[5] The Japanese considered their participation a success. For the Russians it was another disaster.

With the predominantly Russian population in Harbin, the repercussions of the war, the economy, and the politics that took place in Russia were felt by all foreign residents in the city. Vladislav and his friends kept abreast of all developments and kept each other informed.

Vladislav came rushing into the restaurant to meet his Monday night group.

"Have you heard, the tsar has abdicated? March 15, 1917, will go down in history," Vladislav stated anxiously.

"I could see it coming," said Genia, "The devastating war, the millions of wounded soldiers, the financial situation, and the economic unrest. The weekend protests in St. Petersburg clearly underlined the economic and military collapse. Something was bound to happen. The tsar was ineffective in the war and the losses were just too many." They all nodded in solemn agreement.

"It is hard to envision how things will turn out and what is to come next," added Vladislav.

"Russia without a tsar. I wonder how it will be?" They could hear the concern in Genia's voice.

"I heard that a provisional government with Prince Lvov and Kerensky is taking over. Do you think Horvath will continue as commissioner of the railway territory? It was, of course, the tsar who appointed him. Personally, I think he deserves the support and trust of the new government, for he has proven to be very good in what he does," said Misha, thinking out loud.

"What unbelievable times we are living in; war and turmoil seem to be a new norm, unfortunately," added Vladislav.

23 | The Fall of the Tsarist Regime

1917

Because grandmother Helena was Russian, and a monarchist, the negative and depressing news emanating from her homeland was very upsetting. The tremendous losses that Russia had experienced with World War I and the revolution were damaging and created a cloud of despair for all those in Harbin with a Russian connection. Grandmother took this tragedy close to heart. Church services became more solemn and attendance increased, not only for the Sunday service, but every day, with many praying for the departed souls and others turning to the church as their belief and hope of divine intervention seemed to be their last resort. It was natural that everyone was concerned with these events and the uncertain future; after all, many had left behind friends and relatives in Russia.

LEADING UP TO THE RUSSIAN REVOLUTION in 1917 the capital of St. Petersburg became the center of political turmoil and struggle. It started with the abdication of the tsar in March 1917, after his poor leadership as commander of the Russian military in World War I. The abdication of the tsar was a devastating blow to the Mensheviks, monarchists, and other supporters of the tsar. The Russian royal family was a symbol of aristocracy and an elegant lifestyle, but for the Bolshevik Red Russians, the tsar was a reminder of the disparity in the Russian society.

In the unexpected October Revolution of 1917 led by Vladimir Lenin, the communist

Helena in a traditional Russian outfit

Bolsheviks took over Russia from the provisional government in a coup d'état. "Peace, Land, Bread" was their main slogan, as well as other motivating phrases, "Workers' Control of Production" and "All Power to the Soviets."[1] The Bolsheviks stormed the Winter Palace, and the streets of the city were overrun by demonstrators and the military. Many of the wealthy businessmen and landowners were targeted and, in fear, they gathered their belongings and fled the city.

A congress met in late November and approved the coup, electing Lenin as chairman, Trotsky as foreign commissar, Rykov as interior minister, and Stalin as commissar of nationalities. Soviets in other cities quickly met and joined the cause, engulfed by the spirit of the revolution. It was the Bolshevik masses that led the charge. However, there were also many who opposed the Red Bolsheviks and preferred the Whites, who favored a constitutional monarchy. As a result, a civil war ensued between the Reds and Whites, which affected Russia for many years, especially in the eastern part of the country.

Most of the Russians living in Harbin were monarchists, as was Helena and her relatives. Many households had the picture of the royal family on their wall. Keeping track of their relatives back home included following news about the four beautiful, young daughters and how they were doing, and praying for the well-being of the young Tsarevich Alexei. The royal family tried to keep the poor health of their son a secret, yet many knew about the dreaded hemophilia that afflicted him. In Harbin, Russian patriots were more tolerant of Rasputin,[2] as he was said to be the only one who could control the bleeding and keep the Tsarevich "healthy."

In 1918, the new Bolshevik government of Soviet Russia surrendered to the Central Powers (Germany, Austria-Hungary, Bulgaria, and the Ottoman Empire) by signing the Treaty of Brest-Litovsk in March 1918, signaling their defeat and ending the Russian involvement in the Great War. Four months later the tsar, tsarina, four daughters, and Tsarevich were brutally murdered in Ekaterinburg by the Bolsheviks. The residents of Harbin were shocked by the news, and whether people agreed or disagreed with the rule of the tsar, the murder touched everyone. The monarchy was a

The Russian royal family[3]

part of Russia and the tsar and his family were a national symbol, and part of the soul of many of its citizens.

Like many, Ada and Vika had difficulty understanding why the royal family had been killed, especially the beautiful children.

"Why, mamochka, why did they do it?"

No one in Harbin had the answer nor could they comprehend why some in Russia agreed with this murderous act.

By 1922 the war between the Reds and Whites was nearly over. White Russians had been driven out of most of the major cities in the western part of Russia and, in the end, only held small parts of Siberia and the city of Vladivostok. On October 25, 1922, the last stronghold of Whites was besieged and Vladivostok fell. The civil war was chaotic and bloody, and the White leadership, which was divided and inconsistent, did not stand a chance.

In the lead-up to the Russian Revolution and during the uprising itself, life for many of the Russians became desperate, and the political and economic situation in Russia deteriorated rapidly. The most natural escape for many White Russians was the accessible city of Harbin where life could continue in a quasi-Russian environment.

Those who fled Russia and arrived in Harbin told frightening stories about the state of affairs in Soviet Russia and about the cruelties that were carried out. At first many of the residents in cities throughout the motherland thought it was a phase that would pass, believing that normalcy would soon return, but, as time elapsed, it was obvious that the revolution was there to stay. Those fleeing to Harbin grabbed few belongings together with any gold, silver, icons, or jewelry they had.

The new arrivals told of desperate times where bank offices, among them the Russo-Asian Bank, were closed, and factories and businesses were nationalized overnight. Churches were closed, and some were even destroyed. Stories of how Soviet soldiers spat into the faces of citizens were common. The soldiers frequently started fistfights and accosted people for no reason at all. Red army soldiers walked into stores and grabbed what they wanted. They robbed people in the streets with no hesitation. Citizens who held prominent positions were killed or disappeared and were replaced with incompetent, unqualified men. One Russian refugee told a story about a 19-year-old police commissar who was known to shoot citizens who had previously served in the government or who had well-known names associated with the old regime. Shooting them in the face was his trademark and claim to fame.[4] Law and order did not exist, and regulations and decrees changed daily. House raids by the Red Guards and by communist thugs were frequent. Brutal knocks on the door with the rifle butts in the middle of the night would wake up families. Houses were searched and plundered, and families were left terrorized. People became so traumatized that they seldom left their homes and rarely met with neighbors. They didn't know whom they could trust.

The Orthodox churches and religious missions in Harbin played an important part in helping Russians to settle in Manchuria. They offered assistance to the orphans and to the poor and looked after the weak. Vladislav and Helena worried about their families that still lived in Russia. Communication became difficult and in some cases stopped completely. Vladislav did what he could to try to get family members out.

After the revolution, the Soviet Union was closed off. Helena's auntie, Tatiana's sister, and her family were still living in Russia and everyone was concerned when word was received that they were struggling. Helena and Vladislav had heard how difficult it was to buy products. No one had money, and the banks were controlled by the government. Helena thought of a clever way to send money. She took a square of cardboard and carefully cut out a piece. She placed a gold coin in the opening and then took a picture of the family and pasted it on the cardboard. She sent the picture by mail to her relatives in St. Petersburg. In the attached letter she wrote that this was a recent family picture, but that she didn't like the way Tatiana looked in the photo and suggested that they should cut her out of the picture.

The letter took one month to reach St. Petersburg. The reply came back after a second month that they all thought Tatiana looked lovely and that they, of course, will not cut her out of the picture. Helena wrote back saying that she absolutely insisted that they cut Tatiana out. The letter took another month to reach the relatives. Upon receiving the letter, they reluctantly cut Tatiana out of the picture and discovered the gold coin. There was great jubilation when they found the coin, which was appreciated and enabled the family to survive.

The spillover from Russia added flavor to life in Harbin. The city was becoming a boisterous and vibrant metropolis, which stretched past the old town and up the hill to the new town. A popular pastime for residents was to stroll along the tree-lined sidewalks beside the Sungari River, or the cobblestoned main street, Kitaiskaya Ulitsa, where you were sure to meet friends or compatriots. Many of the newly arrived residents congregated in the evenings in hopes of securing work or an introduction for a position in a company. Refugees who had little education had no difficulty finding work in Harbin, but those who earlier held prominent positions in Russia had difficulty finding similar positions. They were often forced to resort to menial jobs. It was not unusual to see a former count working as a doorman or waiter. Those who had specific talents, such as piano teachers or school teachers, were better able to find employment. Many could not find affordable housing and they had to settle in small houses on the outskirts of the city. The refugees often came to Harbin with little or no money. They were known to bring icons and jewelry and pawned them or sold them to the local antique shops. Vladislav refused to buy these "treasures" from the antique stores because he always felt that they were sold with tears and grief.

24 | A Family Outing

1918

Grandfather's forest concession near Yablonia Station became a beautiful and exciting place for family visits and outings. Preparations were made days in advance with many details to arrange. For simpler outings within the city of Harbin, the family enjoyed visiting their dacha (summer home) on the other side of the Sungari River.

The acquisition of the forest concessions escalated Vladislav's business to another level. Naturally, his successes at work translated to his family life. With continued achievements came more privilege. The family was chauffeured everywhere. The girls were dressed beautifully to attend various social functions together with other children, and the large staff including Lenochka made life easy and comfortable for everyone.

Vladislav wanted to make sure that he provided his daughters with the best education. He decided to hire a piano teacher and a governess. A piano was purchased and a teacher came twice a week to give lessons.

The first governess, Mrs. Wardropper, was a British school teacher who worked while trying to get her son and her husband, a rich English fisherman in Siberia, out of Russia. She stayed with the family, teaching the girls German, French, and English. Because of the bureaucracy, it took Vladislav, through his connections, two years to reunite Mrs. Wardropper with her family.

Vladislav left day-to-day house matters to Helena and focused on his business and his life away from the family. When he would join the family for dinner, Helena harangued him with a list of the troubles caused by the girls during the day. Vika remembered being very upset about the onslaught of complaints from her mother and how nervous she was that her father would reproach her, but he never punished the girls and was always patient and encouraging. When Vladislav was home, Helena made sure that he recognized that she had the difficult job of parenting, often through exaggerated performances. At the dinner table Helena barked constant commands.

"Vika, close your mouth when you eat. Chew your food. Sit up straight. Hold your fork properly." With each command, she pushed Vika's arm.

Despite the tension and anxiety that existed between the sisters in the family, for the girls, life was satisfying.

The family frequently went on picnics together with friends, and Vladislav would join when he could. During the summer months, they spent time at their house across the Sungari River. *Solnechnyi Ostrov* (Sun Island), as it was called, was an area where many families had their *dachas* (summer homes) with lovely beaches and a nice social atmosphere. The Sungari River offered many activi-

A visit to the dacha: Barbara, Helena, Ada, Lola, Vika, and Nadia

Chacinsky and Barbara with their children Lola and Nadia

Vika and Ada

Ada and Vika with grandma Tatiana and Lola

ties for the visiting families, swimming, boating, and sunbathing, during the short and beautiful summer. It was a quick, pleasant escape from the daily monotony—like visiting a summer resort, yet it was located near the city.

Alexander and Sophie with a friend (far right) and their son George

Vika, Lola, and Ada

The family on the concession

It was always a special occasion and a rare treat when Vladislav arranged for the family to visit the concessions for "an outing." The children were excited as it was a train trip to a location outside of Harbin and everyone looked forward to the adventure. He was proud of the progress he was making and delighted in sharing it with everyone. He was also equally happy to show off his children to the staff. These outings usually included all the relatives and even a few friends or business contacts. For Vladislav, it was personal and important that the families working on the concessions were able to meet and interact with his family. Helena, Barbara, Sophie, and Tatiana could talk to the ladies' groups and made time to sit with them for a cup of tea and sweets. Helena especially enjoyed the events because so much attention was paid to their visits. Everything was exciting, interesting, and fun, and it was wonderful to be out in the forest, so close to nature.

Stolen Dreams

Vladislav

Barbara and Helena

Vladislav and family waiting for the trolley wagon

In the wagon

Ada and Vika usually included some of their friends from Harbin to enjoy a fun day together. Vika, Ada, George, Lola, and Nadia (Barbara's and Sophie's children) learned new games to share with the youngsters from the concession. They played in designated areas with the other children, who were happy to have the day off from school due to their visit. Sometimes Vladislav took everyone to ride the horses in the corral. Vika, even as a youngster, loved horses and it was obvious that she was a natural and would continue to ride. It was here that Vika honed her riding skills that she came to use many years later when she rode Mongolian ponies out into the countryside. The ponies were small but extremely tough, and one had to be skillful to ride and control them.

The concession had its own railway line, and the highlight of the trip was always the thrilling ride on the fabulous inspection wagon, an adventurous experience for the whole group.

Vika loving horses

Vladislav loved these excursions and was proud to have his two families, his own and that of the workers, enjoying time together. Unfortunately, these occurences were infrequent due to the complicated preparations; however, when they did come together, there was a lot of laughter and enjoyment and the time always went by too quickly. The visits were a reminder to the family and friends how vast the concessions were and what the lumber business entailed.

Vladislav, second row, far left, holding Ada

Ada and Vika with friends: An inspection wagon for the railway on the concession

Vladislav with visiting dignitaries and customers

Vladislav proudly standing along the tracks on his concession

25 | Summer Vacation

1918

Grandfather was a hard worker. He hardly slept and seldom took a day off. He felt uncomfortable relaxing and was always busy. It was with reluctance that he accompanied the family on vacation or on outings, unless it was to the concessions or business related. Coming home for dinner became difficult because of business engagements, and although he made the effort, he often left right after the meal and did not return until late at night. The next morning, he was already gone at dawn.

As Helena got older she complained of pain in her joints, marked by swelling of the fingers and feet. She blamed the cold Harbin winters with temperatures of −40°C, but her vanity and insistence on looking fashionable, even on the coldest winter days, exacerbated the condition as she stepped out of the house wearing dainty high-heeled shoes. Her stubborn habit infuriated Vladislav.

"No one in their right mind thinks of fashion when the temperature plummets to minus forty degrees," he would interject.

Helena ignored his comments. When she noticed slight deformities and when the throbbing pain kept her awake at night, she dismissed the gravity of her condition by simply using different oils to "cure" the ailment. The doctors at that time advised her to move her arms and fingers rather than keeping them still, but she closed her ears to any advice. Instead, she ordered Lenochka and the servants to give her massages and bandaged her arms, knees, and feet to keep them immobile, changing the bandages several times a day.

Dr. Kazem Bek was a prominent doctor in Harbin, a very loved and respected physician. He made house calls at all hours of the night, and Helena took advantage of his kindness and dedication by constantly summoning him

Helena using a cane

Helena riding a pedicab

for her pain. He diagnosed her with rheumatoid arthritis. Vladislav had no say in anything to do with her health.

After having spent many summers in the Harbin area, Helena decided that the family should visit Japan. She had heard about the hot springs located near Kamakura, which she concluded would be an effective treatment for her arthritic condition. The extravagant journey became an almost yearly event.

Helena drew pleasure in telling her curious and envious friends that the holidays to Japan were important as the family needed to get away from the hectic life in Harbin. Vika remembered well the long and exciting journeys to Kamakura. They traveled by train, then by carriage, and when the terrain became too rough, the transporters would appear with chairs supported by two long poles, each chair carried by two men. The entourage usually consisted of Helena, Lenochka, Ada, Vika, the first governess, the second governess, any visiting relatives, and a few servants. They would occasionally stop to look at the beautiful waterfalls, admire the Diamond Mountains in Korea, soak in dramatic landscapes, or just give their mother, Helena, a "rest." The journey by train and on land lasted days until they reached the southern coast of Korea where ships transported everyone to Japan. There was also a less exciting and more direct route by sea, where they traveled across to Vladivostok by train and then took a boat to Yokohama in Japan, but the children preferred the longer passage.

As the entourage made its way through the Korean peninsula, which was now occupied by Japan, the atmosphere and the looming depression was evident. Although Japan exercised domination over Korea since 1904, it was not until 1910 that Japan officially seized the country. There were many factors, the necessity of territorial expansion, war gains, that contributed to this occupation, but one of the major factors was the assassination of the Japanese Prime Minister Ito Hirobumi years earlier. They used the assassination as one of their many excuses to annex Korea using military and marine forces, enforcing martial law and declaring that all Koreans were now Japanese.[1] The Korean population was subjugated to a brutal occupation, which stripped the Koreans of their land, livelihood, language, culture, and dignity. The population was at the mercy of the Japanese occupiers and was subjected to perpetual cruelties and death. With their trip through Korea, the family witnessed the effects of this Japanese occupation. The soldiers' conduct in occupied Korea was abominable.

Vladislav told his young daughters the story about the brave young Korean who assassinated the Japanese statesman and four-time prime minister, Ito Hirobumi, at Harbin station. It was 1909 when the Japanese statesman was scheduled to visit Harbin to meet with the Russian Minister of Finance Count Vladimir Nikolaevich Kokovtsov, and the Russian ambassador from Peking, Ivan Iakovlevich Korostovets. Horvath was present that day to receive them. After Prime Minister Hirobumi inspected the guards, he went over to speak to a group of Japanese. Just as he was walking away from this group, he was shot and killed by Ahn Jung-geun, a Korean independence activist and a protestor of Japan's subjugation of Korea. During the capture and interrogation of Ahn, they received the news that Prime Minister Hirobumi

Prime Minister Ito Hirobumi arriving to Harbin Station minutes before he was assassinated[2]

The young assassin, Ahn Jung-geun[3]

had died. Ahn knelt down on his knees and crossed himself, happy that he had succeeded in accomplishing his duty to his country.[4]

By 1915 Japan had annexed, occupied and acquired substantial territory in Asia. With the appropriation of Korea, the Japanese emerged as a notable colonial power with substantial territory, which included Korea, Taiwan (Formosa), the southern part of Sakhalin, and the Ryukyu, Bonin, and Kurile Islands. With the possibility of expansion and a dominant physical and business presence in Manchuria and much of East Asia, Japan entered a new phase in its ambitions. The occupation of much of the territories was oppressive.

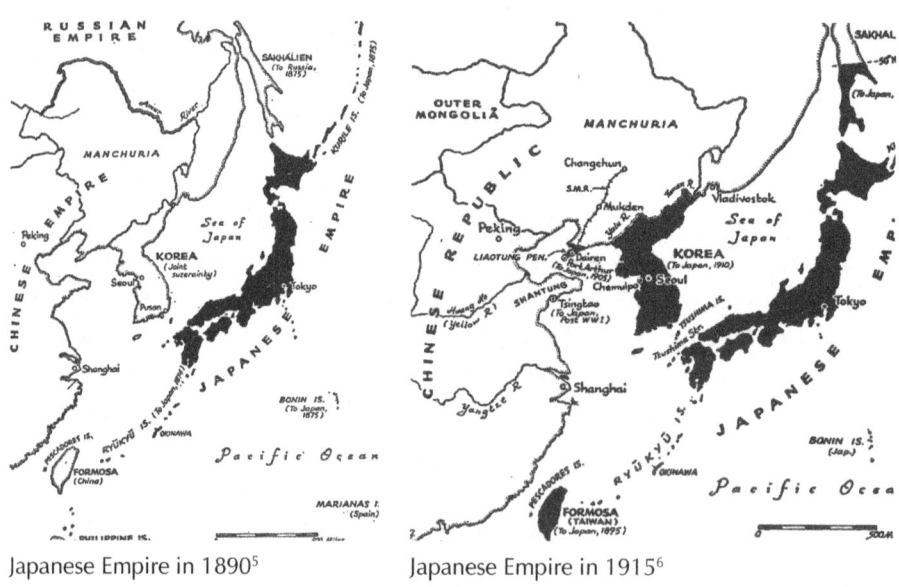

Japanese Empire in 1890[5]   Japanese Empire in 1915[6]

During their trips through Korea, the family witnessed physical abuse, starvation, and forced labor imposed by the Japanese. If a Korean was caught walking on the same sidewalk as a soldier of the Imperial Army of Japan, he was beaten unconscious for displaying such insolence. Even just passing through, the family could sense the fear and oppression the people felt. Koreans were terrorized in their own country, losing their identity in the process. They were forced to speak only Japanese, take Japanese classes in schools, and study their own Korean literature in Japanese. They were also obligated to fight Japanese battles in the confrontations in Manchuria or risk imprisonment and death. The Japanese stationed in Korea were authoritative and callous, but as the entourage came closer to Japan, everything changed.

When the ship landed in Japan, cars and rickshaws were waiting for them to continue the journey to Kamakura along the southern coast. The contrast between the Japanese living in Korea and those living in Japan was astonishing. The courteous ways of the Japanese, the soft-spoken language, and the helpful and generous demeanor made everyone feel welcome. Japan was a beautiful country with spectacular scenery. The countryside was green and lush. As they trekked along

Entourage

the coastline, they stopped in the evenings to stay at a Japanese *ryokan* (hotel), where there was time to enjoy a hot bath, a meal, and a comfortable sleep on a *tatami* (straw mat) floor.

Every year the same bungalow was made available in Kamakura. The lovely beachside rented house was a typical Japanese residence that was large enough to accommodate everyone.

The help showered the children with attention, and constantly hovered with mats, umbrellas, and *obento* boxes (lunch boxes). The summer days were full of activities. The girls spent all their time outdoors swimming in the sea. Just a short distance from the house there was a rocky area near a cove where the girls would spend an entire day diving in and out of the water looking for oysters in hopes of finding a pearl. Despite the many buckets of oysters collected over the years, they sadly only managed to find three pearls, but the anticipation was always exciting.

Ada and Vika playing at the beach

Every trip to Kamakura was a massive undertaking at a high cost, but Helena insisted on making the trip every year. She loved the baths and the hot-spring treatment and believed that they offered relief for her condition. It seemed that Vladislav rather liked the tranquility that came with the family's absence. He could concentrate on his business and enjoy his regular routine with fewer draws on his time.

One summer Vladislav decided to join the family's trip to Japan. He had developed the export business to Japan and he thought it would be a good opportunity to visit and perhaps reach out to some of his clients. He was also curious about Japan and the Japanese because he had never met them in their own country. He always had good dealings with the Japanese and found them to be respectful and business-minded. He also felt that the girls were growing, and as he enjoyed their company, he could use a few days to vacation and be together with them. He made arrangements for Alexander to take the reins while he was gone. This was the

Vika and Ada visiting a Japanese garden

Helena and Vika with baby rabbits

Vladislav touring Japan with the governess and the girls

One of Vladislav's trips to Japan

An outing with the family

The great Buddha in Kamakura

first time he had left Alexander in charge, and he was ready to give him this chance. Although Vladislav was beginning to question Alexander's honesty and dedication, he hoped that Alexander would rise to the occasion. Upon his return to Harbin, he was disappointed to see nothing had changed and that Alexander was still a problem. He continued to lack initiative and simply went through the motions. Vladislav would have to keep his eye on him.

In the summer of 1918 while the family was vacationing in Japan, Vladislav was offered the lease opportunity for his fourth concession. He had leased Hailin two years earlier and now was looking to lease Hundaohetze. He was managing well with the east and west concessions of Yablonia and Hailin, and felt Hundaohetze was a controllable addition. Vladislav knew that to increase his worth, he would have to expand his business and target the export market in Japan, other countries in Asia, Australia, and other cities in China. Vladislav signed the lease documents with the Provincial Board of Finance and the Forest and Mine Tax Office.

Hundaohetze was located along the CER line a few hours north of Harbin. The expanse of land was a good size, boasting beautiful lush forests and rolling hills. Just as in Yablonia, he would build a sawmill and a transport system on the concession with rail lines and cable cars connecting to the main CER line.

Vladislav was expanding, and did so knowing the risks that he was taking. There were many issues that he was already experiencing in Yablonia and in Hailin. The leasing of another concession meant that many aspects of the business required even better coordination.

The company depended on the availability of a responsible workforce. Given that most of the lumbering work was manual labor, good working conditions for the qualified personnel was crucial. Vladislav also had difficulty in securing the technical staff that he needed to work on the concessions. Engineers, technicians, and foremen were scarce, and few of them were willing to work so far from the city of Harbin.

Even though it was difficult to secure good labor and machines, in 1914 Vladislav established the first and only veneer factory in the region and was able to increase his output with this factory. He brought in equipment from abroad and set his ambitions high to eventually establish the possibility to develop a lucrative export business.

The lack of local machinery suppliers for the sawmills and factories created further problems for the lumber business. Good expensive machinery was imported and installed, but maintenance was often a problem as there was an absence of skilled mechanics. Orders of machinery took an incredibly long

Bridge on the siding of Kovalsky's concession[7]

time to be delivered to the concessions. Even after long delays, the delivered machinery was often not suitable. Yet despite these setbacks, the company was meeting all the orders from the railway enterprises and from the local building market; the business was thriving.

Photos of Veneer factory fully functioning in 1922[8]

Photos provided by Grochowski.[9]

Since acquiring the first concession in 1911, Vladislav conducted his business in an astute, profitable way. Years later when he was interviewed about how he grew his lumber business and about his strategy in making his enterprise a success, he stated, "Firstly, I didn't cut costs and invested in the infrastructure. My firm spent more than 800,000 gold rubles [about US$560,000] to build the rail tracks, cable cars, and roads.[10] We spent over 270,000 gold rubles [about US$189,000] on maintenance, repair, and protection money for the Honghuzi. Secondly," he explained, "I allowed laborers to settle in the cleared land adjoining the concessions so that

I would have an available labor force to work on the concessions, sawmills, and veneer factories, which were turning out 3 million cubic feet of wood and 15–30 million square feet of 3-ply veneer."[11] There were immense opportunities for expansion. Vladislav had built a solid foundation based on a good model and he had full control of his business and the knowledge to continue his expansion.

Translation: Cableway on Kowalski concession at Hundaohetze[11]

Train depot in Imienpo[12]

26 | Polish Independence

1918–1922

Living as a Pole in Manchuria after the war, following the independence of Poland and the Russian Revolution, was not easy. With regime changes and transfers of power, difficulties were expected, but the unforeseen nuances for Polish nationals in the case of China was difficult to imagine.

WORLD WAR I AND THE RUSSIAN REVOLUTION AFFECTED HARBIN AND its residents in many unexpected ways. For Poles it was a long-awaited celebration, over a century in the making, as Poland gained its independence from Russia in November 1918 with the armistice and by the Treaty of Versailles. Vladislav and all his Polish friends in Harbin were elated and commemorated the restoration of Poland's sovereignty after 123 years of partition. However, independence did not make life easier for the Poles in Manchuria.

When Lenin took power in Soviet Russia, the Soviets attempted to get diplomatic recognition from the Chinese Republic and at the same time to acquire control over the CER, but they failed. Their claim was that what belonged to tsarist Russia naturally would be carried over to them. Situations changed. The long-standing extraterritorial rights in Manchuria evaporated for the Russians and Poles in the railway zone. Suddenly, all matters were in the hands of the Chinese administration under Marshal Zhang Zuolin, the Manchurian leader, who was a strong anticommunist Chinese warlord.

China would not recognize the new Bolshevik Russian regime. The zone now became the Chinese Special Region of the Northeastern Provinces, where initially there was widespread disorganization and inexperience.

In the spring of 1920 a Polish consular mission was established in Harbin, but did not last long. The Chinese government demanded the closure of this Polish consulate because it did not recognize any government that did not have a previous treaty with China. As Poland was a newly instated nation, it did not qualify in spite of about 3,000 Poles living in Harbin at that time. Poland was permitted to maintain a semiofficial Delegation for Poland Office to look after its citizens' interests.[1] Consul Symonolewicz, who was posted in Harbin, stated in a diplomatic report, "A decline in the presence of Russia in Manchuria left Poland with great problems affecting also a great Polish company—with vast forest concessions of Mr. Kowalski, which were a good 90% of what we, Poland and Polish business, had as national assets and interests of Polish individuals in Manchuria."[2]

With China's takeover of the CER and increased restoration of sovereignty in the CER, issues such as extraterritorial rights, Chinese and Soviet ownership rights, CER budget issues, crime, corruption, and administrative challenges continued to be addressed. It was a learning and adjustment process for the Chinese administrators. A "Special District" of the Three Northeastern Provinces was initiated in 1920, and the administration was taken over from the CER. The Special District secured Chinese restoration and preserved many of the conditions of the previously controlled Russian CER zone.[3]

The atmosphere in Harbin was one of progress and development as many Russians were fleeing the Soviet Union and choosing to settle in Harbin.* Business was booming, prices were increasing, and the population was growing. Employment opportunities were more favorable in Harbin where a teacher could earn between 900–1200 rubles compared to a salary of between 120–300 rubles in Russia.[4]

Harbin life and the standard of living was quite different for every resident. Many experienced a life of luxury and comfort and enjoyed all the privileges that came with it. At the other end of the spectrum were residents who lived a destitute life. There were emigres who lived from hand to mouth and barely survived. Desperate individuals slept in makeshift houses; families made do with whatever situation they could garnish and lived in deplorable conditions.

In this situation, Chinese and Western interests started to cooperate in building new relationships in Harbin and Manchuria. European and American, as well as other consular missions, had opened in Harbin, giving a seal of approval to Harbin in terms of world economic, social, and

---

* The Soviet Union (the Union of Soviet Socialist Republic—USSR) was formed on December 22, 1922, comprising a confederation of Russia, Belarus, Ukraine, and the Transcaucasian Federation.

political standing. The warlord Zhang Zuolin and his economic policy administrators became more involved in managing and administering political and economic ventures in Manchuria. They managed to create a liberal and open economy that stimulated economic growth, and the Fengtian dollar became a popular currency.

Amid what seemed to look like a stable situation in 1922, bandits began to wreak havoc regularly on wealthy residents and on established companies including Vladislav's business, which experienced "forest fires, lack of respect of the legitimate ownership of concessions, lawlessness, corruption, discrimination, blackmailing, and sinister betrayal."[5] These actions were condoned by the administration of Marshall Zhang Zuolin who demanded higher taxes and fees for protection by his troops.

One Sunday morning Vladislav and Helena sat together at the breakfast table, which was a rarity. The combination of her illness and their attitude toward each other added to this situation.

"Many Poles are leaving Harbin, especially those who were working on the CER. I think there is so much uncertainty for the Poles living in the railway zone and in Harbin." Vladislav was visibly upset.

"Perhaps they feel that it is a good time to leave. Poles have been waiting for so many years for independence," added Helena.

"It is difficult to say. Of course, our situation was more secure with the extraterritoriality that we had for so many years. We are not protected as we were before, not by the Russians nor the Chinese and as we don't have a consulate, it makes us vulnerable to compromising situations." Helena could see that he was troubled, voicing his thoughts.

After a brief silence, he added, "Strange how history changes our destiny. Tsarist Russia was the architect, the financier, and the owner of the CER and the leased lands and now it doesn't exist any longer.[6] This certainly will affect the Russians and the Poles living in Harbin and those connected with the railway."

"By the way, did you hear Nadezhda Vladislavna and her Polish husband are going back to live in Poland," added Helena in an attempt to break the mood.

"It's good that she learned Polish while she was here in Harbin," added Vladislav.

"Well, everyone speaks Russian in Poland," interjected Helena.

"I think things will change now. We have our own country again and our national identity. It is important that she speaks Polish. I am sure it will be a great asset," said Vladislav.

"I am worried about the situation for Russians living and working in Harbin. I wouldn't want Alexander Alexandrovich's Russian status to be affected," commented Helena.

"I think Alexander Alexandrovich can concentrate on working a little harder and dedicate himself to the business," interjected Vladislav.

"What do you mean, Vladislav? Alexander Alexandrovich is a very able man," Helena pointed this out in a condescending way.

"Yes, we all are aware of his abilities," added Vladislav with a touch of sarcasm. "Anyway, I must go. I have so many things I must attend to. I probably will not be back for dinner tonight. Apologize to the girls for me." And he walked into his study.

He closed his office door, as he usually did, to discourage any interruptions. He had many decisions to make as the company had grown to a large industrialized operation with many employees. He was a very methodical person and a perfectionist. These qualities brought out the best in him, but at the expense of his time, energy, and health.

It was at this point that Vladislav began to experience serious problems with Alexander. Vladislav was irritated with Alexander and began to exclude him from meetings because he was bothered by his lack of commitment. Alexander arrived late to work, sometimes not at all, his laziness was obvious, and he involved himself with many of the monetary transactions that were not part of his job. He was insensitive to the political situation and all the associated problems and lacked diplomacy. Vladislav needed Alexander to take the initiative and be his right-hand man, but he could see that he had neither the ability nor the desire to do so. Unfortunately, his family relationship, being the brother of Helena, made it awkward for Vladislav to voice his complaints.

27 | Lucia Mikhailovna Solovov

1919

An unimaginable change was about to take place in the family. Who could have thought that the family would grow?

One day the mood and atmosphere changed dramatically. Helena's voice was at least an octave higher. The commands were markedly different. Vika tiptoed into Ada's room. The usual response screeched through the air.

"What are you doing? Get out of here. You know you are not allowed in my room. Get out!"

Vika scurried back to her room and sat on the bed listening for some hints as to why there was so much commotion and her mother's erratic behavior.

It was not until dinner that everyone was informed of the news. Helena announced that she had received a letter from Mikhail Alexandrovich Solovov, the husband of her dear deceased sister. He asked them to look after Lucia, his second child and only daughter, and wondered if she could come to Harbin to live with them. Since his wife Ekaterina had died, he had struggled to bring up the two children and found it too difficult to care for a daughter. He felt that Lucia needed the love of a mother and should be brought up in a normal family setting. His son, Cheslav, would stay with him in Russia. Mikhail admitted that his duties in his new position in the Soviet Government were too demanding and he was in need of their help.

It was decided that Lucia would be "adopted" into the family as a Kowalski, not officially but in a compassionate sense. This was the wish that Helena's dying sister would have wanted. This is what Mikhail wanted and the fact that he turned to Helena to ask for help was what she wanted to hear.

Helena announced, "Mikhail Alexandrovich has asked us to look after his dear daughter, Lucia. She will come to live with us and should be considered as our daughter. Ada and Vika will now have a new sister."

Stolen Dreams

Vladislav just nodded his head and agreed.

Mikhail's letter further stated, "I am sure that both you, Helena Alexandrovna and Vladislav Fyodorovich, will be good role models for Lucia. She needs stability. I thank you for your kindness and understanding." He signed the letter, "respectfully, Mikhail Alexandrovich."

Helena was ecstatic and in her reply to Mikhail she promised that Lucia would be loved and would have a proper upbringing in the family.

Mikhail knew that Lucia would be in good hands living in Harbin together with the Kowalski family. Being a staunch communist, even though he disagreed with their opulent way of life, he felt that it was the right thing to do. Lucia would get a better education in Harbin than in Russia, although the transition would certainly take some time.

The CER offices controlled education and culture and contributed large amounts of money to educate the young Russians living in Harbin. In total, there were over one hundred elementary, middle and high schools, as well as two universities. After the Revolution, there were over 20,000 Russian students studying in the schools in Harbin.[1]

At the schools most of the students were Russian, only 10% of them were Chinese, with only a few students from other countries.[2] In 1915 alone, the CER spent 1,143,000 gold rubles (about US$800,000) on the maintenance of the schools.[3] Approximately 200,000 gold rubles (about US$140,000) was spent on maintenance of the two universities,[4] which were of a very high standard. One was a Law Faculty and had about 800 Russian and 60 Chinese students, and the other was the Polytechnic Institute with 600 Russian and about 50 Chinese students.[5] For many years Vladislav was a generous donator to the Polytechnic Institute and served on its board.

A prestigious school for girls was the M.A. Oksakovskaia Classical Girls Gymnasium where graduates did not have to pass an entrance examination to enter a university.[6] The girls were attending this school, which offered a vast array of subjects to middle school and high school students, including mathematics, algebra, geometry, trigonometry, cosmography, economics, geography, Russian, English, physics, history, Latin, art, and philosophy.[7] The programs were very ambitious.

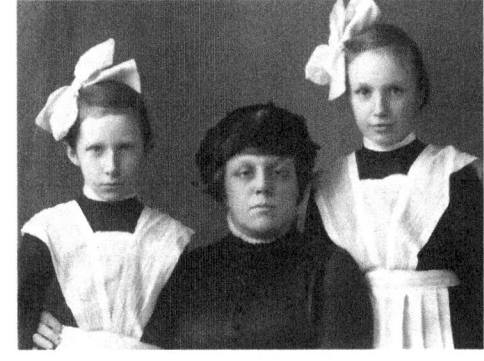

Vika, Helena, and Ada

Harbin's rich cultural life was further enhanced by the large number of intellectuals pouring in from Russia—musicians, artists, and others. The intellectuals thrived in these surroundings where their talents were appreciated and revered. The CER supported cultural organizations such as libraries, institutes, and societies, as well as a meteorological station. The Central Library of the CER in Harbin contained over 100,000 books.[9] Most of the books were in Russian, some in Chinese, and some in other languages.

Polytechnic Institute[8]

Eventually the Chinese assumed control of the educational and cultural institutions except for the Polytechnic Institute, which remained in the hands of the Russians. Nevertheless, the Chinese did not want to jeopardize the Russian interests in the area and encouraged the support the CER was giving to the field of education.

The White Russians were pouring over the border every day due to the problems in Russia. Harbin became the home to a large Russian population. This population in Harbin grew from 34,200 in 1916 to 200,000 Russians in 1923.[10] During one of Mikhail's earlier visits to Harbin it was evident that he did not have any sympathy for the non-Soviet ideology. He would visit Harbin often to try to recruit people with vocational skills, doctors and professors, in the hopes of convincing them to return to the Soviet Union as they were in need of learned people. Over the years Mikhail had changed. He became cold and distant and overly polite. Vladislav tried to convince him to give up on the Soviet government and to come to Harbin where there was a sense of normalcy.

Mikhail quietly answered, "Vladislav Fyodorovich, you don't understand. We have gone through the pains of change. That is behind us. Our future is now ahead of us. But you, here in China, have not yet reached that stage. You will have to suffer and go through the process. It is you who should be joining us."

This came from a man who was from an aristocratic family, had been an officer on the imperial yacht *Standart*, and who had danced with the royal princesses. Vladislav could see it was a hopeless case. Helena just sat there and said nothing.

It took Vladislav some time and great effort to extract 14-year-old Lucia out of Russia. Despite Mikhail's high position in the Soviet government, a payment for the ticket needed to be made to a member of the Soviet government in Petrograd (St. Petersburg was renamed in the beginning of World War I). In addition, he was obliged to ship a railcar load of wheat to a specified destination in Russia before the Soviet government would allow Lucia to board the train for Harbin. After all arrangements had been made, Vladislav sent her the ticket for her trip to Harbin. Lucia received the ticket one month later, owing to the civil war in Siberia.

Sometime later, Vladislav received news that Lucia arrived at the station just as the train was pulling out and had missed the train. All arrangements were canceled by the Russian side and Vladislav had to start all over again—another carload of wheat and another ticket had to be purchased and sent to Lucia.

Lucia Mikhailovna Solovov arrived in Harbin and was warmly met by the family. The journey was long for her traveling alone and she looked a little disheveled stepping off the train. Lucia was not particularly pretty. She was as blind as a bat and wore thick glasses. She was wearing a strange outfit, which was dated and quite unbecoming. Helena immediately took her to the beauty shop for a haircut and styling. It was clear Mikhail had not given her the attention she needed. The next day Helena brought her to the Churin Department Store to buy her suitable clothes. Ada and Vika were not allowed to accompany them as she wanted this bonding time together with Lucia. Helena fluttered around in a state of blissful frenzy. She could see that it would take Lucia a little time to get used to living in Harbin. Lucia, with all the pampering, started to look quite pretty.

Lucia was three years older than Ada, and had a very independent mindset. She did not get along with her father and welcomed a new environment. Quickly, she made up her mind that her situation in Harbin was better than the one she had in the Soviet Union and embraced her new life.

Lucia's arrival was an invigorating lift for Helena and, fortunately for all, the distraction at least temporarily drew her out of her depressive state. She spent a lot of time with Lucia, and kept her father regularly informed about her new life in Harbin. Ada was also delighted with this arrangement as she now had a companion and a "sister" she liked. The two of them soon developed a strong friendship. Vika now was very much alone, but she was able to occupy herself with her own activities and interests.

Lucia Mikhailovna Solovov

28 | On the Concession

1919

Life on the lumber concessions was good but very demanding for the workers. They lived in a family-oriented community that created a secure and wholesome life for the families, and the children grew up in a healthy, stable environment.

The settlements on the Yablonia concession were surrounded by beautiful and rich Manchurian wilderness. The rivers were abundant with fish, and the forests were full of animals and game—deer, wild boars, bears, pheasants, and tigers. The employees on the concessions enjoyed family outings, picnics, and fishing trips, and the men often went hunting and brought home game for cleaning, cutting, and sharing with friends and neighbors.

On Vladislav's concession, workers were treated well and they enjoyed being part of the community. One particular family, the Aksenoff family, recounted in an interview about their life on the concession and told about the many wonderful memories they had. The Aksenoffs had escaped from Vladivostok and arrived in Manchuria as young newlyweds and were happy to find work on the Yablonia concession. They settled in one of the small houses that was provided for the workers. Soon after their arrival, Mrs. Aksenoff became pregnant with twins and was helped and cared for by her new friends. Tragically one of the babies did not survive, but Genia, their surviving twin, turned out to be a healthy and beautiful baby. Genia Aksenoff was born in the small clinic on the Yablonia concession.

On the concession Vladislav needed someone capable of managing money and administrative matters. Since Mr. Aksenoff had worked in a bank and in the gold business, he possessed many of the skills Vladislav was looking for. He was glad to employ him. Aksenoff was hired as the supply manager in the company, with the responsibility of procuring and purchasing all the supplies, machinery, and equipment for the railway, sawmills, and forestry business such as engines, trains, rails, and tools for felling trees and transporting logs. Vladislav was relieved to find such a qualified person.

The Yablonia concession was vast. It had its own railway network that covered the entire concession, providing access to all the areas. In addition to the main station, there were several stations along the line that handled important forestry activities. They had big factories with sawmills to cut logs and prepare planks, and had an efficient logistical network to transport the wood to the veneer factory in Harbin, to construction and building sites, to the CER, and for export.

Loading logs[1]

Preparing logs[2]

Transporting logs

Aside from administrative work, Mr. Aksenoff had experience working with and caring for horses and was happy to take on this responsibility. There were hundreds of horses on the concessions. During the winter months from November to March, the horses were used to drag the felled trees and logs. During the summer, the horses were herded to Mongolia for three to four months where they grazed and recuperated to regain their strength for the next winter felling season.[3]

The logging of the trees usually started in autumn and stretched into the winter months when the frost set in and the countryside was covered with snow. The logs were transported to the banks of the rivers and streams. They were often pulled by oxen and horses. In spring the logs were floated downstream until they reached the Sungari River where they were tied together to make rafts. After reaching their destination, the rafts were disassembled and the logs were taken to the mills and factories for processing.

When Vladislav had worked with Sviiagin on the excavation projects in Pogranichnaia many years earlier, Sviiagin had been in charge of the administration of the workers' camps. Vladislav noticed that Sviiagin was a man of great sensitivity and cared about the well-being of his staff. He made sure the workers had nice accommodations and lived in a comfortable environment. He built a clubhouse for the workers and their families to use for their social settings as well as a small theater at the camp to present amateur performances and encourage in-house productions. Vladislav thought this was wonderful because it created a warm, friendly, and positive atmosphere for everyone. He vowed that he would do the same if he was ever in a position to replicate this, which he did.

Houses on the concession[4]

When he planned the Yablonia concession, Vladislav followed through on engineer Sviiagin's model. He built a stage in one of the buildings and provided a small social hall. He arranged to have performances and organized intermission music using an Ariston, a manually cranked music box. Even though this was a primitive form of entertainment, it was welcomed by the workers who jumped up and danced to the music.

On the concessions, the Aksenoffs lived a secure and happy life as did other employees. Their small wooden house had two bedrooms, a living and dining area, and a lovely small garden surrounding the house. Each house was built using logs and wood from the forest and had windows with a trough along the windowsill to plant colorful flowers. A gardener cared for the garden once every three weeks. Genia was a young boy growing up in these surroundings and remembered the fenced area of

Housing on the Yablonia concession

forty or fifty houses for the families of Russian employees, which was located on the right side of the concession extending to the station. More than 200 Russians lived in their community and another 5,000 Chinese people lived in the nearby Chinese village housed in 600 fanza (huts).[5]

The community was made to be as self-sufficient as possible. Residents were provided with a school for the children, a library, a church, a barber shop, and a dispensary for health care. In the social hall, there were newspapers and magazines that were imported from Russia and Poland so that everyone could keep up-to-date with events. One of the most popular facilities for the families was the traditional Russian bathhouse with separate sections for men and women. The bathhouse would be visited by the family—a time to relax and enjoy being together. Family life and social interaction were important for everyone. It was a healthy, happy environment for the children and the families.

Employees on the concession at an outing

Playground areas on the concessions were fun for children and adults.

Depending on the felling season, Vladislav had between 40 and 300 employees, and between 2,000 and 8,000 workers. Yablonia was the main center for Vladislav's business where he hired an efficient staff of one civil engineer, four forestry specialists, one lawyer, four technicians, five commercial clerks, and seven translators—Chinese, English, and Japanese.[6]

Being on the main CER line resulted in constant locomotive traffic going back and forth, the tracks being quite close to the houses. When the joint

Sino-Soviet administration of the CER started some years later, a special train traveled to stations along the rail line. It carried goods and merchandise from Soviet Russia and stopped at Yablonia at least once a week. These trains had special wagons for the sale of goods. The merchandise was presented beautifully and all kinds of items were displayed—fashion for women, fur coats for both men and women, shoes, cosmetics, Russian tea, and Russian chocolates and candy. The train's arrival was always a special event at the concessions and, although the staple goods were usually the same, people were always excited to see something new. This form of merchandising was a way for the Soviets to earn foreign currency.

Genia remembered how he and his father went to the "shop" to look for a birthday gift for his mother. In an interview years later, he admitted that men were not very gallant during those days. His father felt uncomfortable and looked awkward as he pushed his way through the crowd of ladies to reach the salesperson. He finally decided on a Russian scarf for his wife, Nina Nikolaevna, to wear around her neck during the cold winter months. Genia was always a fan of the Taget brand of hand soap, and he recalled that he managed to slip a bar of soap into the purchase for himself.

The church played an important role for all the emigres in Manchuria, including those on the concessions. As many of the residents were originally from Russia or Poland, they needed to feel a close connection to religion, to traditions, and to their culture. The Russian Orthodox Church and the Polish Catholic Church embraced everyone, giving their respective congregations a feeling of belonging. All the Polish and Russian church holidays were lavishly celebrated on the concessions. The ladies ensured that the food, arrangements for the celebration, and the scheduling were organized down to the last detail. The social aspect of the church was equally valued where they could connect with their friends and build social networks. Meeting each other, having fun with friends, drinking tea, and chatting together were interactions that were always appreciated. Genia reminisced how his mother always gave him 20 kopeks to donate to the church, though he admitted with a smile, "I gave ten to the church and put the other ten in my pocket."[7]

The acquisition of the concessions Yablonia East and West in 1911 and 1913, Hailin in 1916, and Hengdaohezi in 1918 was an ambitious endeavor, but Vladislav continued to increase his holdings when in 1919 he added a fifth concession, signing the lease on Imienpo. He was happy with this last addition of Imienpo because it had no hills and was rather flat, which made it easier to build up the infrastructure.

Stolen Dreams

Vladislav's enterprise contributed considerable revenue or duties to the Chinese government in the form of a stump tax paid to the Chinese by his firm, which would amount to 18 percent of the selling price of the products.[8] The Chinese felt comfortable working with the Kowalski firm since Vladislav was responsible with his payments and deliveries. This was not easy because, at this time, there were wide price fluctuations of timber products, which complicated business transactions.

As the history books on the CER stated, "The most extensive output of building materials comes from the concessions of V F Kowalski near Yablonia Station."[9] He became the largest exporter in Manchuria exporting lumber and veneer to Australia, North and South America, and Japan, employing 10,000 employees.[10] Despite the massive size of the enterprise, Vladislav always tried to maintain respect for the authorities and was conscious about his responsibilities working in the lumber business. He was one of the few entrepreneurs to practice sustainable logging and made sure to replenish the forest.[11] To him it made good business sense in his long-term planning. The importance of preserving and maintaining natural resources was something he learned from his father many years ago in Kozuchow.

Translation: Factory/Firm of W. Kowalski at Imienpo located 162 kilometers from Harbin[12]

29 | General Dimitrii Leonidovich Horvath

1920

When General Horvath (picture on p. 14) visited the house, Ada and Vika were rushed into the bedroom and obliged to change into nice dresses with matching ribbons in their hair. The girls were then ushered out to curtsy and greet the general. Vika, as an 11-year-old, found General Horvath to be intimidating. He was very tall and large and usually wore a cape, which made him look even larger. His voice was low and resounding, yet he had a soft nature about him. His eyes and smile were kind and he warmly greeted the girls with some small talk. Few people have been as important to grandfather and his business career in Manchuria as General Horvath. Grandfather had immense respect for him, for developing and protecting the railway, for creating a safe and prosperous order in North Manchuria and Harbin, and for being such an excellent leader.

GENERAL HORVATH LIVED IN A HOME ON THE OUTSKIRTS OF THE CITY in Staryi Harbin (Old Harbin). He bought a large estate from A. I. Iugovich and his deputy S. V. Ignatsius and renovated their houses where he lived until he and his family left Harbin in 1920.[1] Horvath and his family actively participated in all social and political occasions. Everyone in the city of Harbin and in the Russian Railway Zone appreciated his leadership and held him and his family in great esteem. Horvath had developed the "Russian-Manchuria" Zone with tolerance and equal opportunity for its people, without discrimination.[2] However, the Russian Revolution with the new Bolshevik regime proved an overwhelming challenge for him.

General Horvath had represented the tsar and for a short period served the Provisional Kerensky Government.[3] In response to the Bolshevik coup d'état, he initiated the bold opposition against the Soviet government, and in 1918 he proclaimed Harbin to be an all-Russian, anti-Red government haven, at the same time having close contacts with the Chinese authorities (1917–1919).[4]

He was the leader in a movement to challenge Bolshevism in the Far East, but his attempts were unsuccessful.[5]

He participated from 1918 in the Siberian Intervention (also known as the Allied Intervention and American Expeditionary Force)—the US-led effort by the Western Entente Powers and Japan to dispatch troops to support the White Russian forces in the civil war against the Bolshevik advances.[6] He also established close relations with the US–led forces that launched the Inter-Allied Railway Commission, an initiative to secure the Russian-connected railways, including the CER, under the supervision of the US diplomat John Stevens.[7]

In November 1920, General Manager Dimitrii Horvath was forced by the CER board of directors to step down as head of the CER, but he continued his involvement in the fight against the Bolsheviks. When Horvath came for his last visit to the house to meet with Vladislav, he was already resigned to the fact that the Whites had lost, and that Russia was now a communist, Soviet state that would never return to its former self. The first thing he said to Vladislav was: "My friend, I may not see you again."

"Why's that, Dimitrii Leonidovich?" Vladislav asked, already anticipating the answer. He saw how haggard Dimitrii looked and could see that his uniform was unkempt and loose on his once powerful frame.

"My time to care for the CER and the Russian Railway Zone is unfortunately over, as you have probably understood. I plan to leave Harbin with my family," replied Horvath.

"We are sorry to hear that. The political developments in Russia and Siberia over the last few years have made it difficult for us all," Vladislav replied.

"Dimitrii Leonidovich, you were close to the revolution and understood what was happening here in Manchuria and Harbin. What are your thoughts?"

"I take for granted that you had Bolshevik-inspired workers making trouble in your company, similar to what I experienced in the CER. Truthfully, I didn't feel that it was a real revolution in Harbin and in the railway corridor, Vladislav Fyodorovich. I felt our situation was only slightly affected. What took place here was just a weak echo of events in Russia. It would have been easy to suppress the revolutionary movement here by just appealing to the Chinese authorities, but I avoided doing so. I did not, at that time, want to hand over the CER, our railway, to the Chinese," Horvath replied.[8]

Horvath continued, "Vladislav Fyodorovich, what we experienced in Russia was the fateful collapse of our monarchy. In 1917 Kerensky's power waned and in the State Duma he failed to organize resistance. Still no one expected the Russian people to bring about a coup d'état, and for members of the State Duma to end up at the head of this revolt. In Harbin, I felt I could have taken on the fight with our own railway guards in Manchuria; however, I wanted to avoid armed conflict within the CER leased territory, so I chose not to do that. It was safer, in my opinion, to prevent revolutionary excesses, and I was satisfied that I managed to avoid it. There was no serious or detrimental revolt in Harbin and a relatively peaceful situation was maintained. In fact, there were only a few cases of killings in Harbin during this revolutionary period."

"That was admirable management from your side," said Vladislav. "What more is there about the issues with the CER and Chinese guards on the railway?"

"There were different problems. The Chinese guards and troops were deployed to maintain order as the Trans-Amur Border Guards went to fight in the First World War while detachments of the so-called People's Militia were sent to guard the CER.[9] Also notable was the serious Japanese military troop intervention. A lot of Japanese troops, part of the Allied Railway Commission, appeared and instead of fighting the Bolsheviks, they encroached on CER railway territory by force," explained Horvath. "When the Japanese were first invited to participate in the Siberian intervention, they were not interested, but soon after changed their mind. The Japanese agreed to contribute a number of troops, a maximum of 20,000 (the US leading the operation had 7,000 troops); however, the Japanese in a devious act sent 72,000 troops without informing the other countries."[10]

Horvath continued, "The US diplomat John Stevens, who had established an office in Harbin to lead the Allied Railway Commission work, was shocked when he realized that the Japanese troops acted more like a conquering force than a protective one.[11] Stevens immediately informed his government in Washington, which then made the Japanese government aware that its actions were completely unacceptable. A secret strategy was devised to eliminate all Japanese advisors and troops from participating in any activities concerning the CER, and so far, it seems as if the Japanese activities have been curbed. John Stevens promised me that he would stay on and not conclude the Allied Railway Commission until all Japanese leave the area. His mission was also helping a well-organized transfer of the CER to the Chinese."[12]

"What shocking revelations, I was not aware the situation was so severe and that the Japanese were posing such a threat," sighed Vladislav. "What about your efforts in Russia in the civil war?"

"You know, Vladislav Fyodorovich, I had contacts with Anti-Red opposition and governments both in east and west Siberia. Their army was, in my opinion, just a trashy mob whose heads had been stuffed with ideas instilled by revolutionary demagogues. The military leaders were corrupt and incompetent and lacked coordination. They certainly did not trust me or like my suggestions or my advice. The Reds were extreme and violent in their fight against the Whites in Siberia and determined to win power. One sad example of the violence was demonstrated in the massacre at Nikolaevsk on Amur, committed by a "renegade" group of partisan soldiers not officially sanctioned."[13]

Horvath continued with Vladislav's full attention, "There were Japanese military units stationed in many areas in eastern Siberia, like the garrisons of the Japanese Army operating in Nikolaevsk. This contingent of Bolshevik partisans attacked Nikolaevsk in February–March of 1920 with force and unimaginable cruelty, killing military officers and civilians. The town was wiped out and burned to the ground. Victims were stabbed, shot, drowned, and killed. It was estimated that more than 6,000 Russians were killed during this short period. Not only did the civilian Russians fall victim to this partisan massacre, but also 700 Japanese were killed.[14] As a consequence, the Japanese government demanded North Sakhalin as compensation for its losses, as the Japanese Expeditionary Army garrison in North Sakhalin was part of the Japanese colony stationed in Nikolaevsk.[15] This was, to me, a typical example of how Japan would try to cash in and demand territory, on questionable grounds, even in tremendously tragic circumstances for the Russians."

"Nikolaevsk was an incredible tragedy! Unbelievably upsetting. Such violations by revolutionary Russian peasants against the civilian population and, to think, it is violence against their own people." You could feel the pain in Vladislav's heart.

"I did what I could in Siberia, but the fight was too bloody, and the Bolsheviks were too strong. In the end, I came back to Harbin and the CER. As to the railway, Vladislav Fyodorovich, I think that the complex situation will allow the warlord Zhang Zuolin and the other governors in the Three Northeast Provinces to hopefully act responsibly with the region, the railways, and the Japanese. It will not be like before, and the future is uncertain."

Horvath continued, "The result will probably be that the Bolsheviks will acquire some influence over CER together with the Chinese. In any case, I don't have to worry anymore, there will be two interim managers, Engineer Lachinov and Engineer Kazakevich, who will serve before Boris Vasil'evich

Ostroumov, my successor, will begin next year (1921) in February.[16] He is an able man and will do a good job managing the railway."

"Do you have any advice for me, Dimitrii Leonidovich, I mean, advice to keep up your achievements?" asked Vladislav.

"Vladislav Fyodorovich, support him just as you have always supported me. I have always appreciated you, your assistance, and your cooperation. He will value your friendship during these turbulent times. And thank you for all the good work and good times together. I will miss you and Harbin," Horvath heartfully replied.

Vladislav looked at Dimitrii and felt a twinge of sadness. "Before we break up and say goodbye, let me tell you that I have really valued your friendship and all the help you extended to me and my family during the years. Without you I would not have been able to develop my company and timber concessions in the way that I have. You kept us together, you built friendships and avoided animosity and discrimination in our multiethnic community. You have worked well with and respected men of different opinions, provided they meant business. I wish you could have continued in your CER position."

The two men, both giants in their own right, hugged each other for a little longer than usual, a difficult final goodbye. Horvath turned and left the room. Vladislav could feel the pain of loss deep in his heart.

30 | Acheng (Ashihe) Sugar Factory

1920s

The Acheng Sungari Sugar Factory located outside of Harbin was a mecca for many of the Polish residents who ended up in Manchuria. The factory was owned by a group of Poles and became an important part of the Polish community. Given the unsettling situation for Poles in China, the factory played a significant role in bringing the Polish workers, families, and children together.

THE CITY OF HARBIN HAD BECOME A MULTICULTURAL AND COSMOPOLITAN community that lived in relative harmony. The Russians, Poles, Jews, and other nationalities living on Chinese soil were trying to make a good life for themselves and were ready to put up with the challenges. Life was not always easy for them, but they were ready to confront the difficulties because conditions were usually better in Manchuria than they were in their own country. The emigres had better pay and enjoyed the freedom to do as they pleased. This was a great incentive for many of the settlers.

Despite the political and economic difficulties created by the recent turmoil, Russians and Poles living in Harbin, like Vladislav and his family, had no intention of moving. They were part of the original establishment of Harbin and saw their residence in Manchuria as their permanent home. This was in stark contrast to many of the "new" Russian arrivals who, despite finding the city a suitable place to make a home, viewed Harbin and Manchuria as a temporary place to live before moving on. There was a marked division in the Slavic community. Their differing viewpoints ran deep, with each side possessing strong individual ideologies. Many of those Russians who had settled in Harbin during the early days and those who did not agree with the new ideology in the Soviet Union were White Russians and were anticommunist; however, the "Reds" that came to Harbin after the fall of the Russian Empire, fleeing Russia for personal reasons, still pledged alliance to the Bolsheviks.

Vladislav and Helena tried to make their life in Harbin as normal as possible without entangling themselves in the politics that affected the lives of so many Russians and Poles. They had many Russian friends, yet few of them were Soviets.

"Vladislav, I saw you talking to Tasia Ivanovna Rudakova. You know that her husband is a staunch Soviet working for gospodin (Mr.) Stolovich. What were you talking about?" asked Helena. But before he could answer, she continued. "We asked her if she was planning to attend our church. She said perhaps at a later time. That is what they answer when they are Soviets, you know?"

Vladislav knew that the Rudakovs were Bolsheviks, but he always felt that it was important to be on speaking terms with everyone, in hopes that they may one day change their allegiance. Even in his own company, many of his employees had different beliefs and opinions, and he respected everybody, despite finding some of the demands from the communists problematic.

The entire CER zone, including Harbin, being under the control of the Special Region of the Eastern Provinces was going through a painful process. Slowly the Chinese took control of the police, the military, the CER railway guards, the courts, the Land Department, the Municipal Council, education, and other organizations in the Special Region in accordance with the CER Right-of-Way.[1] The Japanese South Manchurian Railway did not face any similar changes.

As all the Russian diplomatic missions across China were closed, Russian citizens who held imperial Russian passports and Russian Poles under the Russian protection, as well as "capitalists" living inside and outside of Russia, had to reregister if they wanted to become citizens of the Soviet Union. This left many Russians in Manchuria with the choice of returning to Bolshevik Soviet Union, staying in China and becoming stateless, or to try to become Chinese citizens.[2] Harbin was turning back into a Chinese city.

"Larisa Alexandrovna and her husband, similar to many other Russians, are now stateless. What is going to happen to them?" Helena asked.

"Nothing, everyday life will be very much the same," answered Vladislav, trying to calm Helena. "They can continue to live in Harbin as stateless citizens if they choose to do so. That means they will fall under the Chinese legislation, as the Russian extraterritorial protection has ceased. The difficulty, of course, will arise when they want to travel to other countries as they have no passport. We are lucky now that we have our Polish passports."

No matter how hard Vladislav wanted to believe that life would be the same, it wouldn't be.

Mills Sungari Sugar Factory: Ashihe Sugar Mill is also known as the Mills Sungari Sugar Mill. Since 2017 the factory buildings were designated as cultural heritage–protected buildings.[3]

Entry for beets carts[4]

Weighing station[5]

Railway tracks to Harbin[6]

Housing for the workers.[7] The location was used as a summer camp for Polish children and served as a community for the Poles who were employed. Polish families lived in housing provided for the workers.

Apart from his main lumber business Vladislav had diversified his holdings and had invested in different sectors—mining, sugar, flour, and soybean as well as real estate. One of his earlier investments was made in 1907 when he became a shareholder of the Joint Stock Company Mills Sungari, which was located 30 kilometers from Harbin. This was a sugar mill company that extracted sugar from sugar beets. Many of the Poles living in Manchuria were either linked to the lumber business or this sugar mill factory, or, as in Vladislav's case, both.

The Mills Sungari Sugar Factory (Ashihe Sugar Mills), where Vladislav had a substantial investment and where the Russo-Asian Bank was the main owner, was started by a group of Polish businessmen. Vladislav held 3,460 of the 16,000 shares, investing 649,000 gold Russian rubles (about US$454,000).[8]

The Sugar Factory had difficulties right from the beginning. The production cost for sugar became expensive and the company was facing financial difficulties. These challenges occurred at the same time as the Chinese authorities began imposing severe restrictions on Vladislav, other Poles, and the business because of their Polish nationality.

The Russo-Asian Bank, as part owner in the Sugar Mill, found itself in a difficult situation as the ownership of the company was comprised mainly of Polish nationals. The Russo-Asian Bank decided to change its name (and ownership) to the French Banking Company, a clever political move that put the bank under French jurisdiction.[9] The French Banking Company then created a new company, the French Sungari Mills Company, thereby issuing new shares.[10] The conversion to a company with French ownership helped Vladislav and many of its other shareholders, as the French had extraterritorial rights and protection. Though the ownership issue had been circumvented, Vladislav later had conflicts with the bank concerning share dividend profit payments, a matter that could not immediately be solved. As a result, Vladislav's company was forced to go to court to secure its finances.

The conflict over unpaid dividend profits lasted for three months while the bank's business deteriorated, and, finally, it ended with the bank declaring bankruptcy in September 1926. The French government did not take any steps to address the bankruptcy. After a decree by the president of China, the Liquidation Commission was formed to settle the claims. In the meantime, the plaintiff made threats against Vladislav.[11] Vladislav, in desperation, reached out to the Delegation of Poland Office in Harbin, which sympathized with him. The matter proceeded to court, with the assistance of the Polish Consul, and the trial dragged on for a year.[12] The Liquidation Commission's final judgment ruled in favor of Vladislav, declaring that all the claims against him were groundless; however, to Vladislav's surprise and frustration, the judgment made by the commission was ignored by the plaintiff.

The proceedings did not stop, as the Liquidation Commission then appealed to the Judicial Board. Thirty meetings were held in the House of the Judiciary Committee, which required Vladislav's presence for each one. After several months, it was determined, in its final judgment, that the decision "is the same as in the first proceedings was substantial."[13] Vladislav came out the winner again.

Vladislav's business was adversely affected by that time and a substantial amount of money was wasted on the proceedings. The Polish Consul, troubled by the lengthy trials and the impact it had on Vladislav's business, reached out to the Polish Ministry of Foreign Affairs and asked it to take measures against the Chinese authorities. Unfortunately, making this kind of claim was a delicate matter, and as the Polish government had not yet secured official diplomatic relations with China, they chose to avoid the subject. These trials continued until 1928–1929, as was indicated in Harbin newspaper articles that mentioned that Vladislav was sued for $250,000, and he countersued numerous times.[14]

The Mills Sungari Sugar Factory continued its operations, and changed hands several times, eventually being taken over by businessman Leo Zikman. Vladislav sold his shares in the company and, although he lost money with this venture, he had no regrets. It was a meaningful bonding opportunity with the Polish community as so many of the Polish activities centered around this company.

31 | 1 Yi Yuan Street

1921–1922

In 1922 the family moved into a new, big, beautiful house. Vladislav had always told the family that he would build a house perfectly fit for them, but they never expected something so magnificent. It was designed and constructed with copious attention, thought, and love. It was a dream come true for Vladislav and the family, a home where they could live happily for the rest of their lives.

VLADISLAV HAD PURCHASED A PIECE OF LAND IN THE BEST PART OF Harbin. It was up the hill from the main railroad station, close to the St. Nicholas Orthodox Church, which majestically stood on the crest of the hill, and across the street from the main parade ground. The location was meaningful as it was located next to his friend Leon Skidelsky's mansion. Vladislav had contracted a famous Russian architect named Alexander Alexandrovich Bernadazzi to draw up the plans for the house.[1] Bernadazzi was a renowned Russian architect who had designed several buildings in St. Petersburg, all in an Italian style. He had lived in Russia for many years, but fled to Harbin when the communists won control of the country. Bernadazzi, 50 years old at the time, was the son of a famous Russian architect; he was energetic and determined, following in his father's footsteps. After fleeing to Harbin, he had been without a job for some time and was very excited and enthusiastic about the project.

When Vladislav initially discussed the plans with Bernadazzi, he had expressed the desire for a small comfortable home for the family, but Bernadazzi had a different vision and began changing the plans daily, making one addition after another. The blueprints for the house eventually grew into a forty-room, three-story mansion, with a fully functioning basement. Vladislav left things up to him because he could see that Bernadazzi poured his whole heart into the design and construction of the building. As the proud lumber

Stolen Dreams

Kowalski mansion in Harbin completed in 1922

entrepreneur in Manchuria, Vladislav wanted the house to illustrate the richness and the beauty of the forests and the land around them.

He was adamant about using the wood from his concessions to decorate the ceilings, walls, and interior, and insisted on utilizing the talents of Chinese artists to carve the wood. The house was designed in a European baroque style and took several years to build. It was an architectural marvel. Both the exterior and the interior reflected excellent workmanship and talented craftmanship.

The entrance to the house was at the side of the building. It led to a large foyer highlighted by an elegant, deeply rich, wooden staircase leading up to the second floor. At the base of the bannister was a beautiful statue of Diana, the goddess of the hunt, the moon, and nature holding a ball of light that reflected off the shiny wood finish decorating the walls. The foyer led to a well-designed living room, and a dining room that could easily seat a party of twenty people. Off to the side was Vladislav's study.

At the east end of the house was a large semicircular room filled with plants, palm trees, orchids, rose bushes, edelweiss, perennials, and annuals. Something was always in bloom. It was appropriately called the winter garden and was designed with the long, severe Harbin winter weather in mind. Family and friends could sit in the comforts of the floral enclosure, a miraculous contrast to the freezing snow and icy conditions outside its windows. In the middle of the room there was a hole in the floor that had a thick glass

Foyer

Vladislav, far right

The winter garden on the left

The house from the side showing St. Nicholas Cathedral in the background[2]

window. The window was above the billiard table, which was in the room below the winter garden. You could sit in comfort in the winter garden and watch the billiard play in the room below. From the winter garden, one door led to the living room and the other to the dining room.

On the second floor were the bedrooms. Vladislav had his own bedchamber with an attached bathroom and small changing room. He had a small balcony where he often sat quietly reading a book or going over some papers that he would bring up from his office. Like his study, where he spent much of his time when he was home, it was his personal corner of the house. Helena's room was a separate, spacious, and bright room with windows on two sides of the room. She had arranged it comfortably with a bed, a makeup table, and a chaise longue where she could rest and relax her aching joints. Between Vladislav's and Helena's room was a reading room that led to a patio. The patio was made large enough to be able to have the whole family together enjoying the outdoors. During winter the family would gather in the winter garden and in the summer in the reading room, which opened up to the patio on the second floor.

Next to Helena's room were three separate bedrooms for the girls, Vika, Lucia, and Ada. Vika's and Ada's rooms were almost identical, with a few exceptions. Vika's room had a small sink purposely installed, as she was a tomboy and frequently needed to wash her hands. There was also an access door between her room and her mother's allowing Helena to enter freely into the room to check on her. Because of its location at the center of the house Ada ended up with one of the rooms that had a balcony facing the front garden. Though it was not often used, it was a luxury she enjoyed bragging about. The small bedroom next to Ada's was for Lucia. Because her room was rather small, Lucia spent most of her time in the "golden room," next to her bedroom at the end of the hall, reading, studying, and socializing. The golden room was particularly nice as it opened onto a large second-floor balcony. Vladislav ensured the design for the house entailed lots of windows and outdoor space, an attempt to bring nature into the house, as it embodied who he was and what had contributed so greatly to his success.

The third floor was rather plain, but it was functional. It had been designed with a large common area in the middle with multiple rooms around the perimeter. It was built to accommodate guests and any relatives who would arrive after escaping the deteriorating situations in Russia and Poland. Vladislav loved Harbin and hoped that all his and Helena's relatives would come to visit. He knew that it was difficult for the family to travel to Russia and Poland, so he hoped that by offering their relatives a place to stay for an extended period of time, they would make the journey to visit them. There was always room for more guests, even though the rooms were occupied by Tatiana, the governesses, and other relatives.

The entire house was heated by an enormous boiler that filled one of the many rooms in the basement. The lower floor also included the billiard room, a small indoor swimming pool, and the kitchen, which had numerous stations where three cooks could all work at the same time. Behind the kitchen was a wine cellar and a space for food storage, which was large and dark and stayed cool year-round.

Like the winter garden, the grounds around the house were full of trees and flowers. When in bloom, the flower beds were always perfectly manicured, accentuating the gorgeous fountain that highlighted the front yard. There was even a flower bed that was designed and served as a sun clock. In the back of the house was a full-size tennis court, a popular pastime of their friends and family.

Flower bed in the front garden

Pond in the garden

A great deal of thought was given to security and safety in the construction of the house. Vladislav insisted on making it impenetrable from the outside with thick stone walls. On the inside, he had Bernadazzi install a huge iron door and a concrete separation between the second and third floors, a failsafe to seal off the structure and prevent the spread of fire if ever needed. An underground passage led from the basement kitchen to the garage on the other side of the front entrance. It was another way to exit the house if required, but a route that became an appreciated convenience as the family could avoid going outside to get to the car during the cold winter.

In 1922 the house was completed and with its Italian-style architecture stood out as a unique and beautiful landmark. The family moved in shortly afterward. After its completion, Alexander Bernadazzi was able to enjoy the credits of his accomplishment. He died in 1931 leaving behind a masterpiece at 1 Yi Yuan Street (formerly Bol'nichnaia Street). Its beauty, solidity, and uniqueness stands today as an architectural tribute to him.

32 | Mulin Concession

1922

The beautiful mountains and forests of Manchuria contained a wealth of nature and wildlife. Every season would welcome its share of birds, reptiles, and animals that roamed freely. Grandfather loved animals and so did Vika. He often talked about feeling guilty about infringing on "their" territory.

THE FAMILY SETTLED IN QUICKLY AND EASILY INTO THEIR NEW HOUSE. Vladislav used his office more often at home, which meant he could spend more time with the children. He did insist on closing the office doors while he worked because he did not like frivolous interruptions. Helena spent her days reading and limited her socializing to lunches with Barbara.

Ada, Lucia, and Vika were enrolled in the Russian M.A. Oksakovskaia Girls Gymnasium, which was a five-minute drive from the house. Even though the girls could walk that short distance, they were not permitted due to the fear of kidnappings. The Oksakovskaia school was a very prestigious school with an excellent reputation, and the three girls were registered in different classes for the new school year.

When the girls returned home from school, Ada and Lucia did their homework with the assistance of the governess. Vika, being the youngest and with an easier curriculum, was able to finish her work quickly. The governess worked tirelessly to help Ada and Lucia, but they were only interested in getting the answers as Ada generally had a difficult time with her studies. After many hours, the governesses would finally relent and just go through the motions to complete their homework. Ada blamed the governesses, the teachers, even Vika for her shortcomings. For Ada, school was not a priority. She was lazy and knew that even if she didn't study she would be able to pass.

One afternoon Ada came home from school and immediately ran into her mother's room. "Mamochka, I want to go to boarding school in England!

Larissa said that all established families always sent their children to study in England, and I want to go," exclaimed Ada.

Like her mother, Ada was very concerned about social status and the perceptions of others, and if England was where the daughters of wealthy families went to school, that was where she needed to be. She began pleading regularly to her mother to send Vika and her to boarding school. Certainly, the family was able to arrange it, and her mother always supported and reluctantly spoiled her with any request she had. Vladislav, at the insistence of Helena, began to investigate the option of sending Ada and Vika to a school in England.

Early one evening, when the girls were upstairs studying in the golden room, they heard a terrible commotion downstairs. The servants were screaming, and they could hear their mother yelling statements that no one could decipher. Naturally they all jumped up and ran downstairs. Just inside the front door to the house stood their father holding a small bear cub.

A big black bear had wandered into the village on one of the concessions that day, and fearing for the safety of the wives and children, the bear was immediately shot. Sadly the shooter had not noticed a young baby cub following close behind its mother. Vladislav was against killing animals and was devastated by the unnecessary act. He decided to take the cub home, to make sure it was looked after and fed.

The entire household had already gathered. Ada and Lucia stood at the entrance to the foyer, staring expressionless at the animal, whereas Vika was ecstatic, running over to her father and the bear cub. Vladislav and Vika had one passion in common and that was their love of animals, all animals.

Vladislav turned to Vika and said, "I've brought you an orphan, do you think you can look after it?"

"Oh, Papa, of course I can. How cute he is! Papa, I can't believe you found this cub. He will be my baby. Don't worry, I will take care of him. I'm going to name him Misha," she screamed excitedly. Vika ran past her mother and sisters to find some warm milk and blankets for the cub and to arrange a safe place for him to sleep.

"You must be out of your mind bringing a wild animal to the house," screamed Helena. "You are totally crazy. What are you going to do next, bring home a tiger?"

Vladislav did not even look at her. He continued to pet the cub.

From that day on, Vika rushed home from school to care for Misha. She finished her homework quickly in order to spend as much time as possible with him. Nothing was more important to her than Misha.

The cub stayed with the family for nearly eight months. At first it lived in the house, chewing slippers and sliding along the parquet floors. Misha soon became too much trouble to be kept inside, and was relegated to an enclosure in the garden where he was tended by servants and entertained by Vika. As Misha grew, it was obvious that the garden was not suitable and he could not be kept there any longer. Vika was terribly depressed at the news that Misha was being taken away. As a consolation, the day Misha would be transported to the concession, Vika was allowed to accompany her father and the group of helpers. For Vika it was a sad day, but the excitement of visiting the concession and staying over at his private house with him made it easier. Vladislav was seldom able to spend time with either of the girls, so this was a special and memorable day for her.

It was a big ordeal transporting Misha to the concession located along the railway a few hours from Harbin. He was already very large, and the trip made Misha and everyone helping feel uneasy. On the concession, the workers had dug out a big round area in the ground, like an enclosure you would see at the zoo, and installed a huge post in the middle. As soon as they had Misha in the enclosure, they could see this was the perfect place for him. Misha was inquisitive, climbing up and down the post to see what was going on.

Once Misha had been tended to, Vladislav took Vika around the concession. He introduced his daughter to the families and workers, stopping for lunch at the home of one of the administrators, whose wife made a delicious lunch of chicken encrusted with bread crumbs called *Kievskie kotlety*. Cutting into the cutlet was tricky as the butter always squirted out, but Vika managed her cutlet skillfully and glanced over to her papa for a smile and a nod of approval. Vladislav then took her to his office as he had some work he needed to finish.

"Vikachka (as he would call her), do you mind going to the office with me? I have some important things I have to finish before we go back to Harbin." He reached out his hand to walk together with her.

"Of course, Papa. I don't mind at all," she said eagerly. This was special for her, she felt so important.

While he was working, she pretended to read the book she had brought along. She didn't read more than a few lines as everything was too exciting and she wanted to absorb every moment with her father.

Vladislav was clearly busy. He was negotiating the acquisition of another concession, Mulin. This would be his sixth and last concession. With the addition of Mulin, the size of Vladislav's holdings would cover an area of about

Privately Leased Lumber Concessions in Manchuria

Map of the Kowalski's concessions: Top left—Imienpo, Yablonia (East and West); bottom left—Hailin, Hundaohetze, and larger arrow pointing to Mulin[1]

5,400 square versts (2,372 square miles)[2] and became the largest holdings of any lumber entrepreneur in Manchuria. The development of the concessions paved the way for colonization of an entire area. The isolated countryside was transformed into cultivated farmland communities that benefitted the population and the area.

According to the information collected by Vladislav's firm, "In 1921 in and around his concessions they gathered approximately ten million kgs of food, including rice, wheat, soybean, kaoliang, oats, among other products."[3] In addition, they had produced tons of special plants, fostered cattle breeding, and yielded bird-rearing products. A network of roads were built to facilitate communication, and housing was constructed for the workers and their families. Stores with supplies were set up. The population settled in the areas and communities grew.

Although the need for firewood had plateaued in 1922–1923, the demand for building materials continued to grow. Vladislav considered that the Mulin lease would be a profitable investment in spite of political uncertainties. Even though he understood that the export of timber was handicapped by the Bolshevik seizure of the Maritime Province and Vladivostok, the proximity of Mulin to the Russian border and the Vladivostok port was an advantage. He realized that there were more export markets that he could pursue. Vladislav had certain ideas about the direction of his company and had the confidence to make this a profitable and wise decision. Nothing could stop him from moving forward. He continued to get orders through his advertisements and marketing activities.

Cut lumber on the concessions

The trip to the office took a lot longer than expected. As far as Vika was concerned, it could take all night, she did not mind. She wanted time to stop and she wanted the day to last forever. It was a memorable experience for her, one with no interruptions or distraction from Ada, Lucia, her mother, or anyone. It was just the two of them, she and Papachka.

The next evening they arrived home. Vika went upstairs and went straight to bed. She fell asleep with a smile on her face.

Advertisement in Russian and English[4]

Machines and equipment in Vladislav Kowalski's wood factory in 1922[5]

Rail lines on the Hundaohetze concession, 1924[6, 7]

Machinery on the concession

The transporting of lumber down from the mountains on the Hundaohetze concession[8]

33 | Relatives

1924

Grandfather loved to share his home and to have his relatives around him. The whole third floor of the house was designed to accommodate relatives that would come to Harbin. He had managed to get Pawel, his older brother, and his mother to visit. Pawel was so comfortable in Harbin that he remained.

WORD OF VLADISLAV'S SUCCESSES AND HIS MOVE INTO THE NEW, beautiful house had reached the relatives living in Kozuchow and elsewhere. Vladislav's nephew Alex, the son of Adam, was in Russia during the turmoil leading up to the revolution and asked Vladislav for his help to extricate him and his family out of Russia to Harbin.

Alex Kowalski was married to Maria, and they had a lovely daughter, Genia. Vladislav, of course, agreed to help, making the usual arrangements of money and locomotive carloads of wheat. Alex and Genia were to leave Russia first, followed shortly thereafter by Maria. After they arrived in Harbin, the family settled in the apartment over the garage. Vladislav gave Alex a job in his office and was pleased to have a relative from his side of the family working with him.

Vika, too, was very happy, as she had longed for company. When Genia, Maria, and Alex came to live in their house, she gravitated toward them. They were fun, friendly, and very unpretentious. Vika was delighted that she and Genia were almost the same age. They had a lot in common and enjoyed spending time together. The two of them often played hide-and-seek, giggling the whole time. The house had so many hiding places that the girls could entertain themselves for hours. Every once in a while, they would convince Ada to play. Vika and Genia would hide under a staircase or behind an alcove sitting in silence as Ada angrily called for them. These moments made Vika giddy with happiness. Ada would become extremely irritated and would often throw tantrums. The dramatics would end with everyone being sent to their rooms, but for Vika it was worth the punishment as she continued laughing alone in her room.

In the evenings the girls would get together in the small apartment that Alex and his family were using above the garage to play Lotto, a Russian game similar to bingo. Ada, Lucia, Genia, and Vika would sit on the floor in a tight circle so that they could see who was getting close to winning. Maria would bake some *prianiki*, a cookie-type dessert, and the winner of each game would be awarded a treat to eat immediately in front of the disappointed losers.

Vladislav was very fond of Genia and treated her like a daughter, and it was apparent that Genia adored Vladislav. When he asked her questions in his low, even-toned voice, she always perked up, and tried to answer him in the most articulate way she knew. She always felt comfortable and welcomed his kindness, but for some reason Helena always made her feel uneasy. Perhaps it was just her imagination, but she believed that Helena did not warm-up to her because she was a Kowalski and not a Zaharoff.

Alex was a party animal. He loved friends, wine, and women. Maria, on the other hand, was introverted, rather simple and sweet. It wasn't long before Vladislav began to realize that his nephew was irresponsible. As Alex became more undependable, he caused problems in the office and his drinking became a serious issue. He signed bills for drinks using Vladislav's name and often sauntered home drunk. He was regularly late for work and did not take his job seriously. He soon met an attractive woman named Natalie Simonova whose Russian husband was employed on one of the Japanese concessions, a competitor of Vladislav's.

Natalie Simonova accepted Alex as her lover and their affair became so serious that she divorced her husband. Alex's wife Maria became aware of the affair, confronted her husband, and threatened to divorce him. When she explained the situation to her daughter and the possibility of them separating, Genia intimated her preference to live with Alex and Natalie. Devastated, Maria committed suicide three days later in her room by taking poison.

One of the maids found her body and instantly, there was great commotion. Vika, Ada, Lucia, and Genia were whisked upstairs and directed to remain there. Vika held her ear against the door, hoping to hear something. Vladislav saw straight away that it was a suicide. He flushed the poison down a sink and destroyed the cup. He positioned her body to make it appear that she had fallen. Only then did he call a doctor. Vladislav reacted in the way he did knowing that the church would not bury a suicide victim with full religious rites. The burial would, therefore, have been in a potter's field for the poor. Vladislav would not allow this for his elder brother's family.[1] Thanks to his quick reaction, the service was held in the church with the priest presiding. Maria was buried with full rites in the Catholic section of the cemetery in Harbin.

Shortly after the funeral, Alex married Natalie and eight months later a son was born who they named Garrik. Vladislav had ordered Alex to leave his house before the marriage but encouraged Genia to come visit and spend time at the house, which she did. Vika at 13 was too young to fully comprehend what had happened, and it was only much later that she understood why Vladislav hardly spoke to Alex or his new wife.

Vladislav had immense respect for his brother Adam in Kozuchow and decided not to inform him of the circumstances of Maria's death. Instead, he simply wrote to Adam expressing his condolences on the sudden death of Maria, his daughter-in-law.

Alex and Natalie's marriage shortly after Maria's death was a comfort to Genia, as she could count on the love of a "new" mother. However, as she grew up, Vladislav could see that she suspected the truth. She was very mature for her age and was growing up quickly. She became very sensitive and insightful, blossoming into a strong, levelheaded young lady. She began distancing herself from her family and spent more time with Vika. They became very close and spent every day together. Life was easier with a best friend, and Vladislav was glad to see both Genia and Vika so happy.

Vika and Genia often sat on the grass at the far end of the property and chatted about all the secrets they had. Vika could tell Genia anything, unlike her own sister. She confided in Genia the frustrations she had at home with Ada and her mother, and the extreme favoritism her mother showed toward Ada. Genia was very understanding, as she had seen Helena's callousness toward Vika. She also confided in her that she hated her Russian teacher, Dimitrii Grigorevich, who also tutored the girls in mathematics. It was obvious he had assessed the environment in the house, and in order to win favor with Helena, immediately started to praise Ada.

"At first, I couldn't understand what it was all about," said Vika. "He kept praising Ada and advised Mother that he thought Ada was a "mathematical genius." If I ran down the hallway while Ada was studying, I was yelled at and punished for disturbing the "genius" studying in her room. Mother thought he was fantastic."

"But Ada hates mathematics, she even told me so," interjected Genia.

"I know. Isn't it crazy? It was so funny, one day I decided to play a trick on Dimitrii Grigorevich when I had my scheduled lesson with him. I got some sand from the cat's litter box, which was soaked in urine, and put it in a small dish under the desk. Throughout the lesson Dimitrii Grigorevich kept asking if he could open the window, and I victoriously said no, as I was sure I was coming down with a cold. He kept coughing and sneezing because of the smell. It was the best lesson I ever had," giggled Vika. The two of them couldn't stop laughing as they rolled around the grass doubled over.

The two girls enjoyed collecting pictures of Hollywood movie stars. They wrote letters to the stars requesting autographed pictures, and each successful reply was greeted by an incredible screech of happiness and excitement. Vika had been doing this for some time and was so happy to have Genia equally interested in her project, one that everyone else had thought was ridiculous. Her collection included pictures of Rudolph Valentino, Lillian Gish, Greta Garbo, Charlie Chaplin, John Barrymore, Douglas Fairbanks, Mary Pickford, John Gilbert, and others.[2]

"Can you imagine, Rudolph Valentino sent his picture all the way to Harbin, China. He even autographed it. I am the luckiest person in the world," Vika exclaimed. The girls carefully entered the pictures into an album, which they stowed in a box with a small lock and key. They didn't want to take any chances. They would often go to the movies in the city together with the governess or with one of the nannies, as it was important to keep up with the Hollywood scenes and to support their beloved stars.

Genia Kowalska at age 23

One of their favorite games was one that they made up. They would lie down on the grass, look up at the clouds, and try to attribute the shapes of the clouds to something tangible. That shape would be the topic of questions and answers.

"That cloud is shaped like Italy."

"Tell me about Italy," Genia would answer.

"Italy is where I met Georgio. He was a professor at a university in Florence..." and she would continue on.

They would spin fairy-tale romances, of love, life, and happiness.

34 | The Gem of the East

1924

The Gem of the East, The Paris of the East—these were the terms that described Harbin in the 1920s. What a privilege it was for the family to be experiencing this unique and dynamic existence! Life was interesting and exciting. Harbin was changing every day and had so much to offer.

"Harbin offered a Russian-speaking cultural, social and economic world, without the official boundaries and prejudices of the Russian state."[1] It was a bustling Chinese city where you could hear Russian spoken on the streets, as well as in all the shops, restaurants, and administrative offices. The Chinese in Harbin communicated in their form of abbreviated Russian and Chinese. Street names and signs were written in both languages, and you could enjoy a blending of cultures and people. Along the main street in downtown Harbin, there was a mix of Japanese restaurants, Russian bakeries, Chinese jewelry stores, and French fashion boutiques. The main street displayed varying architectural styles ranging from baroque to Byzantine. The atmosphere was unique and added a cosmopolitan flair to the city, which had a prerevolutionary Russian feel to it. Its shops catered to European customers and were designed to fit its clientele. Tearooms and cafés sprouted everywhere, as well as cabarets and nightclubs, which ensured a lively night life.

The Moderne Hotel, which opened on September 14, 1914, was one of the first high-class hotels in Harbin to offer fine dining, dancing, and a venue for social events. Owned by a French national by the name of Iosif Kaspe, it was located on Kitaiskaya Ulitsa (Chinese Street) in the center of town. The three-story hotel housed a restaurant, a coffee shop that served delicious baked goods, and a cinema that could be used as a theater or a concert hall for up to 700 people.[2] The huge ballroom on the upper floor was the best place to hold a function of any significance. Any big occasion had to be scheduled way in advance to secure the date.

The opera performances were usually held at the Railway Club, which boasted the best of the best. The in-house ballet and opera companies performed regularly, and only well-known and accomplished celebrities from abroad were invited to perform. Opera productions were held twice a week and were reputed to be the best in China and comparable to the finest performances in Moscow. Feodor Shaliapin, one of the most renowned Russian opera singers of his time, and Alexander Vertinsky, a famous composer, poet, singer, and actor years later were among the favorite performers in Harbin.

The Harbin audience was a discerning one and did not tolerate mediocre performances. Classical music was particularly popular, and theater, music, and the arts were communally appreciated. In winter, beautiful waltz music was played at the skating rinks along the banks of the Sungari River where seasoned skaters danced in pairs to the delight of onlookers. Open-air concerts were held in the parks during the summer months, and families were entertained with evenings of Mozart and Beethoven. It was often said that Harbin was one of the most cultured cities in the world.

There were several movie theaters, or "picture palaces" as they were called, scattered around the city. The cinema showed productions that kept its audience in touch with the movie stars, fashion, and life beyond the borders of China. They were extremely popular and would have two or three showings a night. The movies were silent films from Russia or Hollywood, shown with the accompaniment of a talented pianist who always stirred up the audience as the actors performed their exaggerated scenes. The family

The Chinese Eastern Railway Club was built in 1911. Concerts were regularly held at the Club[3]

Stolen Dreams

One of several movie theaters in the city[4]

went often. Of the many movies Vika saw, she remembered one in particular. It was a scene of a panic-stricken man in a car stranded on a railway track. The pianist excitedly quickened the pace of the music as the train approached. Everyone was sitting on the edge of their seats, barely able to withstand the exhilaration and anticipation of what would happen next. Women were gasping and some almost fainted from all the excitement. The films were short but intense, and worth every minute.

In the middle of the city, ladies were well dressed and gentlemen elegantly clothed in tailored cuts. Even women from the middle class would copy the ways of the Russian aristocrats, parading in their gowns and high-heeled shoes, carrying parasols to shade themselves from the sun.[5] Shops offered a variety of produce and merchandise for customers who preferred to shop at local stores rather than at Churin Department store. Small Chinese-owned shops offered cheaper prices, but in the Fujiadian districts, where there was a larger concentration of Chinese, you could find even better prices.[6]

Social events, drinks, good food, culture, music, dance, and friendships were an integral part of life in Harbin especially for the privileged class. But like many growing and established cities, as the city grows so does the crime and violence. In addition, the drug trade accelerated, and corruption was more rampant than ever. Warlord Zhang Zuolin was connected to the opium trade and used the lucrative profits to finance his military and himself. He legalized opium in Manchuria and consolidated it under the government jurisdiction, which prompted the opening of government stores in the city.[7]

Japanese and Koreans (as subjects of the Japanese Empire) played a large role in the growing, trading, dealing, and handling of the opium. Utilizing the Japanese Kwantung Army, many of the drug traffickers brought opium and heroin into the area through the Shangdong Province. Many Chinese cities were supplied with drugs from India and Iran, a route earlier used by the British. Tianjin, a city close to Peking, became the center of drug traffic in 1922 where 70 percent of the 5,000 Japanese living there were in some way involved in the drug trade.[8] Drugs were not banned in China, enticing many Chinese and foreigners into the trade. Opium dens were becoming more prevalent, with different classes of dens: some large and elegant with a club-like atmosphere, and some dark, small, and grungy with bodies lying everywhere in delirious stupor.

Vicarious lifestyles flourished during the time of the Warlord Era where prostitution houses became more prevalent in certain Harbin neighborhoods. Most of them were run by the Japanese, but also by the Koreans, and a few were run by the Russians. At this time there were sixty-four Japanese and sixteen Korean brothels where Japanese, Korean, Chinese, and Russian prostitutes worked.[9] Gambling houses were popular where fortunes were won and lost overnight. Harbin offered residents and travelers anything and everything they could ask for, both good and bad.

As bad elements became more prevalent in the cities, the poorer population often became victim to the available forms of escape. Drug addiction offered an escape for those who lived poverty-stricken lives. There was seldom a solution to address the poverty that was very much a part of the city. Certain areas of the city thrived where desperation prevailed, where crowded quarters flourished, where homelessness was rampant, and where beggars often unsuccessfully tried to win the sympathy of a passerby.

Vladislav was a permanent representative of the Harbin Municipal Council and spent many hours at meetings, dealing with issues of public interest.[10] He had an influential position on the Harbin Stock Exchange and was known to spend up to 100,000 gold rubles a year on charitable causes.[11] He was one of the founders of the famous Harbin Polytechnic Institute. He was the cofounder of the Chamber of Commerce and continued to be a prominent member of the Gospoda Polska Association (the Polish Club*), a social, educational, and cultural organization established in 1907, which was

---

* The Gospoda Polska was translated in many different ways: the Polish Inn, Polish Tavern, Polish Club.

Stolen Dreams

an invaluable support for the Polish community. The organization was instrumental in creating programs for Polish children and the Polish community and was active in the fields of education, culture, charity, and sports.

Harbin was a haven to many nationalities. The kinship shared by the emigrants was not unique, as many ethnic and religious groups relied on one another and often banded together. This was especially true for those who had faced persecution or hardships. Many nationalities had set up organizations to service their countrymen just as the Poles had done. Religion was also a natural unifier, and each citizen had his or her own place of refuge. Jews had their synagogues and cultural centers, the Russians had their Orthodox churches and cathedrals, the Muslims congregated at their mosques, and the Chinese Buddhists their temples. In 1923 there were twenty-three churches, houses of prayers, monasteries, and cathedrals and four chapels in the city of Harbin.[14]

Polish Consulate staff, 1925: Consul Karol Pindor, middle front, and Vladislav, second from right, front row[12]

Gospoda Polska Meeting, 1927: Vladislav, sitting third from left, front row; Father Marurus Kluge, fourth from the left with Konstanty Symonolewicz next to him[13]

As one of the most respected individuals in Harbin, Vladislav continued his contribution to the city development. He was among those who felt liberated from oppression or discrimination, a circumstance that always weighed heavily on his heart back in Kozuchow. This liberation evoked his humanistic and generous side, and he was determined to foster his public-spirited commitment in Harbin. He, together with other Poles in the community, contributed to the building of the Polish school, and the Catholic St. Stanislaus church. The St. Stanislav church was built in 1909 and by 1921 the Polish population in Manchuria had grown to 10,000.[15] To accommodate the population, the Catholic church suggested the building of another church, the St. Josaphat church in 1925. It was completed with lumber donated by Vladislav for the building of the church.[16]

The Orthodox Church was the strongest among the many Christian churches in Harbin, and the Kowalski family attended regularly. It was Helena, with little compromise, who insisted that Vladislav attend the Russian Orthodox Church. He was happy to oblige as he was comfortable in both the Catholic and Orthodox churches. He loved the atmosphere and the spirituality of the Orthodox services and felt it was

St. Stanislav Catholic Church[17]

Confucian Temple[18]

important for Helena to maintain the connection to the church.

The close-knit Polish community made sure to celebrate Polish holidays every year. One such occasion was the celebration of Saint John's Night, a traditional Slavonic festival celebrated on the evening of June 23 in the middle of summer, the day before the Feast Day of Saint John the Baptist. The participants would decorate small floats with flowers and a candle, sending them down the Sungari River. It was a breathtaking scene that made for a festive and joyous occasion. The floats were intended to assist in finding a life partner. All the young girls participated in hopes of getting a glimpse into their future.[20] The first garland float to land on the riverbank indicated that that girl would

St. Jozaphatus Catholic Church[19]

Stolen Dreams

Vika, standing far right; Emilia Wanda Czajewska, Jerzy Czajewski's mother (president of the Harbin Club, Szczecin, Poland), far left, sitting in the front row; next to her, Rozalia Kajdewicz, the oldest member of the Harbin Club in Szczecin, who died at the age of 100 in February 2019[21]

be the next to marry. The family made it a point to celebrate this wonderful festival together.

They joined their friends at the Yacht Club to get a perfect view of the floating candles, cheering on Ada's, Vika's, Lucia's, and Genia's floats. The evening lasted well into the night and everyone in the city of Harbin enjoyed the beautiful summer night along the banks of the Sungari River. It was a vibrant, colorful, and a magical evening and time in Harbin.

35 | Lawless Behavior

1924

With the political changes in the region, the former Russian Railway Zone was now called the Special Region of Eastern Provinces and from 1920 until 1924 fully controlled by the Chinese. Thereafter, the CER came again under the joint Sino-Soviet administration and management. This benefitted the Soviets and the Chinese but not the stateless Russians in Manchuria nor the Poles.

CHANGE WAS STILL TAKING PLACE. RUSSIA WAS NOW THE COMMUNIST Soviet Union, and Stalin had taken over after Lenin's death in 1924. Japan's economic and military presence in China and the Manchurian region was strengthening with the continued establishment of *zaibatsu* (a large Japanese business conglomerate) companies in the area. Japan was colluding with Marshal Zhang Zuolin in planning the building of railways especially in the southern part of Manchuria, which would further their influence in the region. China was teetering on the verge of collapse with the continued fight for power among regional and military rulers and warlords. Marshal Zhang Zuolin had won the Second Zhili-Fengtian War, one of the most significant conquests in the Warlord Era, with the backing of the Japanese, defeating the liberal Zhili clique controlling Peking. It was a time of widespread political instability challenged by lawless behavior and the lack of structure and support to control it.

In 1924, the Sino-Soviet joint administration of the CER was established where now the administration and jurisdiction matters would be a cooperative effort between the Chinese Republican Government and the Soviet Union. It was under this joint administration that the Soviet management demanded that all employees and workers on the CER and all its enterprises must be either Soviet or Chinese citizens. This was a dramatic declaration that affected the lives of countless workers on the CER. Many of the workers took Soviet citizenship, some took Chinese citizenship, and the rest who remained stateless were fired. The Poles needed to become Chinese or Soviet citizens to work on the railroad. Polish citizens continued their life "in limbo," a situation that was precarious when it came to working, studying, and living in Harbin. Thousands of Polish CER workers lost their jobs and moved back to Poland, and eventually only 2,000 Poles remained in Harbin.[1]

Vladislav was considerably impacted by these changes, as were his business and lumber concessions. He was not directly working with the CER and thus was able to circumvent the citizenship employment exclusion rules. As an established supplier of lumber, he was permitted to continue his business activities. However, lumber orders from the Soviets to Kowalski's firm stopped and contracts went to those who had Soviet citizenship. Many of Vladislav's competitors like Skidelsky, who became a Soviet citizen, received the contracts and the business.

The Soviets enacted this new regulation, but the CER still needed wood for repairs of the railway and to fuel the trains. Vladislav's firm was a highly efficient supplier and, hence, he managed to continue his business both domestically and by expanding into the export markets. It was widely understood by the Chinese authorities that the Kowalski businesses served "the interest of the colonizing policy of the Chinese government in this province,"[2] and, therefore, his business had the support of the Eastern Provinces Administration and the Chinese government. The situation was not without complications, and the Kowalski firm suffered because it was at the mercy of the Chinese warlord Zhang Zuolin's administration.

Zhang Zuolin's leadership created a liberal business environment and administrative efficiency that fostered economic growth in the country, but it also brought systemic corruption. Vladislav's concessions fell under the jurisdiction of the Forest and Mines Tax Office,[3] which was responsible for permits and collecting taxes. When Vladislav first acquired the concessions, there were very few issues, with the Kowalski firm always making timely payments according to the registered and official concession contracts. As Zhang Zuolin's military engagement and army expenditure skyrocketed, taxes were increased substantially. Vladislav was suddenly forced to increase the amount of tax the firm paid by US$70,000 a year, as a fee for protection money paid to the government against the Honghuzi bandits.[4] This was a superfluous fee because Vladislav had been directly paying the local Honghuzi protection money for years. Though he knew the alleged "protection" carried no merit and this was an excuse to extort money from him as a business owner, he had no choice and paid this extra fee to the government to maintain good relations with the Chinese authorities.

According to the original contract for the lumber concessions, Vladislav paid rent money to the Forestry and Mining Department and, in return, they were obliged to protect the Kowalski firm from any third-party interference.[5] He never had any problems that required their assistance until suddenly poachers illegally began settling on his concessions, claiming that they had the authority from the Peking government.[6] The poachers felled trees, stole lumber, and demanded money. Unable to stop the thieves and unwilling to give in to their demands, Vladislav decided to take the bandits to court for illegal logging. After a lengthy court case, the judgment ruled in favor of the Kowalski firm, but the Forest and Mines Tax Office came up with its own solution. They decided that to ensure better protection, the Kowalski firm had to pay a higher rent to the Tax Office in return for extra protection against poachers and molesters.[7] He was obliged to pay an additional US$50,000 a year, a 75 percent surplus, if he wished to be the only firm authorized to develop the concessions for the next twenty-five years.[8] The new ruling further stated that Kowalski would be responsible for expenses that the military would incur for protection against the Honghuzi.[9] This placed Vladislav in a difficult position. This decision completely violated the original terms of the signed agreement for the concession. When Vladislav first acquired the concessions for the thirty-year period, it was a well-defined stipulation that he would be the only firm authorized to develop them.[10] In 1922, the contract was renegotiated for all the concessions for twenty-five years under the same contractual terms. It became clear that this whole matter and the court dealings were instituted with the ulterior motive of extracting more money from him. Although Vladislav had undisputed and recognized rights to the concessions acquired in earlier years, he accepted the unfair demands and decisions.

After the payments were made, groups of poachers continued to settle on his land, fell the trees, and install facilities to conduct their own business. The Chinese Tax Office did nothing to rectify the lawlessness. Finally, Vladislav was able to get the attention of the sympathetic General Chu Tsintan[11] who arrested the thieves encroaching on the concession.[12] The matter went back to the courts, yet after another lengthy trial, the Tax Office made the final decision that the thieves be freed without punishment. Vladislav would receive all the timber felled by the thieves, but he was obligated to pay them for this timber at a price above the market value.[13] Vladislav had hit his breaking point. He did not want to set a precedent, worried that even his own workers would find this new way of doing business to be more advantageous and lucrative, so he refused to pay. Lawless behavior, extortion, and poaching continued, and the authorities did nothing to implement the laws.

Manchuria prospered during the initial years of Zhang Zuolin's rule as the "Warlord of Manchuria," however, after 1924 the costs of his army engagements and military conflicts in China continued to grow. Though some of the expenditures were covered by the Manchurian taxpayers, including Vladislav's company, he needed more.[14] The cost of maintaining the military and upholding security exceeded the revenue from the provinces, and, to offset the burden, Zhang Zuolin began receiving monetary and military support from the Japanese. Corruption worsened and the Japanese became more confident in their cooperation with Zhang Zuolin.[15] But, as political pressures from the Nationalist Movement within the country and the Japanese imperialistic threat increased, Zhang Zuolin began to change his strategy. He realized that his aspiration to reunite China with the troops under his control was financially impossible, so he resorted to the idea of printing new money. Unfortunately he did so without the necessary backing, and the value of the main currency in Manchuria, the Fengtian dollar, plummeted while inflation and corruption soared.

All these problems were affecting Vladislav's business. He tried to cooperate with Zhang Zuolin's administration and CER officials,[16] but a lack of consistent rules or a supportive ruling body made it difficult. He attempted to resolve controversies in a lawful manner through the courts. However, the outcome was time-consuming, costly, and never in his favor, even though he was in the right. Industrialists such as Vladislav, who were living and working in Manchuria without extraterritorial protection, were usually forced to agree to unjust situations and biased judgments. In almost all cases, the only possible outcome for Vladislav was to make the demanded payments.

Vladislav was looking forward to the Monday night meeting to socialize and relax with his friends. It had been a difficult week and he was feeling unusually drained. He needed a break.

"Good evening Mikhail Alexandrovich, Ivan Ivanovich, you both look like you need a drink. I think we all do. It has been an exhausting and challenging week."

"Vladislav Fyodorovich, I rarely hear you complaining. Is everything alright?" asked Ivan.

"It is tiring dealing with illegal threats causing problems and leading to lawsuits. It is exhausting, not to mention the time, effort, and money that goes into these situations. The authorities are not giving me the necessary protection," complained Vladislav. "Life and business dealings are becoming more difficult. Many of the emigres from Russia are continuing to come to Harbin to live, settle, and make a life for themselves and their families. They don't realize that things are changing in so many ways."

"On the other hand," added Vladislav, "Those who escape Russia are just very lucky. In fact, I met a man at church last week who used to work for me in 1902 during the construction of the flour mill. After a short time, he returned to Kharbarovsk and lived there with his family. He told me how he had recently narrowly escaped from Russia avoiding the wrath of the Russian Bolsheviks in Khabarovsk. The man's name is Sergei Leontievich Sherlaimov." Vladislav continued with the story, "The Sherlaimov family had been kind to their son Nikolai's Japanese classmate who appeared to be an ordinary student at Khabarovsk High School. After graduation in 1920 amid the Russian Civil War, they were surprised to see him walking along the street dressed in a Japanese officer's uniform. He had been studying incognito and only donned his military uniform when the Japanese troops arrived in Khabarovsk to protect the city against the Reds."

"As a gesture of friendship and concern on October 8, 1922, the Japanese officer alerted Nikolai that the Japanese garrison would abandon the city that night and advised that the family should also leave the city immediately. Nikolai rushed home with the alarming news. His father went to confirm this with the young Japanese officer, who suggested that they should leave immediately. It was obvious that something was happening. The Japanese garrison had occupied the main railway station. The Reds were on the other side of the Amur River and were ready to attack. The Japanese expected the Reds to enter the city the next day and did not want to be in a dangerous situation where they could be violently attacked. They had learned their lesson in Nikolaevsk in 1920 where 6,000 Russian civilians and 700 Japanese were killed, a whole garrison of Japanese military was wiped out as we all remember. He reiterated his advice to leave immediately."

"Sergei Leontievich did not need any persuasion, having seen the Reds' dangerous behavior in the city during the civil war and heard about the Nikolaevsk massacre. He went straight to the ticket office at the station, but the night train to Harbin was fully booked. In a panic he noticed an empty *teplushka*, which had been used to transport horses, that was attached to the passenger wagons. The family of eight scrambled to grab a few belongings, abandoned their home and boarded the last train out of Khabarovsk. The train headed south to Pogranichnaia station and then over the border into

Manchuria, to safety. The family is now living across the Sungari River in Zaton and coming to terms with their circumstances. They are so glad to be alive and together."[17]

"Recently there have been so many stories of situations that have put people into life threatening danger. It is nice to hear a story with a positive outcome. The Sherlaimov's were lucky to be able to escape, and really, that was thanks to the young Japanese officer," added Vladislav.

Vladislav's problems continued to mount in 1924, the CER trains gradually began switching from wood to coal, which would lead to a decline in the demand for firewood. Vladislav understood that he must focus even more on expanding the export business and knew that there were more markets he could tap into to export lumber and to maintain a high rate of production. In spite of everything, Vladislav's business continued to expand and he managed to overcome the difficulties. Years later the Polish consul, Konstantin Symonolewicz, who assisted Vladislav through many of these matters, was amazed that he managed to survive in spite of all these pressures.

Symonolewicz was a China authority, who spoke Chinese fluently and who had previously worked with the Russian Ministry of Foreign Affairs until the forced closure of the Russian consulate in 1920. He remained in China, moving to Harbin, and with his experience in the diplomatic field and his background in Chinese studies, he was an invaluable asset and a key figure in helping the Polish community in Harbin. He became a vice consul and continued to support the Polish community until he became the official consul in 1929.

36 | Secrets

1924

The love between a husband and a wife, the love a parent feels for his or her child, and the bond that siblings feel for one another builds strength in a person, in families, and in communities. Looking at the Kowalski family you would think they had it all, but to Vika these fundamental principles of love did not exist in her family.

OVER THE YEARS, HELENA'S HEALTH DETERIORATED. SHE HAD A SERIOUS case of degenerative rheumatoid arthritis, and she had become completely crippled, confined to a wheelchair for the rest of her life. As her suffering intensified, she screamed in pain both day and night. She had never been a positive person, but her poor health and the handicap had made her bitter and demanding. For Helena holding functions at home became trying.

Helena had always had an easy life. She enjoyed regular get-togethers with a few of her close friends and Barbara, and especially loved the afternoons spent with the ladies drinking tea and catching up on the latest gossip. But now Helena's days were no longer filled with lighthearted fun. She pulled away from all friends and acquaintances, seldom left the house, and would limit her activities to a "stroll" in the garden. She was pushed around in her wheelchair, refraining from even the slightest exertion or movement, and had a staff to look after her. She continued to demand attention and was constantly preoccupied with arrangements for her yearly visits to spas in Czechoslovakia, Poznan, and Japan.

Helena did not make life easy. She frequently became irritated, had extreme mood swings, would throw fits and tantrums, and wanted everyone to suffer the way she did.

"I want to go downstairs, get the servants to carry me down." "Where are they, they are never around!" "It's too hot," "It's too cold." "I feel a draft,

Helena in a wheelchair outside in the garden   Helena   Helena with Ada and a nurse

where is it coming from?" "Tell the girls to keep quiet." "Where is my book?" "What's wrong with you? Help me." "Don't touch me!"... this went on and on. Lenochka tried to help. She looked after Helena every moment of the day and night tending to her every need, yet it was never enough.

Helena often acted irrationally. She would summon Vika into her room, ask her to close the door behind her, and call her over to her side. She would then open the drawer to her makeup table and take out an object wrapped in a beautiful, large, hand-embroidered handkerchief. She would slowly unwrap the handkerchief and take out a small pistol. Waiving it around in the air, she would start ranting that she wanted to commit suicide, complaining that she had nothing to live for. Vika would get down on her knees and plead with her mother to stop.

"Please, Mominka, don't do this. Don't even think of it. Put the gun away. Please, Mominka..." Vika begged.

After a lengthy back and forth, Helena would finally put the pistol away, always adding the warning, "Don't tell anyone, but I don't want to live any longer."[1]

On other occasions the rant was less frightening, but no less dramatic. She would call Vika into her room in the same way, sit her down, and tell her that she wanted to commit suicide just like Tolstoy's character Anna Karenina, by throwing herself onto the railway tracks in front of a passing train. Vika grew up with the fear that her mother may take her own life at any moment, which imposed a huge burden on her.

Lenochka was a very quiet, perceptive person, with a kind heart. Though Vika never spoke of the incidents with her mother, Lenochka knew there was something that constantly worried Vika and weighed on her mind. She was sympathetic to Vika's troubles and would show gestures of kindness by placing a candy under her pillow or a pressed flower in the book she was reading in place of her bookmark. These small gestures meant the world to Vika. She admired and appreciated Lenochka's compassion and patience and attributed her tolerance to her strong religious beliefs. She was someone to emulate.

Helena's strange behavior and difficult character created a strained atmosphere in the family. As she was so much younger than her husband, it irritated her that he was strong and full of energy while she was incapable of taking care of herself. At first, Vladislav was very sympathetic to her pain, but he soon grew tired of Helena's nasty habit of blaming him for her ailment. She believed her condition was caused by his insistence to live in Harbin and, hence, he was responsible for subjecting her to the extremely cold climate and taxing conditions.

Vladislav was very busy with the concessions, and did not need the added burdens that were enveloping the family. Yet, deep down he was a family man who loved the idea of being married and having a family around him to take care of. Despite the difficulties in coping with Helena's mood swings, he was always looking for ideas and ways to offer comfort, lighten the atmosphere, and relieve the tensions in the house

One evening Vladislav returned home together with the Polish consul and summoned everyone to come down to the living room. Helena, Ada, Lucia, Vika, Tatiana, Lenochka, and the two governesses were invited for what Vladislav called "an earth-shattering revelation." When they were seated in frenzied anticipation, he brought a box out of his office and proceeded to plug it into an electrical socket. The room was silent. He then turned to everyone and announced that they were all about to witness a miracle. He switched on the "talking box" and began tinkering with the knobs, trying to reach a frequency so that everyone could hear the "voices."[2] The whistles and the whining sounds continued for a long time as he tried, in vain, to catch a frequency. The audience sat in total silence and anticipation. Finally, he was able to tune into a program broadcasting a Chinese opera, but it was very faint and the whistling sound drowned out the background music. The strange sounds continued and soon became almost deafening. The "talking box" demonstration had not gone as Vladislav had expected and after a long while, Helena suggested that the presentation could resume some other evening.[3] The audience marched back to their rooms, and even the Polish consul excused himself to return home to his family. Vladislav continued toying with the "talking box" late into the night. The first commercial radio, which made sounds and voices "magically" travel through the air, had been introduced to the family.

It was the night after the radio demonstration, while Vladislav was working in his study, that Lenochka came banging at the door.

"Something is very wrong with Tatiana Denisovna. Please come quickly. She is not responding. I tried shaking her. *Gospodi Pamiluie* [God have mercy]. Vladislav Fyodorovich, please hurry."

As the two of them ran up to her room on the third floor, he said, "Call for Dr. Kazem Bek immediately. Have the servants help Helena up to her mother's room. Quickly."

It was too late. Tatiana Denisovna Zaharoff passed away quietly while taking an afternoon nap. Helena took the news of her mother's death very hard. She began wailing and sobbing hysterically, calling for her brother. Alexander arrived about the same time as the doctor and did not run to his mother's side. Instead, he focused solely on comforting Helena, taking her back to her room to console her.

Vladislav could not understand the indifferent attitude that Alexander displayed toward his mother's death. It was, after all, his dear beloved mother who had been such a wonderful person and parent. How could he not show any emotion? Vladislav felt that the rift between them was growing. Alexander was self-centered and emotionally insensitive. He brushed off issues and gave frivolous answers for everything, almost as if he didn't care. Vladislav found the feeling disconcerting.

Tatiana was loved and respected by all those she had helped over the years. The poor and hungry in Harbin whom she quietly fed near the house and around the church, and the beggars that found solace in her comforting words and kindnesses were all saddened by the loss. Her funeral was held two days later. As the coffin passed, being drawn by horses through the city to the burial site, the poor, the beggars, and the needy joined the procession. Together they had collected money to buy a metal wreath to place on her coffin.[4] It was a touching scene.

37 | Living the Good Life

1925–1927

Grandfather provided the family with all the comforts that anyone could ask for, and the family enjoyed a privileged lifestyle. It was natural that he seldom spent time with the family as he often traveled from one concession to another and was absent for days. It was always a treat to have him home.

It had been over three years since the family moved into the new house and they absolutely loved it. Often, guests or friends would drop in for late evening visits. Dinners in the dining room lasted for hours, which was not unusual for the typical Russian-Polish meals. The servants created exotic dishes, one course after another, that delighted even the most epicurean guests. After dinner the party moved on to the winter garden where the comfortable setting guaranteed a relaxed and enjoyable evening. It was effortless to entertain in such splendor.

Helena's joints had begun to calcify and fuse. Though it made moving her around more difficult, it reduced the constant and unbearable pain. She tried to subdue her outbursts and even made an effort to join parties, despite having bad days. When the evenings lasted too long she would simply ask the servants to take her upstairs, a frequent occurrence as gatherings usually lasted until the early morning hours given most offices in Harbin did not open until eleven in the morning.[1]

Despite moments of what felt like a return to normalcy, Helena's subdued disposition was only in the presence of guests. The erratic environment, and Helena's difficult personality, made holding on to Russian helpers a challenge. Things did not improve with the arrival of the new governess, Florence Young. But Miss Young's time with the family was short. She left them after one of the summer vacation trips to the beautiful coastal town of Kamakura. She was so impressed by the countryside and people of Japan

Entertaining in the dining room and living room

that she decided to stay behind. Her departure was not due to Helena's antics, but it still meant Vladislav was once again saddled with the task of finding a replacement.

Vika was 14 when their third governess, Georgina Fuller, was hired through the British Consulate to work for them. Miss Fuller was four feet ten inches tall. She had a slim body, short legs, thin curly hair, and big brown eyes. She was cute, possessed a quick mind, and had a wonderful sense of humor. Her personality provided a welcome antidote to the tension and depression pervading in the house. She was always joking and laughing and was like a ray of sunshine. She wouldn't let the girls fight and turned everything into a joke, even managing to thwart Ada's and Lucia's conniving ways. The girls' relationship improved under Miss Fuller's wise direction.

Miss Fuller had a delightful personality that simply tickled Vika. She was always up to something and made life so enjoyable. One night, she came down to the dinner table dressed as Charlie Chaplin. She waddled in and Vika and Vladislav roared with laughter. Helena, Lucia, and Ada forced a polite smile and just continued eating. Miss Fuller's presence changed Vika's life in many ways and helped her through some difficult times. Life was easier and much more entertaining.

Miss Fuller never got on well with Helena and, one day, they quarreled about something rather trivial. It was the last of many disagreements, and Miss Fuller turned in her resignation the next day. She went to work for the married daughter of Boris Ostroumoff. Vika was devastated by her departure. She had begun to rely greatly on her advice, uplifting nature, and even friendship. Helena forbade Vika to see Miss Fuller, but she managed to contact her anyway for the occasional get-togethers at the nearby Ostroumoffs' house, something Vika managed to keep secret from her mother. When they met, Miss Fuller told her about the interesting and wonderful family for whom she worked, assuring Vika that she was happy in her new home. But Vika could tell there was more to the story of her new life that Miss Fuller neglected to share.

Boris Ostroumoff assumed management of the CER, after engineers V. D. Lachinov and D. P. Kazakevich, after Horvath's departure in 1920, and was successfully following in Horvath's footsteps. He was an experienced Russian government administrator, having arrived in Harbin from Siberia and competently supported the Russian community and Russian businesses in Manchuria. Just like Horvath, Ostroumoff was a respected and powerful manager of the CER, despite the many problems it was having.

Boris Ostroumoff had one daughter, Tatiana. Two years earlier she had married Mitya Romanoff and they had a son whom they named after Tatiana's father, Boris. Mitya had arrived in Harbin four years earlier, quite by chance. He was a handsome and athletic young man who had avoided conscription and as a result was wanted by the Bolsheviks. He had escaped to a remote Trans-Siberian railroad station where the CER train stopped for fifteen minutes on its way to Harbin. During a stopover, Mitya approached Olga Yakovlevna Richter, the comely wife of a successful Russian businessman in Harbin, who had briefly alighted from the train for some air. Mitya pleaded with her to get him out of Russia. She sympathetically jotted down his name and address, promising to help. Upon returning to Harbin, she informed her husband that she met a cousin while in Russia and they must get him out. Her husband Karl used his connections to get Mitya out and welcomed the handsome young man into his household as a son.

Mitya learned English and became popular in Harbin society. He was a good tennis player, frequently joining Olga at the tennis court on the grounds of the Kowalski house. Even though Mitya was twenty years younger than Olga, rumors began to circulate that the two were having an affair. The rumors were confirmed when Karl returned early from a trip and found them in bed. He threw Mitya out of his house and banished Olga to a separate bedroom.

Barely a year later, Mitya married Tatiana Ostroumoff. By then Olga and Karl had separated and she moved to Shanghai. Despite his shocking and sordid background, Mitya and Tatiana were welcomed into Harbin's high society.

Miss Fuller was hired to take care of their son. During one of their meetings, Vika remembered thinking how strange it was that Miss Fuller would not stop raving about her wonderful employer, Mitya. "What a handsome and charming man he is," that "she had never met anyone quite like him," and "how lucky she was to work there." Several months later, Vika learned that Mitya's wife Tatiana had committed suicide. Everyone was horrified. Apparently, Mitya and Miss Fuller were having an affair and when Tatiana caught them together, the shock was too great for her.

"You see," Helena said to Vika, "I was right to get rid of her. She was no good."

Vika knew in her heart that Miss Fuller was a decent woman and could only conclude that Mitya must have seduced her. Mitya disappeared after Tatiana's suicide and left the boy with Tatiana's parents, and Miss Fuller moved to Shanghai where she opened a hostel for girls called the Clarenden Club. Vika stayed in touch with Miss Fuller, maintaining their friendship despite the events in Harbin. She even stayed at the Clarenden Club on one of her trips to Shanghai years later. Eventually Miss Fuller adopted a young Russian girl, Marina, and the two of them moved to Australia.

Helena used this incident as an opportunity to bring up the subject of sending the girls to boarding school.

"You see, Vladislav, what indecencies the girls are exposed to here. This is not a good environment for them. In boarding school, they will be shielded from this kind of situation."

"Helena, it is not a situation. What happened with Miss Fuller has nothing to do with the quality of education in Harbin. We have schools here that are of the highest standard and our teachers are recruited from all over the world. There is no reason to send the girls to England; it is an expensive option and ludicrous to insist on a boarding school education in England."

"Vladislav, you are being unusually stubborn. I am insisting that this matter be resolved and that you make the arrangements to send the girls to boarding school. It is our duty to our children," announced Helena.

Vladislav did not answer her. He stared at her a little longer than usual, excused himself, and exited the room.

38 | Setting the Stage

1927–1929

In the minds of the Japanese, the land mass in Japan was not large enough for its growing population. The limited land area and the lack of natural resources was seen as a problem, and expanding their presence in Manchuria seemed to them to be the best solution. In 1924 the population of Japan was around 80 million people and was increasing at the rate of 1 million a year. Japan continued its efforts to get Marshall Zhang Zuolin to support their plans.[1]

Japan experienced a devastating earthquake in 1923, gravely affecting the capital of Tokyo and Yokohama. There were about 140,000 deaths and 576,000 homes destroyed,[2] a tragedy for the whole country. Japan needed to rebuild. For Vladislav, this resulted in a higher demand for timber and building materials, as the Japanese bought all the available timber in Manchuria for the reconstruction of the destroyed capital.[3] Consequently, the prices of lumber increased 30 to 40 percent.[4]

"What a horrible tragedy. From what I understand, many people died in the fires," said Vladislav at the dinner table with the family.

"What do you mean, Papa?" asked Vika. "Wasn't it an earthquake? When we were in Kamakura, I remember how the earth was shaking. It was scary, but it was not so strong that it caused any damage. How lucky that we were not visiting Japan at that time."

"Yes, it was an earthquake. It was a very strong earthquake, but the effects were exacerbated because it happened around noon time, and many people were preparing lunch using their stoves with coal and wood. It sparked fires, which spread over the whole city and destroyed everything. People could not protect themselves or their homes. I think this must have been the worst earthquake Japan had ever experienced," continued Vladislav.

"Why do they have so many earthquakes in Japan and not here?" asked Ada.

"That's more than I know, but I think it is because some cities are more vulnerable while others are sitting on secure earth and mountain rock. China is not immune, there are provinces that have earthquakes here too. In fact, there was a very strong earthquake in the Shandong Province in the mid-1600s. Thousands of people died, but luckily we have not experienced any strong earthquakes in this area since."

"Papa, do you know what causes earthquakes?" asked Vika.

"We should not be giving the wrong information, Vladislav. Perhaps you should do some homework," interjected Helena.

"No, I actually don't know what causes earthquakes," Vladislav shrugged his shoulders. "But, I do know that it takes only a few minutes to cause tremendous damage. I am so happy that you are both so inquisitive my precious children," said Vladislav with a smile.

"I am glad you had the discussion here at home and not in front of your Monday night friends. They think you know everything," said Helena with a touch of sarcasm.

"Truly, I don't want them to know that I am not perfect," he said still smiling.

After a number of years Japan was still faltering. Adding to the financial burden of the devastating earthquake, the Japanese silk industry collapsed in 1927. Silk prices dropped 50 percent and exports fell by 27 percent.[5] Farmers in Japan struggled with this calamity and other challenges, and the jobless rates climbed. The Japanese economy was further impacted by the worldwide depression that followed in 1929. Economic recession, frustration, and panic were widespread in Japan.

The Japanese had been "courting" the Manchurian warlord Marshal Zhang Zuolin for years, planning new railways with him and assisting him both militarily and financially. The Japanese Kwantung Army backed the marshal, as they could see the advantages of his cooperation. Trying to utilize their common hatred of the communists, they furthered their influence and grip on the region; however, the Japanese never managed to make Zhang Zuolin bend fully to their side, nor accede to all their demands. Zhang Zuolin was, at heart, a strong Chinese nationalist, and he was wary of the Japanese and cautious in dealings with them. At the same time, needing their money and financial support, he maintained an open dialogue and received assistance from them over the years.

In 1928 the Polish consul in Harbin, Konstantin Symonolewicz, described in an official report to the Foreign Ministry in Warsaw the Polish position in Manchuria, and more specifically about Kowalski's company and his business. The report stated, "Already since 1922 Kowalski was discouraged by a number of setbacks."[6] It continued to describe a recent development on the Kowalski concession, which again required legal intervention. Kowalski worked at his concession of Hundaohetze adjacent to the concession of the Japanese company Hailinie. He had received a new order from the Bureau of Forestry and proceeded to prepare a large quantity of wood materials. The Japanese sat quietly until everything was completed and ready to be delivered. They then proceeded to charge Kowalski for the material, stating that the wood came from their concession. The Hailinie board declared that the plot belonged to the Japanese and not to Kowalski, thus claiming that the material was their property. Armed Japanese guards prevented Kowalski from making his delivery. To settle the dispute, Kowalski appealed to the Office of Forests, but the office encouraged the parties to reach a settlement on their own. Many meetings were held between the Japanese Consulate and the Delegation of the Republic of Poland, to no avail.

In desperation, Kowalski met with Mr. U Dzin (Wu Jing) who was the deputy foreign minister in the Mukden provincial government and an employee of the Supervisory Board of the CER. Kowalski offered a proposal to Marshall Zhang Zoulin through the deputy minister, as Zhang Zuolin did not negotiate in person.[7] The proposed offer was to form a partnership between the Kowalski company and the warlord. It was agreed that Kowalski would set up a new company in which half the shares of the company would go to Zhang Xueliang, the elder son of Warlord Zhang Zuolin.[8] The agreement stipulated that the Chinese would pay $1 million and, in return, Zang Xueliang would become half owner of a Kowalski company.[9] When the Japanese heard about those discussions, the conflict with Hailinie was immediately settled in favor of Kowalski and the controversial wood material was released.

MEANWHILE, ZHANG ZUOLIN's troops had successfully made advances both in the north and central China, at times with the help of the Japanese Kwantung Army. He had gained strength and had become the head of the Chinese central government in Peking in 1926, controlling four large provinces. He was continually challenged by Jiang Kai-Shek, who moved north in his campaign to unify China. The conflict between the two persisted, and when Generalissimo Jiang Kai-Shek entered Peking in 1928, he defeated Zhang Zuolin and forced Zhang's troops to withdraw.

The Japanese had their own agenda and their eye on Manchuria as a solution to their economic problems. They planned to eventually proclaim the northern part of China as their own, by using the Japanese Kwantung Army to capture city after city, working their way up from the southern part of Manchuria. When Zhang Zuolin failed to stop Jiang Kai-Shek's advances in Peking, and given he was already not fully cooperating with them, the Japanese military demonstrated their disappointment in him, as he was putting a wrench in their plans. The Japanese recommended that Zhang Zuolin return to Manchuria, planning to assassinate him on the journey north.

Intending to continue to keep their plans for Manchuria a secret, and aware that there would be worldwide condemnation of an assassination, the Japanese carefully orchestrated a bombing of the train carrying Zhang Zuolin from Peking to Manchuria in 1928. Their engineers placed explosives on the tracks near the overpass at the entrance to the Mukden station so that the bomb would detonate when the train reached the overpass. In the blast a piece of steel shrapnel struck Zhang Zuolin in the face and he fell unconscious, dying shortly thereafter. The Japanese sent in three Chinese soldiers to check whether the assassination was successful, but as the soldiers emerged from the wreckage they were shot, as a pretext to their involvement in the assassination. Two of the soldiers were killed and one managed to escape, fleeing to the camp of Zhang Xueliang, the son of Zhang Zuolin, to report the assassination and the plot.

Marshall Zhang Xueliang became the leader of Manchuria after his father's assassination. He was determined to show his power as a ruler and to be an able successor to his father. The Japanese urged him to continue his father's pro-Japanese policy, but he had different plans. Zhang Xueliang was more interested in cooperating with Jiang Kai-Shek than with the Japanese

Marshal Zang Zuolin[10]

The wrecked train after the assassination of Zhang Zuolin[11]

who had killed his father. This cooperation was unexpected and did not suit Japan's plans for Manchuria.

With the change in power, there were many questions and outstanding administrative matters. In his official report, Polish Consul Symonolewicz stated that when Zhang Zuolin was assassinated by the Japanese, it was unknown whether Zhang Xueliang had been informed by his father about the deal with the Kowalski firm and whether he would honor the commitment and payment that had yet to be made.[12] Zhang Xueliang went to Paris shortly after assuming his position and the subject of the deal was left unanswered.

Sometime later, Vladislav went down to Mukden to meet Zhang Xueliang and to find out if he had been informed of the deal with his company, which had been discussed. Their meeting was very cordial. They drank tea and had a good conversation, but the subject of the partnership was not raised by Governor Zhang Xueliang. Vladislav felt relieved and the matter could be dropped.[13]

Having reassessed and regrouped, the Japanese continued to move forward with their plan of action for the next incident to "protect their citizens and their interest in China."

39 | A Dream Come True

1927–1929

During the years 1927 to 1929 Ada and Vika traveled to Europe together with their parents. These years turned out to be the best years ever for Vika.

As a teenager Vika was expected to look after her mother. She was taken out of school for long periods of time to travel with Helena to Europe for mud bath treatments that lasted anywhere from three to six months. The procedure was always the same, after the treatment, they would go to Poznan to stay with Barbara while Helena recuperated. Helena's sister Barbara had recently left Harbin and returned to Poland with her husband and two children. During the time in Poznan, Vika would be enrolled in the piano conservatoire although, after all the years of piano lessons, she never displayed any talent or interest. There was no reason to pull Vika out of school and place such demands on the young teenager especially as the family had the means to hire a proper nursemaid.

In 1927 Helena and the two girls went to Dax, a small city located in the southwestern part of France, which was famous for the treatment of rheumatism. Here again it was the three months of treatment followed by three months of rest to prevent a strain on her heart. Helena arranged for Ada to attend the College De Bufomo near Paris during their sojourn in France, while Vika stayed with her mother at the spa to wheel her around the grounds. Vika was 16 and by this time was quite fluent in French, and it was her biggest dream to attend school in her most favorite city in the world, Paris. The plan had been for Ada to enroll in the school first, then the girls would switch after six months. Ada would return to Harbin with her mother and Vika would attend the college. Ada knew that her sister was excitedly awaiting her turn to attend. Finally, when Ada had completed her classes and returned to Dax, she strongly objected to Vika attending because she said, "the girls were smoking at the school." Helena praised Ada for her concern for her younger sister and she decided against Vika going. Instead, the three of them returned to Harbin.

Helena, Ada, and Vika returned to France the next year, traveling to Nice where they planned to remain for nine months. In Nice they stayed at the Negresco Hotel, the most beautiful hotel in the city, located on the Promenade des Anglais. The hotel was built in 1912 and had been a landmark along the Mediterranean Sea ever since. In the grand hall of the hotel it boasted a 16,309-crystal chandelier commissioned by Tsar Nicholas II, who did not take the delivery due to the political situation.[1] The hotel was gorgeous—every room displaying its own sophistication. The marble flooring gracefully reflected the light from the windowed ceilings. The tastefully decorated reception area, the entrance, dining areas, and the social hall displayed classic elegance. The hotel attracted the rich and famous from all over the world.

Ada and Vika shared a room and their mother stayed in a separate adjoining room. The day they arrived they could hear beautiful piano music coming from across the hall. It just happened that Nikolai Andreevich Orlof[2] was staying at the hotel and was practicing on the grand piano in his room. Maestro Orlof was a famous pianist who performed concerts in many countries around the world. The next morning on the way down to breakfast, they happened to meet him and ended up sitting at adjoining tables. Orlof thought Vika was delightful, chatting and making a big fuss over her during the entire breakfast. He invited them all to his room to listen as he practiced; they could

Ada and Vika in Nice, France

enjoy their own private concert. Vika sat on the edge of the sofa and could not wipe the smile off her face the entire hour he played. This was the first time she was happy that she had studied the scales and had made the effort to learn to play the piano.

While in France one hot summer evening, Ada suggested that she and Vika go to a bar to have champagne. Vika was so excited that her sister wanted to do something together that she agreed.

A family friend from Harbin happened to be in the same bar. Surprised to see the young girls in such an establishment, on his return to Harbin, he relayed his encounter to a shocked Vladislav.

Vladislav had been preparing for some time for his company's participation in the Poznan International Trade Fair in Poland, which was scheduled

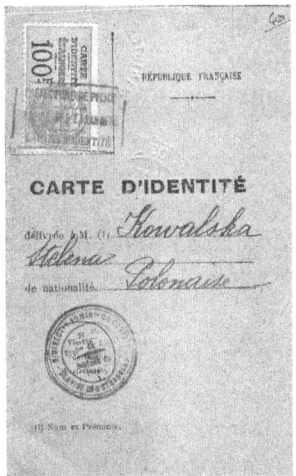

Helena's identity card

Documents for their trip to Europe: Ada's identity card (left) and Vika's identity card (right)

to start in three weeks. It was an international fair organized to support trade, import and export. Vladislav planned to set up a booth at the fair in hopes of furthering his lumber and agricultural exports to European and other markets. As the timing was right, he decided to leave earlier and go to France to check on the worrisome issue with the girls. He immediately asked the staff to make the arrangements for his travel. Prior to his departure, he confronted Alexander in the office about a matter that was brought to his attention earlier that day.

"Alexander Alexandrovich, why have you not followed through on the order to Indonesia that was rejected? I can see that you have totally ignored the matter."

"I talked to the agent here who claimed that the veneer product sent three months ago was defective. The veneer started to break apart because of the climate in Jakarta," explained Alexander.

"And?" questioned Vladislav. "What did you do about it?"

"I told them to just throw it away, what else am I supposed to do, bring it back here to Harbin?"

"Alexander Alexandrovich, are you trying to sabotage my company? What were you thinking? If our other clients find out, each and every one of them is going to make the same claim, asking for a refund. Are you saying that you asked them to throw away the order without verifying the claim? What are you doing?"

"It seems that you are complaining about every action I take," Alexander tried to defend himself.

"To tell you the truth, Alexander Alexandrovich, you are not working to your full capacity. You have become sloppy and you seem to spend more time socializing than working. Your accounts are questionable, and your loyalty is certainly debatable." As quiet and controlled as Vladislav usually was, his patience was running out.

"If you are not happy with my performance, tell me," shouted Alexander.

"You know I am leaving tomorrow for Europe. I need to trust you while I am gone. I need you to uphold the reputation of the firm and to devote your time and energy to your work. Please Alexander Alexandrovich, I depend on you."

Alexander had been caught lying about money matters on several occasions, not to mention taking unauthorized vacations. Funds had been missing but Vladislav did not want to make any accusations until he was a hundred percent sure that the problem was with Alexander. Vladislav could not understand what he was up to, but one thing was obvious, his behavior made

Stolen Dreams

Vladislav uneasy. He decided to leave things as they were until his return, but he would try to hurry back.

Vladislav arrived in Paris and decided to take Ada and Vika to Italy. The original plan was for Ada to attend one of the best schools in Italy and for Vika to go to Poland with her mother to look after her, but this was one of the extraordinary moments when Vladislav injected himself into family matters. The trip allowed for the rare occasion that Vika and her father had a chance to sit down and talk without interference. Vika started to cry and told him how she longed to go to school, but she was always obliged to help her mother. He was sorry that her desires had not been taken into consideration and had been neglected. Vladislav decided that under no circumstance would Vika go to Poland instead he would take both Ada and Vika to England and enroll them into a boarding school he had previously inquired about located outside of London.

Helena was frantic, screaming and crying, accusing Vladislav of taking her children from her at a time when she was traveling and needed them the most. She was not against the decision to place the girls into a boarding school but had wanted it to be under her terms. Vladislav took decisive action. He sent a telegram to Barbara in Poznan, knowing she could help with the logistics of caring for Helena. He asked Barbara to make arrangements for Helena to visit the mud spa for her treatment, and informed her that after taking the girls to London, he would return to France, collect Helena, and deliver her to Poznan to stay with her. He then left to take the girls to England.

Ada, Vika, and their father arrived at the Old Palace School in Bromley, Kent, a majestic manor that looked like something out of a classic Brontë

Vladislav together with the girls in Italy

Old Palace School, Bromley, Kent, England

novel. It was the former summer residence of the archbishops of Canterbury and a place where kings and queens (Henry VI, Henry VII, Queen Mary, and Queen Elizabeth I) visited and stayed.[3]

Vladislav went to the office of the headmaster to arrange everything in accordance with Helena's instructions. With his limited knowledge of English, he was able to get the assistance of a young Russian-speaking teacher to assist in the interpreting. The girls sat waiting in the adjoining room with nervous apprehension. After a long while, he emerged with the headmaster who welcomed the girls to the school. Vladislav hugged his daughters and made haste to travel on to France and Poznan. As he started to walk out of the room, Vika ran up to him to give him a second hug and whispered, "Thank you, Papa, I love you."

Vika was deliriously happy from the first day of school. She had been assigned to share a room with a Norwegian girl by the name of Signe Sundt. Signe came from a well-known family in Norway that owned the Sundt Department Store in Bergen. Vika and Signe connected immediately and quickly became inseparable. They developed a strong friendship based on their similar interests and love for classical music, Hollywood movie stars, and books. She also made many other friends at school and did well in all her subjects. She was blossoming in her new surroundings.

Before Vladislav left for England, Helena made him promise to make special arrangements for Ada since she was so "frail and sickly," of which

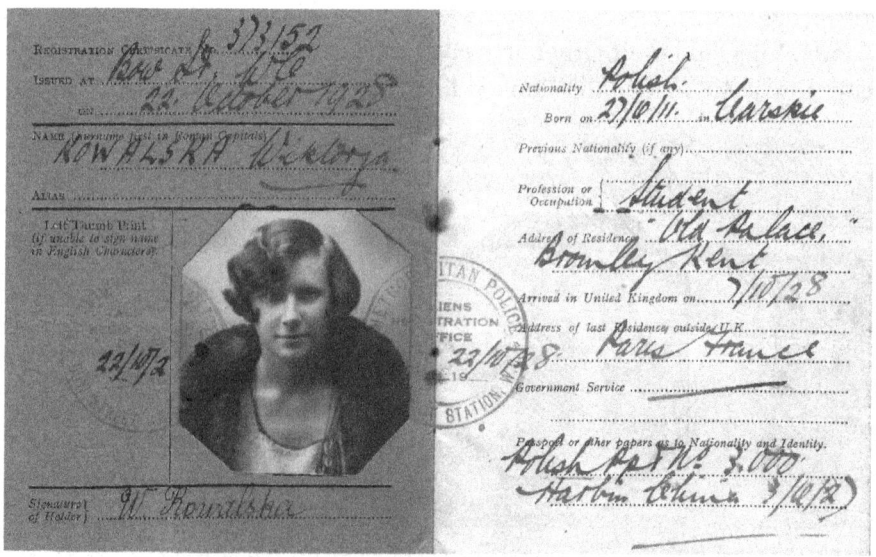

Vika, officially enrolled in the Old Palace School

Stolen Dreams

Signe with Vika   Keeping in touch with the family   Vika as a student

she was neither. Vladislav paid a fortune for the tuition at the Old Palace School and paid an extra fee for Ada to have special treatment. She was given a private room and was served separate meals. Additional arrangements were made for her to eat at the same table as the owner of the school, Mademoiselle Rasinyon.

Ada could keep her own schedule and did not have to attend classes if she didn't feel well, and she could take walks in the garden whenever she wanted for "health reasons." A typical example of her behavior during class was to prop up books in front of her to hide the poetry sheet that was assigned to be memorized. When Ada was asked to recite the poem by heart, Vika cringed with embarrassment as it was clear that she was reading from the page. To make matters worse, she was reading poorly from the page! Ada had hardly any friends and was treated as an untouchable "princess." Vika felt sorry for her father needing to pay all that extra money for Ada to put on airs and act in such a ridiculous manner.

The year that Vika spent at the Old Palace School was by far the happiest experience she had ever had. Signe and Vika became best friends and vowed to maintain that friendship forever. On the day that Vika left for Harbin, the girls decided that instead of saying goodbye, Signe would play Beethoven's *Moonlight Sonata* on the piano and Vika would leave while she was playing. When Signe finished playing the piece, Vika was gone. It would be many years before they would meet again.

Vladislav was running out of time as the Poznan International Fair[4] was to open in three days. He had not expected to spend so much time traveling to the outskirts of London. He was satisfied with his decision to enroll the girls in such a prestigious boarding school and knew that it was the right thing to do, but he now needed to refocus on work.

Vladislav returned to France to collect his wife and take her to Poznan. They checked out of the hotel in Paris and arrived at the station with ample time to board the train. The train ride gave Vladislav time to further prepare for his business meetings and presentations at the fair. Barbara met them at the station together with Lola and Nadia who were now quite grown-up. The plan was to drop Helena off at Barbara's and then go straight to the opening at the fairgrounds where his company display had already been set up.

For Vladislav this was a critical moment in his business. It was important to be represented at the Poznan International Fair and to secure orders to develop his export business further. With the railway trains now switching to coal and construction beginning to plateau, he needed to put more effort into the export business. His production capacity could be enhanced, and he could develop value-added products for the new export markets. Given his Polish background, Poland was a natural choice for him.

40 | A Great Honor

1929

The Poznan International Fair was ranked as the fourth largest European international trade show. Held just before the stock market crash, the Poznan International Fair in 1929 was visited by 4.5 million people and included a series of forty different events, attracting thousands of producers and traders from all continents.[1] Grandfather had participated in 1928 and was planning to do so again in 1929.

When Vladislav returned to Harbin after the first Poznan Fair in 1928, he immediately set the wheels in motion. He went out to the concessions to ensure that the output of lumber was increased to meet the orders he had secured in Poznan. He had single-handedly negotiated several large contracts and was sure that this influx of orders would give his business a new stimulus.

With the increase in his business activities, Vladislav was reluctant to confront Alexander because he needed the extra help. He could not afford to make any changes now and hoped that the problems would resolve themselves, especially as he sensed that Alexander knew his actions were under scrutiny. But, despite Alexander's more cooperative spirit, Vladislav began monitoring him closely. This continued for almost a year and Vladislav was convinced that Alexander was not an honorable man.

Vladislav arranged to return to Poznan for his second participation in the fair the following year. This time he was better prepared for the visit and had made small matchboxes to use as advertisements. He printed the name of his company on the matchbox with all the contact information. It was an original idea and he was sure it would be a great hit.

The opening ceremony of the Poznan Fair was held on May 16, 1929. The event was sponsored by the *Polonia Zagranica* (Poles Abroad) organization and held in their building in Poznan, which later became the medical division of Poznan University. (It is believed that Vladislav partly financed the building.) The exhibition in 1929 commemorated ten years of Polish independence, and hence was an extra special event. Unfortunately, Vladislav was unable to attend the opening ceremony, so he sent his staff ahead to man the booth in the pavilion. The firm erected a large display, stand No. 36, to exhibit their plywood and timber products. They were one of many stands, including a display by the Polish community in Manchuria of a replica of the Gospoda Polska building in Harbin, which received a lot of interest.

Poster advertising the Poznan Fair in 1929[2]

Vladislav arrived by train from Harbin and arranged for the girls to travel from London to Poland. They stayed with Barbara and the family, which was convenient because Helena was already there. This visit was particularly significant, as Vladislav was going to be decorated by the Polish government in a special ceremony taking place in connection with the fair. He would be receiving two decorations. Vladislav received the prestigious Polonia Restituta (Order of the Rebirth of Poland). Władysław Kowalski (Polish spelling of his name) was decorated with the highest civilian honor for his service to Poland, for his dedication and loyalty to the Polish people living abroad, and for his philanthropy in the local Polish community, specifically in Manchuria.[3] It was a great honor to receive this ordinance, issued by the president of Poland, as it was rarely bestowed. The second medal was the Grand Prix Medal of the Polish Industry Exhibition in Poznan for the excellent quality of his firm's products and for his outstanding work. Vladislav's family from Kozuchow was present for the ceremony, as was Barbara, her family, and Helena and the two girls. Despite his modesty, this was an honor he accepted with pride.

The Poznan Fair was a great success and Vladislav was happy with his company's participation. It demonstrated the vitality of the Polish people and their ambition to make their country modern and prosperous. He had instructed his staff to prepare advertisements to be posted in Harbin in order to expand his export business. The trip was gratifying and memorable, and now Vladislav was anxious to return to Harbin to start fulfilling the orders.

Stolen Dreams

On the train ride back to Harbin, he sat admiring the beautiful medal with the crest. It was a simple medal, but one that exuded much meaning. He felt an immense sense of pride to be Polish. Both he and his country had experienced much hardship and he hoped that the future could and would be brighter. Thinking back on his life, his work, and what it had taken for him to achieve all he had in the last thirty-plus years, he felt life was going by too

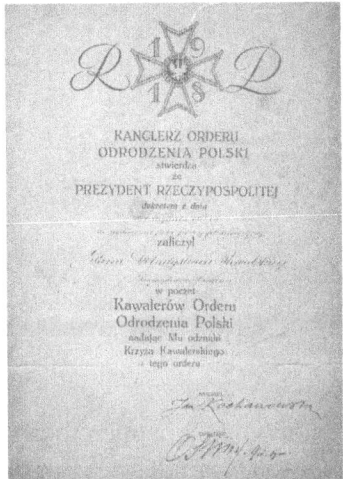

Polonia Restituta (Order of the Rebirth of Poland): Translation of the ordinance: The Chancellor of the Poland Restoration confirms that The President of the Republic by decree of 11th of November 1929 for the work in Philanthropy included Mr. Władysław Kowalski in the rank of Cavaliers (Knights) of the order Poland Restitution bestowing him distinction of Cavaliers (Knights) of this order, Chancellor Jan Kochanowski Secretary—Osinski [sp?][4]

Lumber concessions of V. F. Kowalski on the CER—main office in Harbin[5]

quickly. In an interview a few years later, he reminisced, "I happen to have seen and heard and experienced a lot in life. During one's youth everything is easier, and you have the courage to confront anything, even if it seems impossible. Now it all seems like a dream. It is difficult to believe that during those years I did all of this myself."[6]

He was almost 60 years old and regretted that he didn't have the energy he had in his youth, but he could not slow down, there was too much at stake. Moreover, this great honor and decoration encouraged him to do even more. He had accepted the responsibility with his concessions and he loved what he was doing. He was working in an industry that he appreciated and had friends and business contacts that he liked and respected.

Back in China the political authority of the Nationalist Chinese government of Jiang Kai-Shek was recognized. It was seen as a step in the direction of China's unification. With regard to the CER and the joint administration of the railway there were evident problems. The purpose of the joint Sino-Soviet administration was, in the Chinese view, based on an economic cooperation and lived up to the Soviet promise to give the Chinese control of the railway administration. However, the Chinese frustration escalated because they objected to the Soviet engagement and their spread of communist propaganda along the CER.[7] The Chinese raided the Soviet consulate in Harbin in May 1929, and arrested thirty personnel, closed the consulate, confiscated documents, and arrested hundreds of Soviet citizens with substantial proof that the Soviets were engaged in spreading communist propaganda along the railway line.[8] Soviet consular officers were arrested and in mid-July 1929, under the leadership of the warlord Zhang Xueliang, the Chinese took control of the CER. These developments led to the Sino-Soviet military conflict of 1929 where Soviet troops entered the Manchurian territory and made several successful attacks. The Chinese defeat in this Sino-Soviet military conflict led, at the end of 1929, to the reestablishment of the 1924 status quo and the restitution of the joint Soviet-Chinese management of the CER.[9]

Just two months after the Poznan exhibition had ended, the Great Depression began in the United States with the fall of the stock market in November 1929. The effects were devastating worldwide and between 1929 and 1932 the financial crisis also affected the lumber industry in Manchuria, China, Japan, and other export markets. Luckily, the contracts that Vladislav generated with his visit to Europe were still intact.

On a lighter note, Lucia had met a young man in Harbin, Alex Blumberg, who worked as a customs officer. The two of them fell in love and soon after got secretly engaged. Alex was handsome, manly looking, and very popular with the women. At that time Lucia befriended Galia Svedesiskaya, who excitedly told Lucia about a wonderfully handsome man she met at the border who was coming to Harbin and planned to see her. Galia even showed Lucia letters written to her by Alex promising wonderful evenings together. Lucia never let on to Galia that it was her fiancé. Lucia was furious with Alex and vowed never to see him again. Ludmila Mikhailovna Solovov (Lucia) and Alex Blumberg were married in 1929 while Helena, Ada, and Vika were in Europe.

41 | The Invasion of Manchuria

1931

Even though grandfather would often stay over at the concessions for a few days at a time, he seldom had the chance to visit all the concessions for an evaluation. Once a year he would take three weeks off and travel to every concession, spending extra time at each location. It gave him the opportunity to spend quality time with the administrators and to have an in-depth understanding of the business. It was something he had done for years, which he found to be particularly important in being able to run his business operations efficiently. When grandfather returned from his last visit to the concessions, he was inundated with trouble. It began with continued issues at the office with Alexander and progressed to larger widespread troubles with the growing Japanese military actions and attacks occurring in Manchuria and Harbin. Life in Manchuria and Harbin was about to change for everyone.

AFTER SPENDING THREE WEEKS ON HIS YEARLY EXTENDED TRIP TO THE concessions, Vladislav went straight from the train station to the office. As he walked into Alexander's office, he found it completely empty. He turned to the office staff and inquired of Alexander's whereabouts. They were surprised by his question, assuming Vladislav already knew about Alexander's departure two days after he had left for his trip to the concessions.

"Vladislav Fyodorovich, we presumed this was according to your instructions," Sergei Ivanovich explained nervously. "When we arrived at the office on Monday morning everything was gone. We sent someone to his home to inquire and found that Alexander Alexandrovich had left Harbin with his family early that morning. Nobody we asked had any details or knew about where he was going. We did not realize that this was a decision without your consent. We have not heard anything from them or about them since they left."

"Sergei Ivanovich, please don't worry. I will handle this," assured Vladislav, but he truthfully had no idea how he would take care of Alexander's departure and all the loose ends.

Vladislav was shocked. He never expected this kind of behavior from anyone, especially not his brother-in-law. If you can't trust your family and business partner, who can you trust? He would have to check everything, all the accounts and the contracts. The circumstances and manner of Alexander's exit were unacceptable, and he finally understood that his suspicions about his brother-in-law had been correct. He felt sad and deserted. After checking the accounts, he realized that the extent of Alexander's deceit was far worse than he expected.

That evening Vladislav informed Helena of the matter—of her brother's dishonest conduct and his irresponsible behavior—but his words fell on deaf ears. Instead, to his surprise, hatred spewed from Helena as Vladislav had never heard or seen before. The blame and rage were directed at Vladislav. She stood by her brother and accused Vladislav of ruining her family's good name. She blamed him for demanding too much from Alexander Alexandrovich and said that anyone who would be so unlucky to work under him would have done the same. Helena went days without speaking a word. She would just glare at Vladislav when he entered the room. Her piercing stare, her silence, and her occasional outbursts created a terrible atmosphere in the house. Meals were eaten without a single word spoken and everyone was immediately sent to their rooms when they were finished. Alexander had demonstrated his guilt by running off in the middle of the night together with his family, but to Helena, Vladislav was to blame. Vladislav was suspicious about this whole incident and found it strange that Helena did not know about Alexander's and Sophie's departure. They had always been so close and now, in Vladislav's mind, they seem to be on the same side.

Alexander had embezzled a considerable sum of money. Vladislav was forced to make adjustments, but he was determined not to dwell on the past. He was sorry about the way everything had eventuated but, in the process, felt he had learned a valuable lesson, that he could not trust anyone. He turned to his close-knit network for support. In a strange way, he was more comfortable going to his business friends and even competitors for advice rather than his own family.

Alexander had fled to Shanghai with his family while Vladislav was away for three weeks, to escape any legal action that would surely be taken against him. Before leaving for his trip, Vladislav had entrusted Alexander with ¥400,000 in cash and ¥200,000 worth of products for the pending orders and administrative matters. The money was missing and Vladislav needed to make a police report in Harbin to legitimize the compromised accounts. The law soon caught up with Alexander in Shanghai. Upon apprehension by the local police, the authorities charged him with petty theft. To draw out the proceeding and complicate matters, Alexander made accusations that Vladislav owed him monies totaling ¥40,000. Furthermore, he claimed to be a French citizen, not Russian, to avoid being extradited back to Harbin as was stated in the articles that follow. As a French national, he could exercise extraterritorial rights and could remain in Shanghai.

Иск к инж. Захарову.

Вчера Местным судом был рассмотрен иск к инж. А. А. Захарову. В настоящее время инж. Захаров находится в тюрьме.

Он вчера не был вызван в суд и интересы его представлял прис. пов. А. С. Кабалкин, в то время, как со стороны истца — коммерсанта Фогельбойма, — выступал прис. пов. А. В. Ковалев.

Обстоятельства, предшествовавшия этому иску, таковы.

Еще в прошлом году коммерсант В. Ф. Ковальский взял у Фогельбойма ссуду, обеспечив ее 1.250.000 кв. фут. фанеры. При заключении сделки о ссуде было оговорено следующее обстоятельство: в том случае, если стоимость фанеры не покроет выданной ссуды, то некоторую ответственность принимает на себя инж. Захаров, который выдал поэтому векселей на 25.000 иен.

Как утверждает в настоящее время поверенный ответчика векселя эти были безденежными гарантийными, о чем свидетельствует особый договор о том, что векселя не отделимы от сделки.

В определенный срок В. Ф. Ковальский производит расчет: фанера передается в собственность Фогельбойма и закладывается в банках Чартеред и Трифткор за 70.000 иен.

Теперь же Фогельбойм предъявил иск к инж. Захарову, требуя оплаты векселей на 25.000 иен.

Поверенный инж. Захарова — прис. пов. Кабалкин указывал, что его доверитель не должен отвечать по этим векселям, так как они были безденежными и гарантийными. Тем более, что все расчеты по закладу фанеры уже закончены.

На это последовало возражение поверенного истца А. В. Ковалева.

Последний заявил, что суд должен вынести решение в пользу истца.

— Захаров не маленький, — он знал, что делал, когда выдавал векселя. Раз векселя выданы, то они должны быть оплачены.

Этим дело по иску к инж. Захарову было закончено. Решение суда будет вынесено 29 июля утром.

SUIT AGAINST ENGINEER ZAHAROFF

The article detailing the nature of Zaharoff's crimes appeared in the North China Herald on the June 2, 1931.[1]

After a local court hearing in Shanghai, engineer A. Zaharoff was sent to prison. The plaintiff was businessman Fogelblom whose attorney stated that last year V. F. Kowalski took a loan from Fogelblom, which was secured by 1,250,000 square feet of plywood. Engineer Zaharoff took the initiative to issue promissory note(s) of ¥25,000 in case the price of the plywood would not cover the loan with no intention of ever honoring the notes.

When V. F. Kowalski completed the transactions, plywood was transferred to Fogelblom, but the amount of ¥70,000 was outstanding and needed to be mortgaged. Fogelblom sued engineer Zaharoff demanding payment of the ¥25,000 notes, though Zaharoff claimed that he was not responsible for these notes as they were not issued as a guarantee for payment.

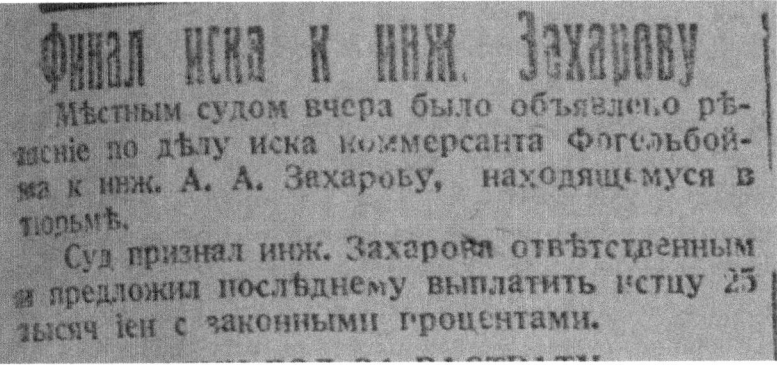

END OF THE SUIT AGAINST ENGINEER ZAHAROFF
When the court announced its decision, it was in favor of businessman Fogelblom and found engineer A. A. Zaharoff, who is currently in prison, responsible to pay ¥25,000 plus interest.* Zaharoff was also charged with theft and detained 60 days in prison.[2]

Vladislav, in his own quiet way, decided to try to end this upsetting matter with Alexander as quickly as possible. Little did he know that the turmoil in the office would soon be dwarfed by greater and devastating political trouble that was brewing.

At about the same time, a fire broke out on one of the concessions, which destroyed a plywood factory, burning forests and stopping plywood production. The timing of this incident was dreadful for Vladislav. It was obvious that it was arson instigated by thugs. Vladislav's financial and personnel problems began to multiply. He was having to take more loans but was not worried as he had substantial assets that he could tap into if necessary.

The political atmosphere in the region was becoming strained, with even military exercises by the Japanese Kwantung Army, as the Japanese had become more concerned to secure what they considered their "special rights" in Manchuria, which included the protection of Japanese businesses, investments, and citizens in Manchuria. These were demands that the Chinese objected to adamantly.

---

* According to the *Tygodnik Polski* archives, the amount Zaharoff embezzled far exceeded that quoted in the newspapers.

Military activity was evident in the areas along the SMR centering on Mukden (Shenyang), which was Japan's main city in its SMR Railway Zone, similar to what Harbin had been for Russia. The situation had become tense between Japan and China, and Vladislav among others became worried that the Japanese could take further steps, even violent steps, in its efforts to win more influence in Manchuria.

The news in September 1931 that Japanese troops had closed the SMR Railway Zone by force led to the belief that this could lead to military confrontations between China and Japan. On September 18, the Japanese reported a bombing that took place the day before on the railway near Mukden, claiming that the Chinese were attempting to sabotage their interests on the railway by exploding a bomb on the tracks. The report stated: "When the explosion site was checked by the Japanese, twisted rail and debris was found scattered in the area. Traffic on the rail line stopped immediately. Two Chinese 'people of suspicion' were killed. The closest Japanese military units were alerted. Those units were on high alert as they were conducting night training and acted immediately. They attacked the Chinese military barracks in the vicinity, which turned into an all-out battle with reinforcements sent in from both sides."[3] On the morning of September 19, the population of Mukden awoke to a city overrun by Japanese troops. The city was occupied by the Japanese military.

Mukden Incident: A dynamite explosion on the railway tracks was blamed on the Chinese but actually was initiated by the Japanese as an excuse to invade Manchuria. Japanese officials inspecting the "sabotage."

Japanese newspaper *Rekishi Syashin*, September 18, 1931

The Reuters news correspondent, Carl Taube, who was the only foreign reporter at the scene in Mukden (apart from the Japanese) and attended the Kwantung Army briefing the following day, reported that it was evident the Japanese fabricated the whole reason for their military intervention. It was a fabricated "incident"[4] by the Kwantung Army to justify its planned military attack and the invasion. The Japanese troops were well equipped and numerous enough to set the invasion into motion quickly and they were well coordinated with great force.[5]

Reporter Taube immediately sent the news "scoop" to Reuters, sending the message through a local Chinese telegraph office. The next day he got a message that unfortunately his communication had only been sent to Mukden and did not get transferred to Peking and London because of a cable breakdown. This telegram was never transmitted as it had gone through the Japanese-controlled communication system.[6]

The Japanese army had attacked the city of Jinzhou under the pretext of protecting Japanese citizens the day before occupying Mukden. The Chinese provincial army under the direction of Marshal Zhang Xueliang was instructed to avoid conflict with the Japanese and assume a position of nonresistance. Zhang Xueliang remained in Peking during this critical time. Similarly, Chinese President Jiang Kai-Shek expressed the same nonresistance attitude from his seat in Nanking. As a result, the Japanese military did not meet any opposition as it proceeded to occupy one city after another along the SMR. Troops continued to march and invade, while the government in Tokyo worked to calm international concerns, falsely assuring everyone that there was no war in Manchuria.

With the outbreak of the Japanese aggression and occupation, the Chinese government in Nanking turned to the League of Nations* to intervene. In reply, the League of Nations declared that "both parties ought to withdraw its troops" and recommended China settle the conflict "by way of negotiations."[7] Vladislav found the response uninformed and strange as Japan was infringing with enemy troops on the territory of China, and, in any normal circumstance, a country had the right to defend its territory. Col. Ishiwara Kanji, chief of the Kwantung Army Operations, commented that "the occupation of Manchuria was essential to Japan's existence and was a vital strategic barrier blocking the southward expansion of Soviet influence."[8] In the eyes of the Japanese, this "incident" would legitimize their ambitions.

---

* Japan was one of the four permanent members of the League Council, where China was not represented.

Soon thereafter, the League of Nations made a new appeal to Japan to withdraw its troops from China, but the Japanese responded that they would withdraw their troops as soon as they had secured law and order. Under the direction of Japan's Foreign Minister Minami, Japanese planes were sent to Jinzhou and, when the Chinese fired at the planes, the Japanese retaliated by bombing Jinzhou "in self-defense."[9] The League of Nations agreed to a Japanese proposal to send the Lytton Commission to China to evaluate the situation, in reply to the Chinese government's appeal. It was over eight months before the commission arrived in Manchuria. Meanwhile, Japan's territorial occupation of northern China continued and escalated.

When news of Japan's occupation of Manchuria reached the United States, specifically Secretary of State Henry Stimson, he said, "Japan was setting on foot a possible war with China which might spread to the entire world."[10] Stimson submitted the Stimson Doctrine of Non-Recognition, which was based on the renunciation of the Japanese Twenty-One Demands of 1915. He was adamant in persuading other powers to condemn this occupation and to allow China to develop into a "modern and enlightened state."[11] However, Stimson received lukewarm support from his own country as well as other world leaders. Britain was going through a financial crisis, Europe and the United States were just emerging from the Great Depression, and the Soviet Union was dealing with its domestic political changes. China and Manchuria were located too far from the Western powers to generate any immediate concern about the Japanese occupation, and the League of Nations was not proactive because Japan was an influential permanent member of its council.

Harbin's residents were feeling uncomfortable with the Japanese with the troops that were advancing. Japanese planes flew over the city spreading leaflets written in Russian and Chinese advising citizens that nothing would happen to them as long as they stayed calm. Residents had heard that similar events occurred in Jilin the previous week, shortly before Japanese troops entered the city. Harbin was bracing for the same.

News alleged that bombs were exploding in front of mainly Japanese establishments in Harbin. Many residents worried that this might be a pretext for Japanese troops to enter the city because they were aware of the Japanese strategy of orchestrating such attacks. Foreign nationals inquired at the Japanese Consulate about the rumored troop movement, and the Japanese Consulate reassured them that no troops would be sent to Harbin unless local disruptions in the city placed Japanese citizens at risk. Both

Chinese and Russian newspapers wrote about the possible entry of Japanese troops into the city at the slightest provocation.

Harbin residents were upset about a Japanese takeover. Many of the residents were worried that a Japanese takeover of railway lines or a large-scale presence would be as alarming as the Japanese occupation of Korea. People in Harbin were suspicious of Japanese excuses and commented that it was impossible for major military action to be launched so quickly in different cities at such short notice without premeditation. Japanese forces retaliated with full readiness at even the smallest incident. Chinese public opinion disapproved of Zhang Xueliang's weakness and his nonresistance to the Japanese invasion. Jiang Kai-Shek also failed to react strongly or swiftly to the Japanese invasion, instead concentrating on boycotting Japanese goods and avoiding military confrontations with the Japanese. Despite the discontent and criticism, the Chinese Kuomintang government remained focused on addressing the growing Chinese communist movement. The timing was advantageous for the Japanese invaders who met limited Chinese military defense and response.

It was the first time the girls noticed how uncomfortable their father was with the troop movement and the feeling that a takeover of Harbin was also imminent. The familiar patterns of the Japanese mode of operation was troubling. Vladislav contacted the Polish consul for any information, but was met with the repeated, empty Japanese rhetoric, officially issued, that there was no threat of war in spite of the fact that a war was already in progress. His friends experienced the same uneasy feeling.

42 | A New Country

1931–1934

This was the beginning of the end for Harbin, for peace within China, for the Three Northeast Provinces, and for many of the non-Japanese foreign residents in China. This time in history became an abominable, regretful, and shameful era.

IN 1931 IN CENTRAL CHINA, PEOPLE WERE CONSUMED BY THE NEWS OF the floods along the Yangtze River that affected millions of people and claimed the lives of almost 2 million.[1] But, up north, all anyone spoke about was the Japanese military advances. By the end of 1931, the family was back together in Harbin. The girls still reminisced about their time at the Old Palace School, particularly Vika who missed all her friends, especially her best friend Signe. The girls sensed the tense atmosphere at home and in the city. They were worried about their father and his business, were stunned by the news of Alexander, and anxious and upset about the impending Japanese aggression.

These troubles did not prevent the family from their yearly preparations for the upcoming Christmas and New Year's holiday on the January 7 and 14 (Gregorian calendar). The gardener brought in a fine Christmas tree selected from one of the concessions. It was a perfect shape and the girls launched into their annual project of decorating the tree. For the first time in a long time, everyone seemed to forget their problems and enjoy the momentary escape. The girls carefully secured each small candle with a clip onto the branches of the tree, making sure they were spaced properly. Helena always insisted on having a bucket of water next to the tree just in case one of the candles caught fire. The project lasted for hours with a lot of laughter and commotion with periodic breaks for tea from the nearby samovar and a chance to indulge in the pastries baked earlier that day. The Christmas and New Year holiday was a very warm and comforting time for the family.

The Japanese troops entered Harbin in February 1932 under the guise of "self-defense."[2] Planes flew overhead in a show of force. Three trainloads of Japanese soldiers had arrived in the city from the south in the middle of the night.[3] Japan's fallacious denial of war did not coincide with the Kwantung Army's advances to occupy Harbin. But yet again, Zhang Xueliang did not fight and continued to order his troops to withdraw. He wanted the world to realize that Japan was the aggressor and hence the League of Nations must act to stop the Japanese occupation and make Japan take full responsibility for the invasion. To the anguish of the Manchurian people there was no help from the United States, Britain, or the League of Nations, and the Chinese response and resistance continued to be too weak.

There were some pockets of resistance from individual Chinese officers. In Heilongjiang General Ma Zhanshan was the only one to attempt a resistance against the Japanese with his small platoon of soldiers.[4] They were ill-equipped and many of them defended themselves with spears. The Honghuzi bandits scattered in the countryside joined General Ma in the fight, but the effort was futile because the Chinese were in no position to defend their cities. In spite of the loss, General Ma won respect and admiration from the people and became a national hero in his opposition to the Japanese invasion.

As the troops entered Harbin, Chinese police stationed along the road were replaced by Japanese soldiers.[5] The Chinese went about their business as normal, seeming not to want to acknowledge what was happening as the army marched through the city. Some Russians were paid and organized by the Japanese to stand along the roadside shouting *Banzai* (Hooray) as the soldiers passed, giving the troops flowers and waving Japanese flags. But for those naive and traitorous supporters, the illusion quickly faded as the Russians realized the intentions of the Japanese troops.

Soon, 150,000 Japanese soldiers, 18,000 Japanese gendarmes, 4,000 secret service personnel, and 100,000 advisors commanded every aspect of life in the eastern part of Inner Mongolia and the Three Northeast Provinces including Harbin.[6] The territory was renamed by the Japanese as *Manchukuo* and became, in their eyes, a separate Japanese state. It was hard to conceive that it had only taken a few months for the Japanese and the Kwantung Army to occupy and control such a vast territory, more than three times the size of Japan. Their planned occupation of the resource-rich land was swift, executed with perfect precision, and aided by the lack of resistance. Life had changed overnight.

The Japanese attempted to calm people by assuring them that nothing had changed. They vainly tried to orchestrate the impression of support from

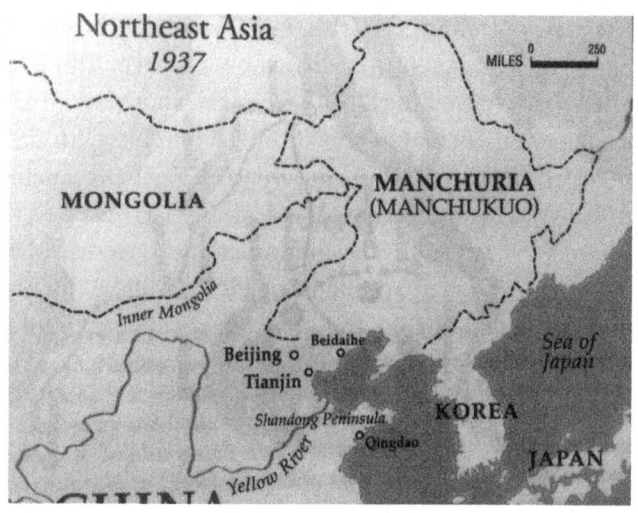
Manchukuo[7]

local citizens, but many in Harbin saw and experienced this Japanese aggression and understood that it was real. Expectations of Zhang Xueliang and Jiang Kai-Shek's troops stopping the Japanese invasion were fruitless due to the lack of financial and military strength. Still, hope remained that the League of Nations would step in and help.

As the occupation continued, Russian refugees by the thousands fled Manchuria. The Chinese were persecuted: "thousands were thrown in jails, hundreds were shot, others were murdered, and women were assaulted by soldiers."[8] Businesses came to a standstill. People remained indoors, and the streets were deserted. Everyone lived in terror and no one knew whom they could trust. The atmosphere in Harbin had changed and it was as though a black, ugly cloud had descended upon the city. Thousands of *ronin* (bandits) were released from prisons in Japan and sent to Manchuria to wreak havoc on the cities and its people.[9] Harbin, once "the gem of the world," became a city terrorized and unrecognizable.

Japan's takeover and declaration of Manchukuo as a separate country was made official through letters issued to foreign missions and written by Chinese officials under coercion. The letters informed different provinces, districts, and governments that the Japanese would "establish an independent Government severing their relations with the Republic of China and create 'Manchukuo,' the State of Manchuria, on March 1, 1932." The declaration continued, "You are no doubt aware that the old military authorities, headed by Zhang Xueliang, that administered the Northeastern Provinces, sought only their self-interest and failed to give adequate consideration to the welfare of the people; that the entire populace was subjected to extreme sufferings through outrageous exactions resulting from the corrupt discipline in the official circles; and that the relations with foreign nations were greatly impaired through the enforcement of anti-foreign policies."[10] This letter went on to justify their actions and was sent to the consular officials and foreign ministers of seventeen countries and to government officials of thirty-five different countries.[11]

In response to China's appeal to the League of Nations the previous year, an investigatory team, the Lytton Commission, arrived in Harbin on May 9, 1932, headed by the elderly British Lord Lytton. The dignitaries were met at the Harbin train station by a delegation of Japanese officials with a full welcoming ceremony. As the group emerged from the station, a young Korean, dressed in a Manchukuo policeman's uniform, stepped forward and gave the British Lord Lytton a letter with grievances. Lord Lytton took the letter and handed it to a Japanese official who accepted the letter with the assurance that he would take care of it. The young Korean, Kim Kwok, was arrested and tortured. Throughout his torture and torment, he insisted that he did this on his own merit, hoping that the commission would assist in Korea's liberation from its long-term Japanese occupation.[12]

The delegation from the League of Nations was driven through the city along streets filled with "Manchukuo" Chinese and Russian police. Japanese soldiers were under strict orders to stay off the streets to ensure the appearance that their presence in the city was not a military occupation. The Japanese surrounded the commission and escorted the group everywhere. A perimeter was set up around their hotel monitored by a twenty-four-hour surveillance team, preventing the members from coming into contact with any resident, but a few participants still managed to arrange some secret meetings under dangerous, stressful conditions to learn the truth. The Japanese wined and

Lord Lytton in Harbin[13]

dined the representatives every night and were convinced they had presented the intended image.

The conclusion of the Lytton Report stated that the League of Nations would not recognize the State of Manchukuo since the territorial integrity of China had been violated. A year later the Lytton Report was ratified in 1933, prompting the Japanese delegation to walk out of the League of Nations and disavow their affiliation. The Japanese conquest of Manchuria continued without any changes.

Just after the occupation, Harbin was hit by a destructive flood in August 1932. Three weeks of torrential rains turned the entire downtown area into a sea of water, causing the banks of the Sungari River to overflow. Boats floated down the main street rescuing stranded residents. Many people were evacuated to Novyi Gorod (New City) away from the low-lying areas, yet despite rescue efforts hundreds of people died in the floods and in the cholera epidemic that followed. While the city's residents were busy rebuilding and looking after one another, the Japanese further exploited the city's vulnerable state to exact control and implement their takeover.

The Japanese were devious in their attempt to try to create a positive image to the outside world that this was a legitimate takeover. In 1932 they appointed Pu Yi as the supreme ruler of Manchukuo, and enthroned him as the "puppet" emperor of Manchukuo (i.e., Manchu Empire). He was installed as the head of state, but given no power or authority, instead he served the Japanese and played the role as a figurehead. Pu Yi was placed in this role

Postcard of flood conditions in downtown Harbin, 1932

to give the appearance that the Japanese occupation was in some way validated by China and the Chinese people. The city of Changchun was declared the new capital of Manchukuo, where Emperor Pu-Yi would now live with his wife, and, at the same time, a new national flag was instated. They even went so far as issuing Manchukuo-Japanese commemorative friendship stamps to celebrate their claim.

It was not only in Harbin where the relentless aggression brought tragedy and devastation, it was all over China. Vladislav came home one evening with news about an incident in Shanghai in the district of Zhabei in January 1932. The Japanese were enraged by the murder of a Japanese monk and sent in seventy planes from an aircraft carrier to bomb the city and the Chinese civilian population of Zhabei, killing thousands of people.[15] The many foreigners living in Shanghai were horrified. Word spread quickly and anti-Japanese sentiment swept across China. Nevertheless, it did little to stop the Japanese.

Pu Yi, the last emperor of the Great Qing Dynasty[14]

In opposition, Honghuzi guerilla groups, who the Japanese called bandits, burned down Japanese houses, derailed trains—to create havoc—and killed Japanese soldiers. These acts of violence often backfired, as the unacceptable level of cruelty by the Japanese was exercised to the limit. When one soldier was killed, the retaliation was ten- or hundred-fold, even more. The soldiers were the imperial officers of the Japanese Army and demanded that everyone acknowledge and respect them as superior beings.

To escape persecution, many Russians and individuals from other countries began working for the Japanese in Harbin. On the Japanese payroll foreigners enjoyed a comfortable life. They seldom complained about the conditions and were the first to defend the Japanese presence, saying that the Japanese were instrumental in building up the area economically, politically, and socially. They praised the Japanese for building roads and railroads and for bringing a sense of security to the city. The faithful residents who could identify those sympathizers made sure to avoid them because no decent human being would support such atrocities.

With Japan's ambition to turn Harbin into its own city, it did not take long for the Kwantung Army's occupying officers to identify a house in Harbin they desired for their Security and Intelligence Officers' Club. It was the Kowalski mansion at 1 Yi Yuan Street. The Japanese needed this prominent house because it was next door to the Military Intelligence Headquarters, now housed in the former Skildelsky residence. The Skidelsky family had sold their house some years earlier in 1918 or 1919 and had moved into a beautiful house on Ashiheskaia Street.

At the end of 1933 into 1934 the Japanese pressured and ordered Vladislav to give up to the Japanese the house he had built and lived in for only twelve years. The terms of the "purchase" imposed on him were absurd and not negotiable. Despite the orders by the army, Vladislav refused to sell. He contacted the Polish consul for assistance, but the consul was powerless to do anything. The house was "sold" and taken over for nothing, basically a token. The Japanese turned the Kowalski mansion into the North Manchurian Railway Assembly Hall. The underground passage to the garage was lengthened for direct underground access from the Kowalski house to the Military Intelligence Headquarters next door.[16]

Being forced out of the house was painful for the family. They had come to love everything about it, and it was the one thing that was currently holding their family together. For Vladislav it meant so much more. It was a symbol of his accomplishments; his love and connection to the city, the people, and his workers; a place where all his friends would gather and where relatives could come to live. He knew that this was the final straw and that their lives would never be the same.

The family was given hardly any time to move out and leave their home. The soldiers and special forces were ordered to help with the move and stormed into the house picking up pieces of furniture and boxes. Many nice pieces of furniture were left behind, including an old grandfather clock,[17] as they would be moving to a smaller house. The family moved back into the eleven-room house on the corner of Artilleriiskaia and Aptekarskaia Streets where they had previously resided. Vladislav had cleverly used the house as an office during the years, fortunately, as they now had somewhere to go. When the family began unpacking they noticed that some of the boxes and many of the smaller valuable items were missing. Again, the family's complaints were ignored and no action was taken.

43 | Manchukuo

1934–1936

Successful Chinese and internationally established businesses in Manchukuo were impacted and industrialists like grandfather did not stand a chance. All non-Japanese businesses would now be controlled and manipulated by the Japanese themselves and the Manchukuo authorities. Every action, step, or decision was made with the backing of the Kwantung Army, the state-owned SMR, and the government of Japan. Japanese capital poured into Manchukuo, but all of it went to fund Japanese projects and Japanese companies.

MANCHUKUO BECAME JAPAN'S "GOLD MINE" PROVIDING VAST RAW materials and resources for its accelerating economic, industrial, and military strength. Agriculture also became an important industry suppling farm products for Japan and the growing empire. The Japanese built up their army and naval forces, with its priority on the shipbuilding industry. Their ambition to match the US military force in the Pacific resulted in a formidable fleet that was "better armed than their British and American counterparts."[1] In 1930 before the State of Manchukuo was established, the Japanese population in Manchuria comprised less than 1 percent, totaling 233,749 Japanese.[2] By 1935 the Kwantung Army alone had grown to 164,000 men.[3]

To improve its military standing, in July 1935 Japan announced a five-year armament modernization plan, allotting ¥900 million (about US$263 million[4]) for expenditures.[5] This plan allocated ¥500 million (about US$146 million) for aircraft, ¥20 million (about US$5.8 million) for improved armaments—specifically for Japan and Korea, and ¥200 million (about US$58 million) to be used for Manchukuo.[6] These amounts were in addition to the regular budget for the army and navy. The special purpose of these increases was earmarked for war against the Soviet Union, which they now felt posed the biggest threat to their newly acquired territory.[7]

The Soviet Union was dealing with its own internal problems and could not afford a conflict with Japan. As a removal of a possible pretext for a Japanese attack, the Soviets engaged Japan in dialogue to sell them the CER.[8] Japan offered to buy the CER, with terms particularly favorable to them. The Soviets were worried about the negotiations because of the enormous CER debt that existed and ended up selling the important CER from Manzhouli via Harbin to Pogranichnaia in 1935 for only ¥170 million (US$49 million/70 million gold rubles), nowhere near its true value.[9] Vladislav observed with regret thirty years of progressive and successful Russian economic policy, with the CER as the golden key to the East, transferred to the jubilant Japanese railway officers. The deal was concluded, and the Japanese renamed the CER the North Manchurian Railway. Together with the SMR, the railway network in Manchukuo was now able to support Japan's business interests, as more railways continued to be built. Step-by-step the Japanese secured their presence, power, and total control.

Economically, the big Japanese zaibatsu companies were dominant and had political and financial influence both in Japan and in China. For many years, there was a close relationship among the Japanese government, the Kwantung Army, and the leading Japanese enterprises in Manchuria. Both Mitsui and Mitsubishi had become part owners in the state-owned railway company and held the most extensive private concessions in the SMR Zone. The mining development of coal and iron resources made steelmaking possible for them in Japan. The zaibatsu conglomerates were amenable to the idea of territorial expansion with their bankers—Mitsui, Mitsubishi, and Sumitomo holding a quarter of the Japanese finance capital—and each bank tried to outdo the other to raise the funds for this.[10] Nissan, Meiji, Mitsubishi, and other companies constructed factories, mines, and businesses in the area and controlled a large percentage of the import and export market.

Japanese government rules and regulations were enforced under the military rule of the Kwantung Army. They were implemented as a special law drawn up between Japan and Manchukuo and regulated by the Japanese Manchukuo government, structured so that all companies would be under Japanese control.

The Japanese had devised a shrewd scheme to take control of all private and government businesses and industries of any importance in the region. Government workers, businessmen, and officials kept their jobs, but were assigned two to three Japanese advisors to form "partnerships." There were 100,000 Japanese advisors in Manchukuo appointed to penetrate and take control of every aspect of these businesses and the government.[11] English- or

Russian-speaking Japanese were candidates to become advisors, irrespective of their limited language skills.[12] Once placed in control, they were given the power to give orders and make all decisions on behalf of the company and/or departments.

This system of military suppression and government control was applied to Vladislav's business. He was appalled at the thought of needing to take on a Japanese "partner" in a company he had poured his heart into for the last thirty-five years, but he realized that he had no say in the matter. His industries and concessions were too important to escape the hands of the Japanese occupiers.

Shortly after his arrival in Harbin, Shigeshi Kondo was appointed as an advisor to Vladislav and Takahashi as the manager.[13] It was Polish Consul Aleksander Kwiakowski, consul in Harbin from 1932–1938, who recommended Kondo. The Japanese authorities may have influenced this decision because the consul was an agent of the Polish military intelligence, which developed a close relationship and had intelligence cooperation with the Japanese. Both Poland and Japan's military considered the Soviet Union to be their common enemy and major threat.[14] The selection of Kondo was certainly not in the interest of the Kowalski firm.

Kondo was a small-time Japanese businessman who had made his way from Vladivostok. He had no experience in the lumber industry, and lacked business acumen, but that did not matter. Because of the size and importance of the timber resources for the Kwantung Army, Japan wanted all the income and assets from Vladislav's company. They demanded full control, and as Kondo was backed by the Kwantung Army and the SMR company, Kondo, of course, was ready to oblige.

Kondo, as an advisor to the Kowalski firm, was soon in charge of all business decisions. All files were at his disposal and Vladislav was denied access to the company's financial accounts.[15] The bank contracts were changed and reissued under Japanese banks.[16] Kondo would hold meetings and refuse to allow Vladislav to attend them. The only documents in Vladislav's possession had been collected two days prior to Kondo's confirmation. Polish Consul Kwiatkowski had come to the office with a suitcase and filled it with as many important documents as he could. They then went to Vladislav's home and into his study, closed the door, and spent the whole night in discussion over the papers.

According to an article in the *Harbin New Evening News* written by Liu Yannian, Kondo arrived in Vladivostok as a 19-year-old.[17] After sixteen years he founded the Merchant Shipping Company in Vladivostok. In 1932 he learned that with the Japanese occupation of Manchuria, Minami Jiro, a person who came from the same town as he did, became the commander of the Kwantung Army and the Japanese ambassador to Manchukuo, serving both positions concurrently. Because of this connection, Kondo moved to Harbin and shortly thereafter became the advisor to Vladislav's firm. At that time, Kondo opened his own business, Kin Do Forestry Company, even though he had no experience in forestry, and registered it at 106 Diduan Street in the Daoli District of Harbin. Once he became the advisor to Vladislav's firm, he stopped payments to the Kowalski business and began transferring assets to his own company.[18] Vladislav fiercely objected, but to no avail. Kondo was very confident in his role as an advisor because of the friendship he developed with Japanese Manchukuo Commander Minami Jiro.[19]

With the "partnership," Vladislav's financial situation deteriorated. His debts were growing and his situation was becoming grave. Kondo took over everything and did not allow Vladislav to make decisions. It had reached a point where if he had something to discuss, he was now obliged to call the office for an appointment to see Kondo.[20] Kondo did not address the debts of the company and pocketed the money from the business. He prevented Vladislav from reviewing the books and, when questioned about the money that Vladislav was entitled to, Kondo promised to pay him later, refusing to give him any promissory notes in writing.[21]

Vladislav was a quiet, modest, and levelheaded man and avoided unnecessary confrontations. He didn't have an enemy in the world. Vika mentioned years later that the only time she saw Vladislav truly enraged was with Kondo. He used to complain that Kondo completely shut him out. Her father was always proud of the way he managed his business and he respected professionalism, but he described Kondo as a conniving, money-hungry crook who was only interested in his and Japan's self-serving gains. Vika said it was the first time she saw her father hate anyone as much as he did Kondo.

It was a critical situation that Vladislav was put into. The Japanese were taking everything from him—his money, his assets, his house, and his livelihood. He could not protect himself. In 1932 his concession at Hundaohetze was seized for the debts that he incurred according to a Japanese-controlled newspaper article.[22] Clearly, Vladislav did not acknowledge this action as legitimate because in 1933 he leased out this property, Hundaohetze, to a third party. The original creditors demanded his arrest and had him guarded. It is not certain if he was arrested at the time that the newspaper article was published on January 13, 1934. On February 2, 1934, three weeks after the demand for his arrest, Vladislav was put in prison for not being able to pay off a debt of 500,000 rubles (about US$350,000).[23] There are no records of how long he spent in the Japanese-administered jail.

Vladislav was frustrated and desperate. He realized that the consequences of confronting the Japanese could result in grave repercussions, but he was running out of options. He appealed to Polish Consul Litewski for legal advice, who recommended the claims against Kondo be brought to court, which he did. The Japanese Military Mission in Harbin investigated the claim for a year and a half, confiscating all accounting books, papers, and documents from the office.[24] Multiple court hearings were held for discussions and disagreements.

One account at a court hearing in Harbin illustrated Vladislav's desperate situation. "The Japanese military authorities had robbed him of all he had, and he, seeing himself unable to pay his debts, declared himself bankrupt. Both the state and city police stood by him and maintained that he was an honorable man, above all suspicion: whereas the Gendarmerie (Japanese Army Police) insisted that he was nothing but a rascal capable of committing any sort of crime."[25] There was a general laughter of disbelief from the audience in the courtroom when this contradictory Japanese remark was read.[26]

The final verdict stated that Kondo was to pay Vladislav the money he owed him for the last year and a half, a fraction of the total he actually owed.[27] Kondo was released from detention and remained as the Japanese advisor to Vladislav's firm. After the initial payment, he continued to pocket the profits and resumed his deceitful actions without any fear of retribution.[28] The Japanese made their own rules and had taken the Kowalski firm and its assets without any ownership, investment, and business consideration or compensation to Vladislav. It was worse than highway robbery. His continued appeals to the authorities were futile as the police, the government, and the courts were all in the hands of the Japanese. Without power or clout behind his demands, the Japanese authorities were not even respectful.

In the *Harbin New Evening News* article, it was stated that in a little over two years Kondo's company, Kin Do Forestry Company, became Harbin's largest timber trader.[29] He also built a sawmill factory in Majiago at Xiehe Street in the Nangan District. Kondo eventually bought a piece of land, close to St. Nicholas Cathedral, invested ¥1 million, and built a hotel, the New Harbin Hotel, in 1936. The hotel was designed by a famous Russian architect, Petr Sergeevich Sviridov (1889–1971). The hotel was completed in 1937 using the money he stole from Vladislav's business. After the liberation of Harbin in 1945, the hotel and the sawmill were accepted by the People's Government. The hotel was later renamed the Harbin International Hotel.

Vladislav's situation and life had changed radically with the Japanese occupation. The freedom to continue his business activities, to lead his company, and to develop his vast concessions were severely challenged by the occupation and the Japanese military interference. His life became a struggle for his properties, his business, and his family's existence in Harbin. Their lives were characterized by the Japanese war, the occupation, and the oppression of Chinese and foreigners in Manchuria and Harbin. Vladislav was not alone in his struggles. People lost control of their businesses and many fled to other cities in China or, in the case of many of the foreigners, returned to their home countries.

44 | Another Life

1935

My mother, Vika, had a strange relationship with her mother. Her mother never showed her any love and refused to give her any encouragement or signs of affection. She thrived on criticizing Vika, and even at the age of 24, in her mother's eyes Vika could still never do anything right. Vika had struggled with the feeling of rejection her whole life. Adding to the hurt was her sister Ada's puzzling support for her mother's mistreatment of her. Why did they both demonstrate so much antagonism?

LUCIA AND ALEX BLUMBERG HAD LIVED IN HARBIN FOR A NUMBER OF years. Alex worked for the customs office, and in late 1934 they were transferred to Wuxi, a city along the West River in Jiangsu Province north of Shanghai. Wuxi was located between Nanking and Hong Kong. The city was in a remote area of the country with hardly any buildings and the only way to reach the city was by boat.

Lucia and Alex

Photo provided by the Jonckheer family,
Lucia's grandchildren

In 1935 Vika and Ada visited the Blumbergs in Wuxi. Lucia, Alex, and their 3-year-old daughter Ada had just moved into their new apartment, a comfortable dwelling with ample room for guests. Ada and Vika had planned to stay for a short time, but their visit lasted longer than expected. Life had been so trying as of late, and Wuxi was a welcomed escape. They spent many hours sitting in the living room talking about Harbin, the Japanese occupation, the family, and the uncertainties of life, but also about the good old days of growing up in Harbin. While it was pleasant to be together, the news from Harbin created a worrying atmosphere. It had been seven months since they arrived in Wuxi when Ada returned to Harbin and Vika decided to travel on to Hong Kong.

Vika was reluctant to return home. She had been happy in Harbin but was not content with her life at home with her mother and with Ada. She felt unwanted and dejected and longed for the feeling of unconditional love. She had been inspired by the kindness and righteousness of Lenochka, and her thoughts had turned to joining a convent and becoming a nun. In Hong Kong, Vika visited the Cannosa Convent and met with one of the nuns, Flo Nunas, to discuss and explore the possibility of joining the nunnery. She decided to enter the convent and to devote her life to God.

Vika started her training, living at the convent in a semiconfined arrangement. While she was there, she ran into Judy Citrin and Lita, friends from Harbin. They were staying at the convent as boarders during their visit to Hong Kong, as it was safer for young girls traveling alone to live in the secure

Vika, 24 years old in Hong Kong

surroundings. Judy and Lita described the recent changes in Harbin and how the Japanese occupation of Manchukuo continued to influence life in the city. They praised Vladislav for his strength and determination to tolerate the oppression and not to concede.

From 1935 to 1936 Vika lived in the convent, praying every day. Word had already reached the family that she had chosen to become a nun and would not be returning home. The family wrote to her encouraging her to give up the idea and return to Harbin. She did not miss her mother nor Ada, in fact, it was a relief for her to be away from them. But, she missed her father terribly and worried about him. She had already seen how the issues with his business and the Japanese occupation had affected him before she left and could only imagine how much worse the situation had gotten. He always took problems with his work and life so personally, and now this stressful environment must be devastating for him. Although Vika was concerned for her family, she felt at home in Hong Kong and had no intention of leaving.

While at the convent she received a letter from her classmate Elenora from boarding school in Bromley, Kent (England). Elenora was planning to visit Macao and would be there for only one night on her way to Australia. She asked about the possibility of getting together and invited Vika to stay overnight at her hotel in Macao. Vika was ecstatic. It immediately brought back so many wonderful memories of her time in England. She continued reading the letter, and even reread parts of it to make sure she did not miss any details of Elenora's plans. She read the section that stated the date and rushed to a calendar to clarify her suspicion. It was so! Oh no! Not Saturday

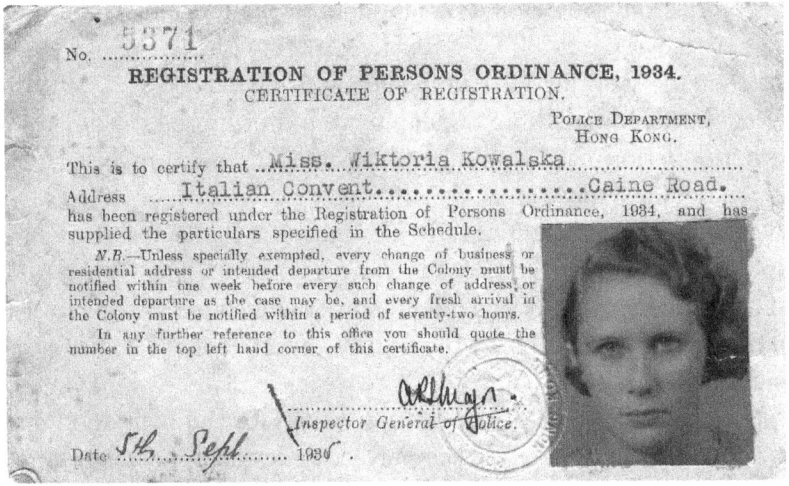

Vika's registration to enter the Italian convent

to Sunday. She was sure Mother Superior would not allow her absence from the convent on Sunday. How would she manage? She sat on the side of her bed in despair. There was nothing to do but ask.

Vika immediately went to see Mother Superior to request permission for her to leave the convent for one night and go to Macao. Mother Superior read the letter, handed it back to Vika, and took off her glasses.

"You know Vika, when we enter the convent we give up all our attachments to our family and to our friends. We become a servant of God and everyone becomes our sister and brother. I understand that you have lived under unique circumstances. I am going to let you go under one condition. You must promise to attend mass on Sunday morning and take communion, and you must return after the church service."

Vika thought she was going to explode with happiness.

"Thank you, Mother Superior, I give you my word." She had a hard time walking back to her room, her heart was beating so fast. Vika arranged for the travel on the ferry to Macao for the following month.

Vika arrived at the pier in Macao at three in the afternoon and made her way into the small city, clutching the printed address in her hand. When she approached the hotel, she spied Elenora waiting outside the entrance. They ran to hug each other. It had been years since their time in England, and they had so much to catch up on. Vika had not eaten lunch, so they decided to go to the local bakery to buy some jam and bread and eat it in the room.

They began chatting and continued to talk late into the night, even forgetting about dinner. There wasn't a moment of silence until they both fell asleep midsentence during one of the discussions. In all the excitement, they had not realize the time. It was already four in the morning when they fell asleep.

At ten in the morning Vika jumped up with a bolt.

"Elenora, I've missed the Sunday service. I promised. I gave my word to Mother Superior that I would go to mass." She was ready to start crying. "What am I going to do?"

"Go to high mass, Vika. You can leave right after the service. I am sure she will understand."

Vika hurriedly dressed, hugged Elenora, thanked her for the most wonderful time together, and ran to the nearby church that she had spotted the previous day.

Vika took a seat in the last pew and waited for the high noon mass to begin. When the service started she prayed harder than she had ever prayed before. She asked for forgiveness and prayed for her parents and Ada, for the people in Harbin, for the peasants in China, and for the whole world. She recited over and over the Hail Mary with her rosary in hand.

When it came time for the communion, she walked slowly toward the front of the church from the back pew, her head down in repentance. She knelt down on the stair in front of the priest, vaguely sensing the absence of any other parishioners.

The priest bent down and quietly whispered, "The High Mass communion is only for the governor and his wife, so please come back after the service, my child, and I will give you communion."

Vika had been denied communion. She had to stand up, turn around, and face the whole congregation as she walked back to her pew in the last row. She was very upset, and felt so ashamed. She was sure everyone was looking at her. As she walked back to her seat, she could feel herself shaking, and could hear the pounding of her heart in her ears.

Vika did a lot of thinking on her way back to Hong Kong. That night she couldn't sleep. She was so bothered by the fact that she was denied communion, yet the governor received it. In the eyes of God, we are all equal, she thought.

Three days later she asked to see Mother Superior and told her of her reservations about becoming a nun.

"Don't pursue this, my child, unless you know that this is your calling. You must be sure in your heart that this is what you want. This is a commitment for life and you must be 100 percent sure that you will give yourself fully to God. If you have the slightest hesitation, you should rethink this."

Vika packed her meager belongings, said goodbye to all the dear sisters, and returned to Harbin. On her way back, she stopped at Wuxi to visit Alex and Lucia. She was surprised to learn that Lucia was not there and that she had gone to Harbin.

Even though Alex enjoyed his rendezvous with the ladies from time to time, people in Wuxi thought he and Lucia had a solid marriage. She was indifferent to all of Alex's ways and never exhibited any jealousy. It was quite by chance that Lucia befriended Kostia at a Sunday afternoon picnic that was arranged to celebrate their friends Sergei and Luda's five-year wedding anniversary. Like Lucia, Kostia was married, but that did not stop them from spending time together. Lucia fell madly in love with him and they had an affair that lasted for four months. Lucia eventually realized that she was so much in love with Kostia that she was ready to give up everything just to be with him. Kostia professed his love to her as well, so she soon asked Alex for a divorce. She decided to leave her two children and returned to Harbin.

There, she would wait for Kostia to divorce his wife and then she would go to Shanghai to marry him. Her choice was certainly going to draw criticism, but she did not care as long as she could be together with her new love.

Vika was surprised to hear that Lucia had left Alex to care for 4-year-old Ada and their second child, George, who was only 6 months old. She was in Harbin when Vika arrived, and said and did nothing each day, just waiting to hear word from Kostia. As time passed, she realized that Kostia had no intention of divorcing his wife and marrying her. Lucia was at a loss as to what to do next.

Everyone was relieved that Vika had surrendered her plans of becoming a nun, especially Vladislav. They respected her decision and not much was spoken about this topic.

45 | The Imperial Way

1930s

The Japanese soldier was a topic of conversation during many meals. Although wars and incidents had taken place in Manchuria for many years and foreign spheres of influence existed, the mentality and the mode of operation of the Japanese soldier was different. The soldiers had a thirst for power and passion for superiority that was unstoppable. Those under Japan's occupation were at its mercy.

THE JAPANESE SOLDIER WAS THE SOUL OF JAPAN—THE LAND OF THE Rising Sun and the emperor was his guiding force.[1] The soldiers believed that Japan was the center of the world and that their sole duty was to show their dedication to the "Imperial Way" while expanding the Japanese empire.[2] Soldiers had extensive training in strategy.[3] Students who graduated from the army academy were trained in Bushido, the ways of the warrior, with mastery of martial arts thereby generating an enthusiasm for war and the philosophies of the samurai; in the case of the naval academy the concentration was on education.[4] Principles of this samurai philosophy included dishonesty and lies in dealings with the outside world, actions that were not only allowed but encouraged because it was a sign of intelligence.[5] The officers insisted that the soldiers always attack and not act defensively. This mentality was evident in all Japanese war actions also in Manchuria. The soldiers were tough and were trained to endure anything in the name of the emperor, where to die for the emperor was an honor and a privilege.[6]

Japan's aggressive actions and repression in occupying Korea had given it the confidence of a conquering force. The soldiers were emboldened to do anything in the interest of the emperor, Japan, and the Japanese people. As a colonial power, Japan hated having equal treaties forced upon it and believed that an aggressive policy was necessary to safeguard its investments as it was in the case of Manchuria.[7] It wanted to show the world that it was not a country to be dealt with lightly.

The Japanese Kwantung Army was shaped by the many political incidents and wars that occurred in China—the Sino-Japanese War, the Boxer Rebellion, the Russo-Japanese War, World War I, and the Mukden Incident, which allowed them to take control through aggressive means, often in violation of existing treaties and often with the pretext that they were protecting their citizens. With the Japanese occupation of Manchuria, the Kwantung Army became the absolute power and aspired to further expand in Asia and even take over parts of China and the Soviet Union. The decisions made by the army in Manchukuo were seldom questioned by the government in Japan; they had free rein to conduct, defend, and administer their rules as they saw fit.[8]

The Japanese occupiers made efforts to address the anti-Japanese sentiment that was rampant among the Chinese and foreigners living in China. They implemented very stringent censorship on the press, so that all the news would have a positive, pro-Japanese spin. Newspaper articles and radio broadcasts would substitute names, change stories, and fabricate events to make the Japanese look good, relaying stories of heroism and gallantry, glorifying the Japanese soldier.

To specifically target the Russian residents, the Japanese created an organization called the Bureau for the Affairs of the Russian Emigres,[9] which broadcast Japanese propaganda in Russian. It was established in December 1934. It was not only Japanese propaganda that was broadcast but it also served as "an obedient tool" for the Japanese military mission in Harbin as well as in the settlements along the railway line. It was an effective way for the Japanese to monitor and control Russians as well as other nationalities and be able to report this back to the Japanese.[10]

After its creation, the bureau increased its activities to include newly formed Japanese-controlled associations and clubs. By 1938, through the bureau, the Japanese had managed to indoctrinate Russians who were recruited to engage in activities to support the Japanese defense of Manchukuo.[11] The Asano Detachment was an offshoot of the bureau and a special detachment of the Kwantung Army; the bureau recruited young Russian men to serve in the Japanese military.[12] Residents in Harbin were cautious not to express any anti-Japanese or pro-Soviet opinions. The consequences were often extreme, as people were killed or would disappear for even the smallest infraction.

The Japanese wanted to maintain an atmosphere of fear and unease, allowing them to further gain and keep control in Manchuria. To do so, they used a common, strategic tactic to create disruptive situations in the cities and throughout the region. They employed Russian, Korean, and Chinese "bandits" to do their dirty work, activities that included kidnappings, bombings, killings, crimes, and deceit. This allowed them to divert attention away from their wrongdoings and maintain a more favorable image. But, despite their attempts, the local population was not naive as to who was behind the terror.

The Japanese military expansionism gave Vladislav an eerie feeling of familiarity. Years earlier he had experienced the Russian occupation in Poland and was familiar with the imposing indoctrination that an oppressing force inflicts on its victims. With the occupation of Manchukuo, the Japanese had a similar strategy of enforcing their ideology and identity, and this was done through brutality, terrorism, and demoralization. The Japanese were victimizing the population of Manchukuo, and exercised a degree of cruelty, ruthlessness, suppression, and intimidation that broke the rules of acceptable wartime practices.

What Vladislav found most perplexing was the contrast between the Japanese he had met in Japan and those who now lived in Manchukuo. He had been in Japan and had experienced their kind, soft, and gentle mannerisms. He knew that Japan was a nationalistic and homogeneous nation that for many years was isolated and intolerant of foreigners, but this felt like something much greater. Now in Manchukuo the Japanese demonstrated an extreme degree of self-confidence and arrogance that was calculated to bring its victims to their knees. Vladislav could see that their expansion was not to integrate but to impose and to annihilate all things foreign to them. The Japanese military in Manchukuo even wanted power over Japanese ministries and decision makers at home in Japan. Vladislav could see that to them war was a "game" with their own established rules. All means were acceptable if the end result was in their favor.

The Japanese military was strongly supported by the Kempeitai soldiers who acted as the military police of the Japanese armed forces, dealing with intelligence and counterintelligence espionage.[13] The Kempeitai was a secret force of the Japanese Imperial Army and Navy that "got things done," at any cost. They wreaked havoc with full authority to do whatever they felt necessary with no questions asked.[14] Their philosophy was based on the principles of Bushido and their brutality was notorious in the territories occupied by the Japanese, Korea and China among them. They exhibited unimaginable cruelty against millions, using torture to kill, maim, and humiliate their victims. Of all the atrocities at the hands of the Japanese occupiers, none were as terrible as those that occurred in the city of Pingfan at the Epidemic Prevention Research Lab, located a short distance on the CER from Harbin, which covered a two-square-mile area with 150 buildings known as Unit 731.

The Epidemic Prevention Research Lab in Pingfan was created and implemented by a bacteriologist, Shiro Ishii, who was a graduate of Kyoto Imperial University and was married to the daughter of the head of the university.[16] While in Japan, he was able to convince the War Department and lay the groundwork to set up a human experiment facility in China. He pressured the military for the establishment of a division that would base its activities on the development of germ warfare. His aim was for "the development of bacteriological research as a weapon for offensive warfare," finally convincing the Ministry of the Army and the Kwantung Army to sponsor such a program.[17] The research centers would be able to manufacture and produce large quantities of bacteria such as "glanders anthrax and other pathogens" raising rats and collecting fleas for the spreading of the bubonic plague as well as other diseases while experimenting on the thousands of imprisoned victims.[18]

Shiro Ishii, orchestrator of the biological warfare program in Harbin and Unit 731[15]

This facility in Pingfan was the notorious Unit 731, a biological and chemical warfare unit of the Imperial Japanese Army, funded by the Japanese government.[19] The facility was officially known as the Epidemic Prevention and Water Purification Department of the Kwangtung Army. It was actually a research and development unit where biological and chemical warfare experiments were performed on thousands of innocent victims and where medical experiments were performed on humans.[20] The Pingfan facility in Harbin was the main, central unit with other facilities in Peking, Nanking, and Guangzhou. Statistics showed that there were about 20,000 personnel working at these facilities.[21] It is believed that during the five-plus years of its operation, thousands of men and women (many pregnant), children, and infants were victims of unfathomable cruelty and death at Unit 731.[22]

The victims of Unit 731 were never just killed, they were tortured, subjected to experiments, often meaningless experiments, to satisfy the curiosity of the Japanese perpetrators, under the guise of medical research for their biological warfare program. Victims were used as guinea pigs, injected with germs of different diseases to see the effects. They were subjected to frostbite and body extremities were amputated. Organs were removed, victims were shot in torturous ways, and body parts were removed and sewn back onto opposite sides of the body to see if functions could be generated.[23] All the experiments were conducted on the patients without anesthetic, and vivisections were common.[24] Most of the victims were Chinese but Russians, Koreans, Americans, and other nationalities, some POWs, were among the victims.[25]

Canisters of plague-infected fleas were released from low-flying planes on the Chinese cities of Ningbo, Shanghai, Changde, and other cities, and disease-carrying microbes were thrown into rivers, wells, and reservoirs, killing between 1.5 million to 6.3 million Chinese.[26] The intention was to expand the biological warfare program that could inflict disease and kill hundreds of thousands of people in their germ warfare program even extending to other parts of the world.

The Chinese who "disappeared" were often victims and were never heard from again. Similar units were created in other areas, but the Unit 731 near Harbin was believed to be the most brutal and active. The tortures and experiments were condoned by the rulers in Japan and "General Hideki Tojo, who was Prime Minister of Japan and Minister of War for most of the conflict, was so pleased by General Ishii's test results that he saw to it that the Emperor awarded Ishii a high decoration."[27]

46 | Story After Story

mid-1930s

It was frightening to see the perilous state of Harbin since the occupation. It brought such negativity, suffering, and unimaginable circumstances that affected the core of the society and the country as a whole. Why Manchuria? Why Harbin? Why was this allowed to happen? Father tried hard to continue to bring normalcy into his life and that of his family, as he did in 1937 on June 26 when he invited guests from the Polish community to our summerhouse on Sunshine Island to celebrate the Day of the Sea. It was a memorable day, a happy time amid all the gloom. We all decorated the cottage with the Polish colors, white and red flowers with an artistic depiction of a boat with sails that we displayed over the entrance. It was very festive. Three boatloads of guests from the Polish community arrived by motorboats and were greeted by the Polish Consul Kwiatkowski and other members of the Polish community. It was one evening where we all forgot about reality and enjoyed the festivities late into the night. The event made it into the newspaper the next day.[1]

VIKA WAS PLEASED TO SEE THAT DESPITE THE STRESS AND TERRORS THAT had become part of their daily existence, Vladislav still made it a point to continue his Thursday night bridge games. He was a strong bridge player and loved the game. He also treasured his friendship with his playing partners, and they all found solace in this distraction. He often said that he had to have this enjoyable diversion to keep his sanity, but even during the many hours sitting around the bridge table it was hard to escape discussions and the realities of life in Manchukuo.

One Thursday evening as the hands were being dealt, Sergei turned to Vladislav, "Vladislav Fyodorovich, I can see that there is a lot of activity in your former house," commented Sergei.

"Well you know, the Japanese Imperial Railway Headquarters is next door. A lot of high-level intelligence and military activity seems to be centered in that building. We try to keep our distance. It is still very painful to imagine that our house is occupied by the Japanese Kwantung Army and that we no longer live there. Just the thought of the Japanese using it to advance their agenda is very difficult to take. As hard as it is, I have difficulty getting it out of my mind," said Vladislav with such noticeable pain and sadness that the room became eerily silent.

"We have not come here to lament. Who dealt this hand?" Vladislav changed the mood.

The former Kowalski residence hosted many high-ranking visitors after the Japanese took over the house. Important meetings took place there or at the Military Headquarters next door.[2] Manchukuo's Emperor Pu Yi lived in the house when visiting Harbin as did the prominent Japanese visitor, Prince Konoe Fumimaro, who was appointed prime minister of Japan in 1933.[3] The prime minister was well known for his imperialistic Japanese rhetoric and had a close relationship with Emperor Hirohito, so his 1935 visit to Manchukuo and Harbin was a major event, where he was surrounded by intense Japanese security.[4] His visit indicated the Japanese government's strong approval of the Japanese invasion of Manchuria and the Japanese establishment of Manchukuo.[5] This support continued throughout his administrations as prime minister.

"Did you hear about what took place at the Marco Polo Bridge in July? It seemed that Prime Minister Konoe Fumimaro gave the command for the military escalation.[6] It is obvious that the Japanese are getting more and more involved in expanding their war efforts in China," interjected Andre. "Did you ever hear the details of the military encounter?"

"I heard some stories, but I am not aware of all the details," said Boris.

"The Marco Polo Incident started with the Japanese Army's military exercises near the town of Wanping, southwest of Peking. They sent a message to the Chinese commander requesting permission to enter the town, which was surrounded by a stone wall, as one of their soldiers, a private named Shimura, was missing. The Chinese commander refused access,"[7] explained Sergei.

"Of course he did," answered Dimitri.

"It was not surprising that they refused them entry, as the Japanese had gotten many troops together and were in the middle of their military exercises in the surrounding area. But the Japanese didn't take no for an answer, and they mobilized troops to break through the wall and the Chinese defenses. To stop this aggression, the Chinese sent their mayor to negotiate, which didn't resolve anything. Shortly thereafter, war broke out at the Marco

Polo Bridge between the Japanese and the Chinese troops. Oh, in the meantime the soldier Shimura, who they had reported missing, showed up at the Japanese camp," commented Sergei.[8]

After the Marco Polo Incident, as the Japanese called it, the fighting continued and led to confrontations all over China, marking the beginning of the Second Sino-Japanese War, which lasted from 1937–1945. During the war, clashes between China's National Revolutionary Army and the Japanese Kwantung Army were frequent. Already, since 1936, there was a joint Chinese front against the Japanese aggression, after Governor Zhang Xueliang and the communists, under Chairman Mao Zedong, joined forces. President Jiang Kai-Shek was persuaded by Zhang Xueliang to join their efforts and stop his national military campaign against the Chinese communists. The combined forces were determined to save the country from the Japanese, but it was a long, slow battle.

From December 1937 to early 1938 still under Prime Minister Konoe Fumimaro's government, 50,000 Japanese soldiers went wild in the capital city of Nanking.[9] During a six-week period more than 260,000 (some figures are as high as 350,000) Chinese were tortured, raped, and killed.[10] An estimated 20,000 to 80,000 women were raped or mutilated.[11] Soldiers disemboweled women, forced parents to rape their children, performed castrations, and subjected victims to tortuous, agonizing deaths.[12] Westerners had cordoned off an International Safety Zone to offer Chinese a refuge, which the Japanese respected, thus saving many lives, but the carnage was still considerable. This inconceivable event, with an unimaginable degree of cruelty, came to be known as the Nanking Massacre, or Rape of Nanking.

The Japanese tried to keep the news of the Nanking Massacre a secret to avoid worldwide condemnation. Foreign clergy, however, had hidden cameras in their hats to photograph the atrocities.[13] These pictures were smuggled out and published around the world.

As they sat there recounting the brutalities that had occurred in the last year, Vladislav looked down at his bridge table and smiled, taking a moment to escape the conversation. It was a new, custom-designed table that he had received on July 9 as a birthday gift from his three bridge partners. The table had caricatures of their regular bridge foursome on each corner of the table. The scenes brought Vladislav memories of laughter and happiness, and an appreciation for the wonderful friendships and the pleasures of life. He treasured this present as one of the most precious gifts he had ever received. How sad it was that these simple joys now seemed so isolated.

Stolen Dreams 235

These are the illustrations on the four corners of the bridge table. The family still has the table today.

When news of the Nanking Massacre reached Harbin, the citizens were terrified, and this further empowered the Japanese soldiers, an army that by 1937 was 280,000 strong in northern China.[14] For Harbin's residents, the violence had become very personal. People they knew were affected, making it hard to disassociate and ignore what was happening around them. One of the most recognized of these events was the kidnapping of Simon Kaspe, which took place years earlier in 1933 to the son of Iosif Kaspe. Iosif Kaspe was a French businessman who owned the Moderne Hotel. He had two sons who were educated and lived in Paris. One of his sons, Simon, was a gifted concert pianist, who occasionally came to Harbin to perform. He was an excellent pianist and his performances were always an event that everyone looked forward to.

During his last stay in Harbin years ago, playing to sold-out crowds, Simon Kaspe had become romantically involved with a married woman. On the night before his departure back to Paris, the kidnappers approached Simon and his lover as they were returning from an evening together.

He begged the kidnappers to let her go, which they did, but he was not as lucky and they whisked him off.

Iosif Kaspe began receiving ransom letters demanding a payment of US$300,000 to release his son, but he was suspicious and cautious to agree to any exchange of money.[15] He was not sure if the ransom demands were from the actual kidnappers, and so he chose to ignore the letters. Iosif Kaspe was alone in making the decision as his wife was in Paris at the time. She tried to find passage on a ship to "rush" back to Harbin, but her voyage would take over a month. Also contributing to the delays in responding to the mandates were the assurances Iosif Kaspe received from the French consul that nothing harmful would happen to his son as he was a French subject, even though at this point diplomacy was nonexistent. The payment demand and negotiations continued.

"That was such a tragic crime," said Vladislav.

"What a terrible experience for any family. Kidnappings are so cruel, I cannot imagine going through something like that," lamented Sergei.

After ninety-five days in captivity they finally found the body of young Simon Kaspe, his fingers were severely frostbitten, his ear missing, his hair gray, he was literally skin and bones and looked like a hundred-year-old man. His father had gone mad with grief and guilt for not having taken stronger action. Iosif Kaspe left Harbin shortly after that.

There were accounts that the Japanese were after Kaspe to sell them the Moderne Hotel, which he refused to do. It was maintained that the Japanese and Russian thugs from the Russian Fascist Party were hired to kidnap Simon as "revenge."[16]

The court case for the accusers of the kidnapping went on for some time. Finally the court declared that the kidnappers would be set free due to the benevolent pardon that Emperor Pu Yi had bestowed upon them.[17] They were released by the Japanese authorities as it was declared that they "acted as patriots."[18]

"We are all living under the fear of kidnappings and killings, and even though this tragedy happened in 1933 the tragic story of Simon Kaspe continues to haunt all of us here in Harbin," said Sergei.

"What crazy times we are living in," added Vladislav before dealing the last hand.

47 | Annulment

1936

The Japanese occupation and the Japanese rulers of Manchukuo caused grandfather more trouble than anyone could ever have imagined. The occupation attacked his business and his holdings. He could feel the rug being pulled out from under him. The Polish authorities supported him as best they could, but it was insufficient in spite of Poland's recognition of Manchukuo. Diplomacy and the rule of law did not exist.

After the Japanese had established the state of Manchukuo in 1934 with the powerless puppet Emperor Pu Yi at the helm, the situation in Harbin as well as areas outside the city continued to deteriorate and safety was a concern. The Japanese soldiers concentrated their efforts in the cities and along the railway lines, near the large railway stations. Their presence, particularly in areas previously controlled by the Honghuzi, led to many clashes between the Japanese soldiers and the resisting Chinese "bandits." The Japanese casualties were mounting as the anti-Japanese bandits blew up trains and derailed them. It was more important than ever for the Japanese to exert their control.

The Japanese living in Manchukuo were bleeding it dry. To them, all residents, from the peasant worker to the wealthy entrepreneur, were fair game. An average salary of a general or an admiral in the Japanese military was about ¥550 a month, about US$125.[1] Yet one observer noted, "There are relatively few Japanese officers garrisoned in Manchuria who, when their time is up, return to Japan with less than US$40,000 or $50,000."[2]

Edgar Snow, visiting Harbin, wrote, "Probably in no other city of the world is life so precarious. Harbin residents, including about 100,000 White and Red Russians, risk their lives if they go unarmed anywhere, even in broad daylight. Hold-ups, robberies, murders, kidnappings are common occurrences."[3] Even small-scale rackets were endemic. When Emperor Pu Yi was instated as the puppet emperor, the racketeers printed pictures of the emperor at a cost of two cents and sold them to the Chinese farmers for one dollar.[4] They threatened the farmers and residents with severe punishment for being "unpatriotic" if the picture was not framed and displayed. One dollar for a Manchurian peasant was a substantial sum of money, but the fear of the ramifications for not buying the picture was much greater.

The timber concessions that the Japanese had were small and few, nothing compared to the vast resources that they could access through the Kowalski and other foreign-owned forestry concessions. The lumber business was an important commodity because the Japanese were building railroad lines throughout Manchukuo. Between 1933 and 1934 there was a total of 665 miles of new railways laid by the Japanese, all managed by the SMR.[5] In 1935 with the purchase of the CER it added 1,072 miles of tracks to their railway holdings.[6] There was also a strong demand for wood after the Japanese occupation, to build new houses for their population migrating to Manchukuo. It was important for the Japanese to have access to the lumber business and to have it in their hands.

In 1936 a shattering declaration was made by the Japanese government in Manchukuo annulling all lumber concessions.[7] The annulment was made abruptly and without consideration to the existing contracts. The concessions were Vladislav's most important assets. In 1922 the agreement for the lease of the concessions was renegotiated for a period of twenty-five years. With the Japanese-instigated annulment Vladislav had eleven years left on his renewed contract, an agreement that was made with the owners of the land and with the approval of the Chinese authorities and Bureau of Taxation.[8] The Japanese offered no compensation for the unlawful annulment. Vladislav was not about to capitulate without objection and was ready to fight for his legitimate ownership rights.[9]

In Poland the Kowalski enterprise was viewed as a private concern of economic importance to Poland because of its size and value. From the start, the Polish government had pushed for diplomatic relations, first with China, and then with Manchukuo, to protect its Polish interests, the Kowalski properties being one of the main ones. Now, with the annulment of the concessions, Vladislav turned to the Polish consul who approached the Japanese Consulate in Harbin.[10] It was to be a long process stretching over several years.

Vladislav's appeal to the local court was fruitless as the courts were controlled by the Japanese. The Polish consul took it a step further, appealing to the Polish embassy in Japan for support and demanding it issue formal objections to the aggressive and illegal Japanese actions against Kowalski's forest concessions.[11] The claims covered different aspects, primarily related to monetary compensation. The Polish embassy was not successful in persuading the Manchukuo authorities to reverse the decision. Kondo continued to usurp what he could from the business to his advantage, which went on for years.

Vladislav had invested a substantial amount of money, a total of 10,100,000 gold rubles,[12] (about US$7 million) in equipment and infrastructure, which he was unwilling to hand over to the Japanese without reimbursement. He had bought equipment from abroad, from Germany and the United States, and owned railway engines, locomotives, wagons, trucks, and cars on every concession. He had established fully functioning sawmills and veneer factories. The construction of Vladislav's private railroad alone had cost him $1,751,274, for which he still owed a debt of $138,000.[13] The annulment of the concessions in his opinion required the Japanese to honor the remaining years of his original contracts and compensate him for his equipment and investments. He was resolute in this, but the claim was ignored and the Japanese began to use the railway lines on the concessions and exploit the forest industry facilities and machinery despite his objections.

Through his company, Vladislav presented a claim to the Japanese government for the final unpaid invoices for the railroad ties and timber that Japanese customers had ordered and received. The amount of this delinquent payment was $408,963 (gold Gobi).[14] The Japanese in Manchukuo and in Tokyo disregarded this demand, claiming that this payment should fall under the annulment umbrella.

The new regime had affected the lives of the Chinese workers on the concessions. They received minimal wages and at times received no pay at all. Most of them had nowhere else to go and so stayed on. Their lives were radically different from the days when Vladislav was the chief operator and employer. Even though he was no longer in a position to care for their livelihood, he visited the concessions with Toubin to try to keep in touch with some of the administrators, former managers, and workers, and assisted them in any way he could. Aksenoff, among others, always received money when he or others turned to Vladislav for help.[15]

Workers from the concessions also visited Vladislav to report on their desperate conditions. The workers were in dire situations and had no means of survival. Even when they tried to find other means to support their families, they were quickly shut down. Aksenoff had described an instance where he wanted to sell the milk from his cows to make ends meet, but that was not allowed as the Japanese Meiji company had the monopoly in Manchukuo to sell dairy products.[16] Options were limited and commercial opportunities were closed for non-Japanese.

The annulment was devastating as it took away Vladislav's assets and left him with the debts. The process took its toll. Vladislav fought for his rights despite the negative effects on his health. He refused to accept the Japanese decisions and was determined to contest them for his rightful compensation. The consul provided encouragement and support, but there was not much else he could do. The Japanese were in no hurry to open discussions as the concessions were now in their hands and it was in their interest to ignore the matter. Kondo continued working with the concessions, legitimized by the involvement of the Kwangtung Army, the South Manchurian Railway Company, and Japanese police authorities.

48 | Stolen Dreams

1938–1939

With everything that grandfather had achieved over the years, he was disillusioned with the way it had turned out. He was a good, honest person who deserved to enjoy the fruits of his labor and investments. In every attempt to rectify the situation, he was confronted with barriers and problems. Why is it that bad things happen to good people?

DURING THE OCCUPATION, THE CITY OF HARBIN FUNCTIONED MORE AND more like a Japanese city with Japanese restaurants, drinking houses, and shops. In this environment they established a good and profitable situation for themselves. They developed a lucrative opium trade monopoly that was thriving. The Japanese in Manchukuo mandated that all the products sold in the stores should be from Japan and manufactured by the Japanese. When other foreign goods were imported, customs officials created problems for the importer. Food was left to spoil, wine bottles were broken, canned goods were punctured, and machinery was "fixed" so as not to function. Everything was geared to self-serve the Japanese.[1]

Despite what was going on in Manchukuo and the questionable conduct of the Japanese, some countries diplomatically recognized Manchukuo as a separate state. Between 1934 and 1943 Manchukuo was recognized by approximately twenty-three countries, including Japan, El Salvador, the Dominican Republic, the Soviet Union, Costa Rica, France, Italy, Spain, Germany, Hungary, and Poland.[2]

When diplomatic relations between Poland and Manchukuo were established, Vladislav was convinced that he would receive protection from unlawful dealings. But since 1936 the Polish embassy in Tokyo was unsuccessful in persuading the Japanese authorities to reverse the decision of the annulment of the concessions. For the next couple of years Vladislav fought for his rights and demanded compensation for the loss of the business and machinery worth millions of dollars. After considerable pressure and because of the diplomatic ties, discussions finally commenced between the governments of Japan and Poland to compensate Kowalski for the factories, the equipment, and the lumber business that had been seized.

Negotiations between the two countries dragged on for some time. Polish Consul Jerzy Bogumil Litewski (consul in Harbin between 1938–1941) was instrumental in trying to further the discussions. Complicating matters, a law had been instituted in Manchukuo limiting the amount of money that could be taken by departing residents from Manchukuo. Shanghai was a free port so Vladislav understood that any negotiated money should be deposited directly into a bank in Shanghai outside the perimeter of Manchukuo.

While the sum of money was being discussed and negotiated, Vladislav started to make the arrangements to deposit the money into a bank in Shanghai. Vika offered to go to Shanghai to receive this money. Vladislav did not want her to leave Harbin again. At that time, they had a heart-to-heart talk.

"Papa, you know that I am not happy here at home. I irritate mamachka all the time, and Ada absolutely hates me. She is at me constantly," Vika confided to her father.

"I know things have not been easy for you. I am sorry that I have not been around to protect you, but I see everything. I know this has been going on for years," admitted Vladislav.

"I just don't know why my own mother and my only sister are like that. It has been difficult for so many years. I was too young to understand many things, but know in my heart that it was something out of my control. That is why I wanted to become a nun, I thought God would have all the answers," Vika could feel the tears welling up in her eyes.

"I am sure he has the answers. You know we have to forgive your mother, as her life in her disabling condition has not made it easy for her. It has been difficult for her to accept," explained Vladislav.

"Dear Papa, I am so sympathetic to her condition. It is something I would not wish on my worst enemy. But you know, she hated me my whole life, even

Polish Consul Litewski[3]

when she was not ill. I have tried to be there for her, but I know she does not love me. Do you know what your sister, Felia Fyodorovna, told me during one of our visits to Poland? She said, 'Vika, you know, your mother does not love you.' At that time, I was so shocked. I told her it was not true. I never thought it was possible not to love your own daughter." Vika felt a tinge of guilt as she did not want Vladislav to think badly of his dear sister.

"Your mother is a complicated person. I don't have the answers." Vladislav reached over to give Vika a hug.

"Lucia, who is still here in Harbin, is terribly sorry for the problems she created and for leaving Alex and her children. She wants to return to them but feels nervous about it. As you mentioned, the Japanese need to make the payment for the concessions to a bank outside of Manchukuo as in Shanghai. I would be happy to help you. I can travel with Lucia and go to Shanghai to accept the money in the bank if you want me to," explained Vika, hoping in her heart that a payment from Japan would be made soon.

"I have thought about that, but I am reluctant to let you go away again. Businesswise it would be a good solution. I don't know whom to trust anymore, and it would be prudent to have you handle this. I'll talk to Consul Litewski tomorrow," Vladislav said with a heavy heart.

Travel arrangements were made for Vika and Lucia to go to Shanghai, and he made provisions for her to receive the payment once an agreement was reached. All these discussions had to be secretive. Vladislav bought the train tickets to Shanghai. Bank contacts were made, meetings arranged, and travel plans were progressing.

In 1939 Vika and Lucia arrived in Shanghai and, with Lucia's insistence, Vika agreed to stay with them. Lucia felt that Vika's presence would ease her return to the family after she had caused such awkward complications. The Blumbergs lived in a small two-room apartment with Alex's in-laws, the Vidiapins (Alex's mother and stepfather and their daughter, Tanya). There were eight people living in one small apartment: Lucia, Alex, Ada, George, the Vidiapins, and Vika.

Vika waited in Shanghai to hear from her father in Harbin to confirm the banking arrangements. As the weeks passed without any word, Vika decided to sign up for a crash course in nursing, which would be a good, needed distraction. It was a free course run by the French embassy headed by Madame Barrow and was conducted in the French language by a French medical team. The students were trained in Shanghai hospitals, treating Chinese beggars and attending surgeries. The French Red Cross issued the diplomas.

Vika had been attending classes for months and was worried that the negotiations for the payments were taking too long, but her father reassured her that things were moving in the right direction and that a suitable settlement would soon be reached. The delays were mainly due to the Japanese stalling and bickering about the final amount. Has the agreement finally been made? What amount has been agreed upon? Will it be possible to make necessary transfers of money to Shanghai? These were questions to which Vika eagerly awaited answers. Instead, discouraging news was emerging from Europe.

On September 1, 1939, Nazi Germany attacked Poland and broke through the Polish defense lines and stormed Warsaw. The Germans and the Soviets had a nonaggression treaty, and the Soviets invaded Poland from the east. It was a brutal, violent, and ferocious invasion with mass executions of Polish citizens and a death toll of over 150,000.[4] Poland fell in three weeks. On September 27, Warsaw surrendered to the Germans and Poland was wiped off the European map. Japan, a German ally, celebrated the victory and Poland found herself the devastating loser. With the invasion, again Poland was not recognized as a country and was taken over by Hitler's Germany and Stalin's Soviet Union.

Vladislav lost everything with the outbreak of the war—a war that came as a surprise to everyone in the Far East. This was the beginning of World War II where Japan, Germany, and Italy became allies. The discussions about compensation were the last resort that Vladislav had. The Japanese had already taken everything—his house, his business, his lumber concessions with all its equipment and infrastructure—without any compensation. This

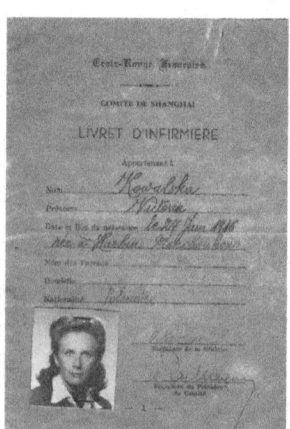
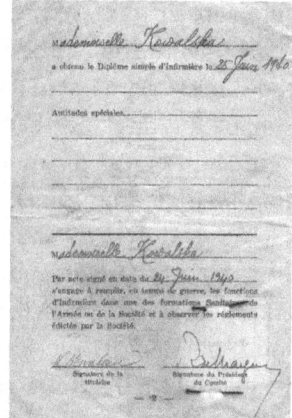

Vika's nursing school certificate; she received her diploma on June 25, 1940. When Vika enrolled in the course, she changed her date of birth to 1916 because she was afraid that she may have difficulty finding a job being 29 years old.

now meant that there would be little hope for any demands and that the Japanese had successfully taken all that he had worked so hard for.

The Japanese-Polish negotiation concerning compensation and payment for Vladislav's business was discontinued. The Japanese delegation immediately left Harbin and no longer saw the need to honor any compensation to Kowalski or Poland.

Vika was desperate when she heard the news. "What is going to happen?" "Papachka must be beside himself." "How can I help him?" "What am I going to do?" Vika could not decide whether to hurry back to Harbin or continue her wait in Shanghai. She rushed over to the Polish consulate in Shanghai. She banged and banged on the door. There was no answer.

Vladislav insisted that Vika wait in Shanghai where she remained for months while her father tried to salvage the situation. She communicated regularly with her father and he assured her that he would manage to resolve the matter.[5]

49 | The Legacy

1940

On November 1, 1940, Vladislav suffered a massive stroke while he was visiting the Hundaohetze concession. He was transported back to Harbin accompanied by a local doctor living in the area. He miraculously managed the journey back to Harbin, and was immediately attended to by the best doctors upon arrival to his home, but the prognosis was bleak.

After his stroke, Kondo and his associates would dress up in suits and top hats and come to the house to inquire every day, "How is Mr. Kowalski doing?" waiting to hear the news that they had achieved their final victory.

Vladislav lay in bed, delirious, in and out of consciousness, for almost two weeks. He repeatedly asked to see Vika. He wanted Vika by his side. Word had been sent to Shanghai and Vika immediately prepared for her trip. She applied for a visa to enter Manchukuo and was frustrated by the process that took several days. Finally, she was given a three-week visa to enter Manchukuo.

The train ride to Harbin was the longest trip she had ever experienced. She couldn't sleep and prayed that everything would be alright and that he would survive. The train arrived early in the morning and she rushed home from the station. Vladislav was delirious and repeatedly asked for her even after she entered the room. Ada insisted that Vika was there, but he repeated over and over that it was not so. Vika clutched his hand, holding it against her face, kissing his hand and calling his name, talking to him, hoping that he would recognize her voice. It was obvious that he never understood that she was there. Shortly after Vika's arrival, he slipped into a coma.

Vladislav died at his home at 7:30 p.m. on November 22, 1940. It is hard to tell whether it was the stress of the negotiations with the Japanese, the horrific conditions imposed by the occupation, or the invasion of Poland—the annihilation of its population and its ultimate surrender—which caused Vladislav to suffer this stroke. His love of Harbin, the pride in his lumber business, and the love of his country, Poland, were all taken away from him. The devastating circumstances were more than he could handle.

The next day Vladislav was transported to a chapel and the following day to the church. November 25 was the official burial ceremony. He was taken in a procession from the church to the cemetery for the burial. Light snow was falling that day as hundreds of mourners filled the road to the cemetery where they walked in total silence under the gray sky. The crunching of packed snow under their feet was the only audible sound as the procession followed the main road from the church to the cemetery in the center of Harbin. When they turned onto the cemetery grounds, it was like stepping

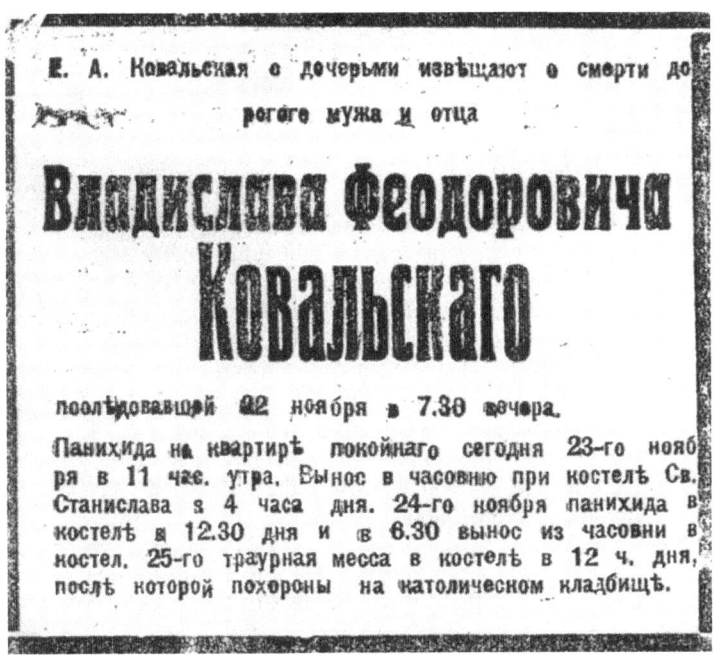

Not sure which newspaper published the Russian notice. Translation: Vladislav Fyodorovich Kowalski passed away on November 22 at 7:30 in the evening. Memorial Mass took place at the residence of the deceased on November 23 at 11:00 a.m. He will be transferred to the St. Stanislas Church at 4:00 p.m. On November 24 a special mass will be held in the church. The body will be transferred at 2:30 p.m. and at 6:30 p.m. from the chapel to the church. On November 25 a special memorial service will be held in the church, and at noon the burial service will take place at the Catholic Cemetery.

> Dnia 22 Listopada o godz. 7.30 wieczorem po ciezkich cierpieniach opatrzony Sw. Sakramentami zasnał w Bogu
>
> SW.P.
>
> # Wladyslaw Kowalski
>
> Kawaler Orderu „Odrodzenia Polski", członek zalozyciel St-nia „Gospoda Polska", członek Zarz. Polskiej Izby Handlowej.
>
> Eksportacja zwlok z domu do Kaplicy pogrzebowej przy Kosciele Sw. Stanislawa w Sobote. 23-go Listopada o godz. 4-ej po pol.
>
> Przeniesienie zwlok z Kaplicy do kosciola w criedziele, 24-go b.m. o godz. 6 30 wiecz.
>
> Nabozenstwo zalobne w poniedzialek, 25-go b. m. o godz. 12-ej w pol., poczym eksportacja zwlok na cmentrz katolicki.

Published in *Tygodnik Polski* weekly: On November 22 at 7:30 p.m. after receiving the Holy Sacraments, Wladyslaw Kowalski passed away. The late Wladyslaw Kowalski was a recipient and knight of the Polonia Restituta medal, a member-founder of the Gospoda Polska Association, and a board member of the Polish Chamber of Commerce. The body will be transferred to the funeral chapel at St. Stanislas Church on Saturday, November 23 at 4:00 p.m. He will then be transferred from the chapel to the church on Sunday, November 24 at 6:30 p.m. A memorial service will be held on Monday, November 25 at noon after which the body will be transferred to the Catholic Cemetery.

out of China and into a European maze of elegant tombstones of carved marble, statues, angels, crosses, engraved icons, and carved images, each depicting love and sorrow.

Vladislav was laid to rest in the Harbin Catholic Cemetery located across the street from the Orthodox cemetery. The Catholic burial grounds was part of a United Cemetery of Seven Countries.[1]

Vika was so proud of her father's accomplishments and knew that his love of Harbin had driven him all those years. The funeral procession following his coffin to the cemetery included representatives of the thousands of Chinese employed on his vast timber concessions and sawmills. Toubin, dear distraught

Stolen Dreams 249

There are no pictures of the original tombstone[2]

Entrance to the Roman Catholic Cemetery in Harbin[3]

Toubin, had to be carried all the way. Genia, Lenochka, Ada, the staff, grandfather's friends, and Russian aristocrats who had escaped the Revolution, French, German, British and the entire Polish community followed with their heads bowed in mourning. Far from his humble beginnings, he had become a legend. He was unofficially named the "Polish Forestry King of Manchuria."[4]

Behind the coffin walked a Japanese delegation in black tails and top hats, their faces in false postures of grievance. Now, in their moment of triumph, the Japanese were huddled together bowing, eager for the final takeover of the business.

Two years earlier, Vladislav had completed the mausoleum he chose as his final resting place, explaining jokingly in his deep voice that he wanted his many Polish, Chinese, and Russian friends to visit him. He built a special stone bench in front of the tomb for his friends to sit comfortably and "talk" to him. In life, he loved to have his friends around him. Little did he realize how soon his final resting place would be called into use.

Vladislav had been a pillar of strength. To Vika he was larger than life. He had built a timber empire in a remote area in northern China that would enter the history books. His unusual character exuded both strength and sensitivity. Respected and valued for his professionalism, he was loved and cherished. The many hundreds of mourners present on that cold November day were a testament to his standing.

Vladislav loved Harbin and he loved China. He appreciated and praised the talents and character of the Chinese people. He was proud of a city that brought together people of different nationalities, religions, and backgrounds to live and work in an atmosphere of respect, friendship, and collective determination. He lived to fulfil his dreams and never faltered when they were shattered or stolen along the way. He accepted all the challenges and hardships, of which he had his fair share, and tackled failures head-on. He knew that this came with the territory.

He had weathered wars, rebellions, migrations, lawlessness, pressure, and political unrest. The journey had been long and hard with constant challenges in every aspect of his life. He accepted it all and bore the pain that came with it, choosing to quickly move on.

The Japanese occupation of Harbin in 1932 left him disillusioned and devastated. He tried to maintain his business and keep his family together. He refused to give up on Harbin. The outcome for most of Harbin's politically, socially, and economically successful residents had tragic endings.

These and other conditions destroyed industries that were not directly Japanese. It wiped out fortunes established over many years. Harbin was morphed into a shell, devoid of the dreams and ambitions of its founders. Everything became a memory of bigger and better times without repressions, discriminations, confiscations, robberies, rapes, and shattered dreams.

How could this have happened? How could the dreams of such a glorious city be smothered and obliterated?

On the day of Vika's departure, she said farewell to her mother, Ada, and Lenochka and was then taken to the Harbin railroad station by Japanese soldiers and escorted onto the train.

On the train looking out the window at Harbin and at the life she was about to leave behind, Vika felt an emptiness.

The whistle sounded for everyone to board. Last goodbyes were shouted from the platform outside. Conductors urged passengers aboard and ensured doors were closed. The whistle signaled—a final blast. The Harbin to Shanghai journey began as the train started to move and to spew its smoke. The Japanese officers made their final bow and suddenly their images disappeared into billows of steam when the train pulled out of the station. At that moment Vika's world seemed to end—gray low-lying clouds, dark November depression, and a mourning city—Vika wanted to die.

Alone now on the train, the events of the past three weeks in Harbin hit Vika with an almost physical blow—she had just lost the only person in the world who loved her. A desperate overwhelming emptiness triggered her desire to scream and plead to bring him back. Tears flooded her soft cheeks and she sobbed, covering her face with her hands.

The clacking of the train and the incessant back-and-forth motion was tiring. The whistle was sounding annoyingly often. Vika sat alone in the first-class compartment, the hard seat being cushioned only with a thin layer of worn red velvet. The two upper births that dropped flat against the wall during the day banged irritatingly with the train's movement, the dirty gray wisps of curtains serving no purpose. The Chinese conductor was curiously opening and closing the compartment door, trying to catch a glimpse of the distraught redheaded foreigner in the compartment while making the intrusion look official.

Finally, exhaustion and reality set in and through the blurred vision of tired bloodshot eyes, she stared blankly at the countryside—the forests, the rich green forests, the beautiful rolling countryside, the lovely white-stemmed birch trees that her father loved, and the rich vegetation around the trees.

There, in the wilderness, among the tall trees and untamed bushes along the rivers she could see the image of her father walking, as he always did. Through the blur of the forests and the mountains and fields she could see him bending occasionally to feel the soil, reaching up to break away the bark of an elm, touching the flaky layer of a cypress to sense its health. His figure was tall and stately, with his flowing red hair and distinguished beard and moustache. He had a commanding posture, truly a handsome man. A man in control—who had owned lumber concessions in China the size of the country of Luxemburg. He was such an authority that government leaders befriended him and requested his advice and support. He was an amazing person, a good, humble, honest, and incredible person. The memory of Vladislav Fyodorovich Kowalski will live on forever through my mother, Vika, and through me and my family. Grandfather is a part of us and will always be...

Epilogue

After the death of Vladislav in 1940, what was left of the family wealth and business was all taken by the Japanese, and the family basically fell apart. Vika continued to live in Shanghai and made a life for herself there. She experienced World War II in Shanghai, subjected to bombings from the Japanese and the allied forces. During wartime as a Polish citizen she was treated as a "friendly enemy" by the Japanese as Poland was annexed by the Germans. Vika married a diplomat and had one daughter, Julie, but she struggled with her marriage, work, and her situation. Life was not kind to her. She ended up alone bringing up a child in a time and place and under circumstances that were challenging.

After Vladislav's passing, Helena and Ada, who continued to live in Harbin, tried to contact Kondo but he avoided them. They continued to demand compensation from the business and for the confiscated equipment. They were told by the Japanese government to wait until the end of the war. In 1945 when the war ended, the Soviet army entered Harbin and Kondo and his large family were kicked out of their house, which was located close to St. Nicholas Cathedral, and moved to Majiagou (Majiagou Timber Storehouses) on the outskirts of the city. As was the case with other Japanese, the Soviets and later the Chinese needed his services for his knowledge regarding the management of properties, which included concessions. Kondo cooperated with both the Russians and the Chinese and began working for them. One day in September 1948 he mysteriously disappeared on his way home from the office. Kondo's family and the Chinese police continued to search for him but he disappeared without a trace. There were many rumors about what may have happened to him, but he was never found.[1]

In 1945 after the surrender of the Japanese at the end of World War II, Harbin and China were liberated from the Japanese. Poland became a Soviet-influenced communist country, and the plight of the Kowalski family did not win any sympathy.

When the communists took over in China in 1949, many of Vika's friends had already left Shanghai, and she did not know which way to turn. She was pregnant and was left alone because of personal circumstances—she was stranded in Shanghai. Her closest friends in Shanghai, John and Mary Besford, left for Japan in the beginning of 1949—he was British and she was Canadian. Before leaving, they promised Vika that they would secure a visa for her to immigrate to Japan. She did not hear from them for some time and figured that they had not managed. Suddenly after two years she got word from the British Consulate in Shanghai that she had received a visa for Japan. If it wasn't for them, she would not have been able to leave.

Vika and Julie in Japan

Vika together with her young daughter Julie left China with almost nothing—two large camphor chests with a few personal belongings, no money and no clue as to how she would manage to live in Japan and among the Japanese people. They arrived in Yokohama in 1951 as Polish citizens, and as there was no Polish representation in Japan at that time, they were given the option of becoming stateless citizens or returning back to Poland. Vika and Julie lived as stateless residents in Japan for the next twenty years.

Ada, Helena, and Lenochka remained in Harbin. After Vika had arrived in Japan, they began writing to her, pleading for her assistance to get them out of China. At that time, Japan was under the US allied occupation and it was extremely difficult to get visas for people with a communist country passport or to have the possibility of immigrating to Japan. It took Vika two years of paperwork to accomplish the task, with multiple visits to government offices and with Vika's promise to house and support them in Japan, though she herself was not in a stable situation. She finally managed through the World Council of Churches to get them visas to come to Tokyo. In 1953 Helena, in her wheelchair, Ada, Lenochka, and Ada's dachshund dog, Mimi, arrived by boat to Yokohama Harbor. Vika

Lenochka and Julie in Tokyo in 1955

had been looking forward to seeing everyone again and was hoping that now it would be a new start for the family. The first thing Ada said as she walked off the boat was, "You don't owe me anything and I don't owe you anything." Vika understood that nothing had changed.

Vika supported and housed everyone until her mother died in Tokyo in 1955. She was buried at the Yokohama Foreign Cemetery. Shortly after that, Ada and Lenochka got their papers to immigrate to the United States. Lenochka wanted to stay behind to help Vika with her young child but was afraid that at 78 she would be a burden to her. In 1955 Ada and Lenochka went to the United States with the promise that Lenochka could enter the Calistoga Monastery outside of San Francisco. It was her lifelong dream to become a nun, and shortly after their arrival she was ordained as Mother Sophia. Ada lived in San Francisco and became an American citizen and ignored all contact with Vika, despite numerous requests from her. She refused to help Vika and Julie immigrate to the United States.

Mother Sophia (Lenochka)

Lucia's daughter, Ada, and Ada Kowalska visiting Lenochka

Genia visiting Lenochka

Mother Sophia passed away at the age of 99 at the convent in Calistoga, California.

Lucia and Alex moved to Australia. Lucia's daughter, Ada, married and settled in the Philippines as her husband Bill Jonckheer was head of the Bank of America office there for many years. Ada died in 2008, Bill died some years earlier in San Francisco, and their three children continue to live in the United States.

Alex and Lucia

Happy Lucia

Pictures provided by the Jonckheer family.

Alexander and Sophie's son, George (Lola), married Floria Paci (Fofi), the daughter of a famous Italian pianist and conductor working in Shanghai. They eventually moved to New York. Vika thought highly of George and often said he was her favorite relative, stating that he was the most personable, kind, and amazing person. Their son Lex continues to live in the United States with his family.

Genia met Cliff Getchell in Shanghai. They married and settled in Oregon in the United States. They never had any children and lived a simple happy life together.

Genia and Ada in San Francisco

Ada and Mel in Arizona

In her later years, Ada Kowalska met Mel Rice and they married. They moved to Arizona and had only a few years together before he passed away. Ada passed away in Arizona in 2002. She never reached out to her sister or to Julie and purposely ignored their existence.

It took time for Vika to feel comfortable in Japan. In the beginning she felt desperate and lost. She didn't speak the language and had difficulty separating herself from the memories and experiences in China that haunted her. By nature she was a forgiving person and after some time was able to put the negativity behind her. Eventually, she came to love Japan and the Japanese. She understood that the Japanese occupation of Manchuria was a different time, a time of Japanese imperialism, ugliness, and war—a different mentality—and always felt that it was a terrible breed of Japanese that lived in Manchuria. The Japanese people, her dear friends in Japan, were not from that "other" evil time and world, they were her friends who were kind, gentle, sensitive, and helpful.

Vika's daughter, Julie, grew up in Japan and to her that was "home" for twenty years. She married a Swedish diplomat, Ulf Erik Sormark, who was posted in Tokyo. They lived in many countries around the world in their diplomatic capacity and were blessed with three lovely children, Jeanette, Kristina, and John, who had the privilege of growing up and living together with their grandmother, Vika.

In 2004 Vika passed away in Hawaii and is buried in San Francisco at the Colma Cemetery where her daughter, Julie, and her three grandchildren, Jeanette, Kristina, and John, look after her grave, remembering the life she led, all the years they spent with her, and the fond memories of the wonderful and amazing person she was. Knowing and listening to the stories about all her experiences in life it always amazed the family how she managed to get over the difficult memories, and not to harbor any grudges, bitterness or regrets. She was always a positive and kind person who wanted to help everyone. We have all agreed that she took after her father. She emulated all the wonderful characteristics he had, and through her, his person, his spirit, and his legacy lives on. She was happy to have had many opportunities to visit China and Harbin.

Kristina, Vika, Jeanette, and John in 2000

The memory of Vladislav lives on at the Revolutionary Leaders Visiting Heilongjiang Memorial Museum at 1 Yi Yuan Street. This is the house that Vladislav had built, and it has stayed intact and became a museum in 1975 due to the fact that Chairman Mao Zedong, making an inspection visit to Heilongjiang in 1950, stayed there for one night on his way back from the Soviet Union. Chairman Mao's visit is well documented. He arrived in Harbin on February 27, 1950, at 2 p.m. After touring a Repair Plant and enjoying a dinner with dignitaries at 1 Yi Yuan Street, he worked and read until midnight, writing some sayings, which today are displayed at the museum: "Study Marxism and Leninism," "Develop Industry," "Struggle," "Study," "Do not become contaminated with Bureaucratic Style of Work." He left the following morning at 8 a.m. Chairman Mao established the fate of this building. It has been looked after well for all these years and continues to be the Revolutionary Leaders Visiting Heilongjiang Memorial Museum.

Brochure introducing the museum in 1985: Commemorating Chairman Mao Zedong's visit to Heilongjiang with a picture of the house and the room that he stayed in

In 1985 Vika and Julie visited Harbin, traveling from Beijing by train. This was Vika's first visit back to Harbin in forty-five years and it was an emotional and exciting experience. Vika and Julie spent days visiting the house, the factories, and the churches and had a chance to meet the foreign residents who had remained in Harbin. They had a chance to befriend Edward Stokalski, a Polish citizen who told them in detail about his life and his experiences since the day he attended Vladislav's funeral forty-five years earlier.

Stolen Dreams 259

Beijing to Harbin train: Julie and her mother in 1985.

Sleeping wagon on the train

Vika together with the museum directors and staff in 1985

Visit to Vladislav's old sawmill and factory

Edward Stokalski, the last surviving Pole and one of the last foreign residents of Harbin

Vika reflecting on the past at the Sungari River in front of the Yacht Club

Nina Arfeziva Davidenko together with Richard Mohr, visiting US researcher

Gathering after Russian Orthodox church service in Harbin

The longest surviving foreign resident, Ms. Nikiforova

In 1990 Vika made another trip to Harbin together with her daughter Julie, her son-in-law, and her grandchildren.

Edward Stokalski, Ulf Erik, Vika, Julie, and Valya Han (one of the Russian/Korean residents)

Mrs. Kang Yu, Ulf Erik, Julie, Vika, Mrs. Wang (Director of the Museum), John, Jeanette, and Kristina

After staying in touch with their new friends in Harbin, in 1998 the Heilongjiang Cultural Relics Bureau invited Vika and Julie back to Harbin. They were planning to renovate and restore the building at 1 Yi Yuan Street and wanted to learn about the original interior of the house. Vika tirelessly spent days explaining to the eager staff of the museum every detail she remembered about the house.

Vika and Julie together with the leaders and staff of the Heilongjiang Provincial Cultural Bureau and Museum

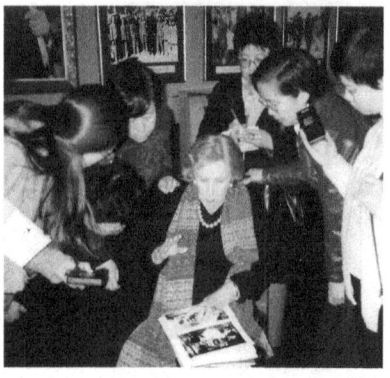

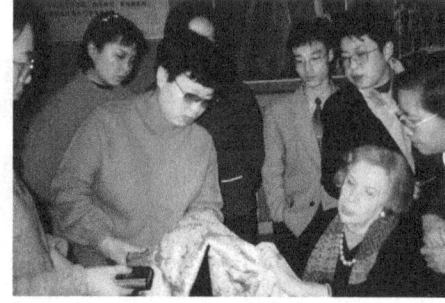

Vika explaining to the staff about the interior design

Stolen Dreams

After the cemetery was destroyed during the Cultural Revolution, a new cemetery was built by the Harbin City Government in Huangshan especially for foreigners. During the same visit, Vika and Edward Stokalski arranged to erect a monument for Vladislav in the new cemetery. Edward Stokalski immortalized the memory of Vladislav Kowalski. He kept all the pictures and newspaper cutouts of Vladislav and idolized him as the kindest and most supportive Pole in all the years in Harbin. Edward built a new tombstone with a hammer and chisel with his bare hands and transported the tombstone to the cemetery in Huangshan. The tombstone remains today as a monument to Vladislav buried among his other friends from the Harbin community.

Edward Stokalski, Vika, and Ms. Nikiforova at the cemetery

Vladislav's tombstone made by Edward Stokalski

Vika visiting the house

Vika in the garden

In 2009 the Heilongjiang Cultural Relics Bureau and Museum had an exhibition on the second floor of the house. The exhibition was the 1 Yi Yuan Street Architectural History Exhibition, which was attended by Julie, members of her family, and other foreign guests. This exhibition lasted for eight years. The house has seen 2 million visitors since 1975 when it became a museum.

Opening day of the exhibition: Ulf Erik, Kristina, Natalie Ermakoff, Julie, Ariana Dolgoff, and Vladimir Ermakoff ([Harbin] *New Evening News*, 2009-5-18, page A05.)

Ivan Voiloshnikov, Grigori Voiloshnikov, Lydia Anikieff, Ulf Erik, Julie, Kristina, and Tania Sherlaimoff

Stolen Dreams

15 日，在位于哈尔滨市南岗区颐园街一号的革命领袖视察黑龙江纪念馆内，房子的原主人外孙女，来自瑞典的茉莉亚女士等 10 名亲友为"颐园街一号建筑史话展"揭牌。当日，茉莉亚及亲友参观了纪念馆，在讲解员的介绍中，回顾这座欧洲古典主义巴洛克风格为主的建筑近百年的历史。

□ 记者 白林鹤

Newspaper article commemorating the event—Britta Kinnemark, Ulf Erik, Kristina, Julie, Ariana Dolgoff, and the Museum staff (*Heilongjiang Morning Post*, 2009-5-16 page 4.)

In 2017 Julie and her husband, Ulf Erik, visited Harbin on the occasion of the International Conference of Former Residents in Harbin sponsored by the Harbin Foreign Affairs Office. At that time the renovation of the Museum had been completed. Julie had the privilege to make a presentation about the legacy of her grandfather at the seminar at the event. Her speech was very well received and appreciated. It inspired her to finalize the project that she had been working on for many years, to write a book about her grandfather and his family, about his fascinating and adventurous life in Northeastern China and Harbin.

Visit in 2017—Director of the Museum, Liu Qiangmin, Deputy Director, Xu Yujiao

Presentation ceremony

Friendship photo

In 1996 the museum at 1 Yi Yuan Street was designated and approved by the State Council as a Historical Monument and Cultural Relic under State Protection at a national level for its architectural, historical, and cultural value in the Peoples Republic of China. The house stands as a testament to Chairman Mao, Zhou Enlai, and other State leaders who visited and worked in the house during their trips to Heilongjiang and to the passion and love that one Polish resident had for the city of Harbin. Today, Harbin is a modern city of over 10 million people and is growing every year. The streets, preserved buildings, restored churches, and distinctive atmosphere in the city tells the story of the rich, unique, and incredible history of this city. As the granddaughter of one who participated and experienced this transformation, my attachment and love of Harbin will always remain, and it is something I proudly pass on to my children so that this legacy will live on in them for generations to come.

Notes

Names: Grandfather was Polish, and his birth name was spelled as Władysław Kowalski (in Russian, Vladislav Fëdorovich Kovalśkiĭ)—according to the transliteration of Russian names in the US library systems (ALA-LC 1997).

Having been brought up in a Russian-speaking environment, he eventually adopted the Russian spelling of *Vladislav*. In different printed documents the spelling varied between *Wladyslav* and *Vladislav*, and similarly, his family name was spelled *Kovalsky* in Russian and *Kowalski* in Polish. In this story he is referred to as Vladislav Fyodorovich Kowalski.

As a gesture of respect, Russian first names include the name of the person's father as Vladislav Fyodorovich. I refer to my grandfather by his first name, Vladislav, throughout the book, rather than using the traditional Russian patronymic. Furthermore, Russian or Polish names are often used with the informal, diminutive form, often changing the name completely, which I have chosen not to use except in the case of my mother Vika and her sister Ada.

Linear and Metric Conversions:

Tael: A unit of weight used in China. Most measurements of tael were worth 1.3 ounces of silver depending on the scales used.

Li: A traditional unit of distance used in China. It has varied over the years but is standardized to measure as half the length of a kilometer. One li equals 500 meters or 1,640 feet.

Verst: A measure of length used in Russia years ago, obsolete today. One verst equaled .6629 miles or 3,500 feet.

Money Conversions: The issue of money conversion and Manchurian currency exchanges is challenging for many reasons. China did not have a national currency until 1933. Earlier Spanish and Mexican silver coins were used as tender for many years, and in 1914 the silver dollar was used as a currency. There was a lack of consistency and the currency was often different from one city to another. That is why many of the larger transactions, costs, and transfers of money were done in other currencies—rubles, yen, dollar, gold, or silver. When a monetary figure is mentioned in the book, it is stated in the denomination that was found in the source.

Photos: Photos that are not noted or sourced are from our family's personal collection.

Story Line: This story was told to me over the years by my mother, Victoria (Vika). Our family has many personal documents that were used to generate the timeline and authenticate the story. Many of the facts were also confirmed through the Polish and British Foreign Service archival material, the many papers and newspaper articles that were published about Vladislav Kowalski, and material that he had written himself. I have tried to keep the facts as accurate as possible.

Names of People Spelled in Different Ways: Rather than include the transliteration of names, in the book I have chosen to stick to the spelling of the Russian and Polish names as they were referred to me by my mother over the years. I hope I do not offend any readers, scholars, or countrymen, it is not my intention. The following are the names as they appear in the book, followed by the different transliteration or spelling forms.

Aksenoff, Eugenia (Genia)—Aksenov

Bernardazzi, Alexander Alexandrovich—Berna Datti (Russian architect of Swiss Italian origin.)

Chacinsky, Nadia—Nadezhda

Chacinsky, Vladislav—Lola

Chacinsky, Wladyslaw—Chacinski

Fogelboim—Fogel'boim

Garrik—Henryk (Henry/Harry)

Honghuzi—Hunghuzi/Huntutze/Khunkhuz

Horvath, Dmitrii Leonidovich—Dimitrii Leonidovich Khorvat

Iugovich, Aleksandr Iosifovich—Yugovich, Aleksandr Iosifovich

Jiang Kai-Shek—Chiang Kai Shek

Kowalska, Ariadna Vladislavna (Ada)—Ariadna Vladislavovna Koval'skaia (Ada)

Kowalska, Helena Aleksandrovna—Elena Aleksandrovna Kowalska

Kowalska, Wiktoria Vladislavna (Vika)—Viktoriia Vladislavovna Koval'skaia (Vika)

Kowalski, Gerwasi Fyodorovich—Gervasi

Kowalski, Pawel Fyodorovich—Pavel

Kowalski, Vladislav Fyodorovich—Vladislav Fedorovich Kowalski/Wladislaw Kowal'skii/Kowalsky

Kuropatkin, Aleksei Nikolaevich—Alexei Nikolaevich Kuropatkin

Kwiatkowski, Aleksander—Kviatkovskii

Lenochka—Akilina Semenova (She preferred to be called Lena—Lenochka is an endearing form.)

Natalie—Natalia

Orlov, Nikolai Andreevich—Orloff

Ostroumoff, Boris Vasilevich—Boris Vasil'evich Ostroumov

Pu Yi —Pu-Yi; Puyi

Russo-Asian Bank (Name used in historical accounts in English)—Russo-Asiatic Bank/Russo-Chinese Bank

Skidelsky—Leiba Solomonovich Skidel'skii (The father was Haim Leiba Shimon Skidelski, known by his Russified name of Leontii Semenovich Skidel'skii. He had four sons, whose Russified names were Iakov Leont'evich, Moisei Leont'evich, Solomon Leont'eich, and Semen Leont'evich.)

Solovov, Mikhail Alexandrovich Solovov—Solov'ev

Solovov, Lucia Mikhailovna—Solov'eva

Sviiagin, N. S.—Sviagin

Three Northeast Provinces—Dong Bei, Dongbeisheng

Zaharoff, Alexander Alexsandrovich—Aleksandr Aleksandrovich Zaharov/Alexander Alexandrovich

Zaharoff, Barbara Alexandrovna—Varvara Aleksandrovna Zakharova

Zaharoff, Olga Alexandrovna—Ol'ga

Zaharoff, Sophie—Sofia Zakharova

Zaharoff, Tatiana Denisovna—Tat'iana Denisovna Zakharova

Zhang, Xueliang—Chang Tso Liang

Zhang, Zuolin—Chang Tso Lin

NAMES OF PLACES SPELLED IN DIFFERENT WAYS

Ashikheskaia Street (Ashihejie)—Azhikheiskaia

Changchun later renamed Hsinking (Xinjing) by the Japanese

Dalian—Dalien/Dal'nii/Dalny

Fujiadian—Fuchiadian/Fujiatian

Harbin—Kharbin

Hundaohetze—Hengdaohezi

Imienpo—Yimianpo

Manchukuo—Manzhouguo/Manzhou-di-guo

Nikolaevsk—Nikolaievsk/Nikolaevsk

Novyi Gorod—Novy Gorod (New Town)

Podol'sk Province—Podol'skaia Guberniia (District)

Pogranichnaia—Pogranichnaya

Pristan—Pristian/Pristan

St. Nicholas Cathedral—Sv. Nikolaevskii Sobor

Staryi Harbin—Staryi Kharbin/Staryi Gorod (Old Town)

Sungari River—Songhua River

Xing'an Tunnel—Khingan Tunnel/Hingan Tunnel/Ghingan Tunnel

Yablonia—Iablonia

Yi Yuan Street—Yi Yuan jie/Yi Yuan 1/Yiyuanjie/Bol'nichnaia Ulitsa (Hospital Street)

Bibliography

I. UNPUBLISHED AND PRIMARY SOURCES

Aksenoff

Dr. Genia Aksenoff. Interviewed in Harbin in 2008 and in Tokyo in 2010.

Bakich

Dr. Olga Bakich (Emeritus, University of Toronto) sent comments on the manuscript in several emails in November 2018.

British Consulate, Harbin

Kowalski Timber Concession. Registry no. F420/420/10. From Sir R. Macleay (Peking). Despatch no. 130 of November 27, 1925, pp. 223232. 11 p. including various reports. [This report can be found in the Confidential British Foreign Office, Political Correspondence. China: Series 2, 1920–1931—Part 1, 1920–923. Microfilm reel 75.]

Concession Contracts

Three documents concerning the leases for the concessions in the Sormark family archives.

Czajewski

Jerzy Czajewski, President of the Harbin Club in Szczecin, Poland, May 2010. Spent three days in Szczecin interviewing Jerzy, visiting libraries, and working in the archives. Also met with former Harbin residents. Jerzy graciously allowed me to use materials in his private collection, which includes postcards, newspaper articles, and other documents. Also, article "Roman Catholic Cemetery in Harbin (1903–1958)," submitted for publication in 2019 to a magazine published in China.

Horvath

Dmitrii Leonidovich Khorvat/Horvath (1858–1937) Memoirs. 1 box.

Lt.-General Russian Imperial Army. General Manager and Administrator of the Chinese Eastern Railway, 1902–1921. Held at the Hoover Institution Library and Archives, Stanford University, California. "Introduction" by W. Klemm, 6 p.

Kang

Interview in 1985 with Mrs. Yu Kang by Vika about the Confucian Temple in Harbin.

Koval'skii, V. F., "Vladislav Fedorovich Koval'skii: o samom sebie," *Kharbinskaia starina: izdanie Obshchestva starozhilov g. Kharbina i S. Man'chzhurii*. Kharbin: 1936, pp. 15–17. [Translated from Russian by J. Sormark: *Vladyslav Fyodorovich Kovalsky: About Himself.*]

Kowalska, Ada

[Testimonial] by Ada. This is regarding Kondo and the concessions.

Kowalska, Elena and Ada

Document [Memo Po pretenziiam naslednikov umershego pol'skogo grazhdanina V. F. Koval'skogo k Pravitel'stvu IAponii] submitted by Elena and Ada Kowalska. March 20, 1947. In the personal collection of Julie Sormark.

League of Nations/Lytton Report

Appeal by the Chinese Government: Report of the Commission of Enquiry Signed by the Members of the Commission on September 4, 1932. Geneva: 1932, 148 p., includes 14 maps on 13 folded leaves. [Series: League of Nations Publications VII Political; 1932, VII, 12. Also: US Department of State Publications, 378]. Official no. C.663.M.320.1932. VII. This is also known as the Lytton Report, prepared by Victor Bulwer-Lytton, Second Earl of Lytton (1876–1947).

Loukashkin

Anatolii Stepanovich Loukashkin (1902–1988) Papers, Series 2, 53 manuscript boxes.

Held by the Museum of Russian Culture, San Francisco.

Sherlaimoff

Personal communication from Dr. Tatiana Sherlaimoff on May 6, 2018, in Honolulu. She recounted their family story as told by her late father Nicholas Sherlaimoff in Sydney and by her late aunts Eugenia Hawkins and Tatiana Kalousek in San Francisco.

Stevens

John Frank Stevens (1853–1943) Papers, 1917–1931, 1 box.

American civil engineer; president, technical board, Inter-Allied Railway Commission for the Supervision of the Siberian and Chinese Eastern Railways, 1919–1922. Includes memoirs and correspondence. Held at the Hoover Institution Library and Archives, Stanford University, California.

Stokalski and others

We spoke to Edward Stokalski, Nina Davidenko, Ms. Nikiforova, Mikhail Mikhailovich Miatov (1912–2000) and his brother, and Mrs. Valya Han during our visit to Harbin in 1985. Their stories and conversations were very helpful.

Symonolewicz

Konstantiny Symonolewicz (1884–1952), Polish diplomat "started his career as an employee of the Russian consular service in which he worked as an official in the Russian diplomatic mission in Beijing (1912). Between 1913 and 1920, he served as a consular official in Qiqihar. In the same year, he began working for the Polish foreign service. He was entrusted with the following functions in Harbin (1920–1930): Secretary of the Consulate, Vice-consul, Deputy Delegate of the Polish Republic in China, Head of the Polish Delegation in Harbin, and de facto Head of the Consulate in Harbin (1928–1930)." [From Borysiewicz, "Wladyslaw," p. 90, footnote 52.]

In the Polish Archives of the New Ministry of Foreign Affairs [*Archiwum Akt Nowych*], Ref. 11686, k. 3–16, there is a typescript: Secret report of Consul Class II Head of Delegation of the Republic of Poland in Harbin, Konstantiny Symonolewicz for the Ministry of Foreign Affairs of November 19, 1929 (No. 2559/29)—"In addition to my cipher telegram dated 15 November 1929, which I sent on request by local Polish industrialists, in particular on request by Mr. Kowalski. We had to send it in order to forestall his position and interests and to directly ask the President and the Lord [M]arshal to assist, which we already had determined to do." The author has an English translation of this report that is 20 pages. It is this version that is cited in the endnotes.

II. PUBLISHED SOURCES

Arsen'ev/Arseniev, Vladimir Klavdievich, *Dersu the trapper*. Translated by Malcom Burr. Kingston, NY: McPherson & Co., 1996 (1941), ix, 351 p., illus., map. [Series: Recovered Classics.]

Bakich, Olga, "Émigré Identity: The Case of Harbin," *South Atlantic Quarterly*, 2000, v. 99, no. 1, pp. 51–73.

Bakich, Olga, "Origins of the Russian Community on the Chinese Eastern Railway," *Canadian Slavonic Papers*, 1985, v. 27, no. 1, pp. 1–14.

Bakich, Olga, "Russian City in China: Harbin before 1917," *Canadian Slavonic Papers*, 1986, v. 28, no 2 (June), pp. 128–148.

Bakich, Olga, "Russian Education in Harbin, 1898-1962," *Zapiski Russkoi akademicheskoi gruppy v SShA*, 1994, v. XXVI, pp. 269–294.

Bakich, Olga, "Russian Emigres in Harbin's Multinational Past: Censuses and Identity," in Ben-Canaan, Dan; Grüner, Frank; and Prodöhl, Ines, eds. *Entangled histories: The transcultural past of northeast China* (pp. 83–99). Heidelberg, Germany; New York: Springer, 2014. viii, 238 p. (Transcultural research: Heidelberg studies on Asia and Europe in a global context)

Beck, Sanderson, "Imperial Japan 1894–1937 and Japan's Growing Military 1894–1903," in *East Asia 1800–1949: Ethics of civilization*. Goleta, CA: World Peace Communications, 2008, xii, 637 p. [Series: Ethics of civilization, v. 21.] See also http://www.san.beck.org/21-8-ImperialJapan1894-1937.html#a1

Bickers, Robert, Christian Henriot, and Keqiang An. *New frontiers: Imperialism's new communities in East Asia, 1842–1953*. Manchester, NY: Manchester University Press, 2000, xiv, 290 p., illus., maps.

Borysiewicz, Mariusz, "History and Historiography of the Polish Diaspora," *Scripta Historica*, Rok 2016, nr. 22, pp. 85–124.

Borysiewicz, Mariusz, "Wladyslaw Kowalski (1870–1940): Polish Pioneer of Industrialization the Far East," *Scripta Historica*, Rok 2017, nr. 23, pp. 83–108.

"Boxer Rebellion, Russia and 1899–1903," v. [2?], in Dowling, Timothy C., ed. *Russia at war: From Mongol conquest to Afghanistan, Chechnya and beyond* (pp. 145–146). Santa Barbara, CA: ABC-CLIO, 2015, 2 v.

Breuillard, Sabine, "A New Review of the Kaspe Affair: Documents Reported and Published," 2001. English translation: [24] unnumbered leaves. [Author (Sormark) used the section entitled "The Historical Background," pp. 1, 2, and 4. This was available on the web: CIBOX 2004. Ofer Dror/Sources for Yeshivat Mir in Kobe, Japan during World War 2. Internet publication: Yigud Yotsei Sin, Israel. 2004: http://jewsofchina.org/JewsOfChina/communities/publications_item.asp?cid=1051&iid=12952 But it cannot now be found. Breuillard first published this in French: "L'Affaire Kaspé revisitée: Documents publiés it présentés," *Revue des Études Slaves*, 2001, v. 73, nr. 2–3, pp. 337–372.]

Bunting, Tony, "Battle of Port Arthur: Russo-Japanese War," *Encyclopedia Britannica*, September 8, 2017. https://www.britannica.com/event/Battle-of-Port-Arthur

Brynner, Rock, *Empire and odyssey: The Brynners in Far East Russia and beyond*. Hanover, NH: Steerforth Press, 2006, x, 331 p., [64] p. plates.

Chang, Iris, *The rape of Nanking: The forgotten holocaust of World War II*. New York: Penguin Books, 1997, xi, 290 p., [24] pages of plates, map.

Chang, Jung, *Empress Dowager Cixi: The concubine who launched modern China*. London: Vintage Books, 2014, xvii, 436 p. [32] plates, some in color, map.

Chiasson, Blaine R., *Administering the colonizer, Manchuria's Russians under Chinese rule, 1918–1929*. Vancouver: UBC Press, 2010. x, 286 p., illus., maps.

China, diplomatic and consular reports for the year 1911, commercial conditions in North Manchuria and the trade of Harbin, London: Harrison and Sons, 1913.

Chinese Eastern Railway, Economic Bureau. *North Manchuria and the Chinese Eastern Railway*. Harbin, China: C.E.R. Printing Office, 1924, xvii, 454 p., illus., maps. Chapters have individual authors and titles: E. E. Yashnoff (Evgenii Evgen'evich IAshnov, 1881–1943): Chap. III: "Administrative Division," pp. 26–33; Yashnoff, Chap. IV: "A Brief History of the Railway," pp. 34–44; V. N. Kasatkin (General Vasilii Nikolaevich Kasatkin, 1886–1963): Chap. X: "Forest and Lumbering Industry," pp. 173–208; V. I. Surin (Viktor Il'ich Surin, 1875–1967), Chap. XIII: "The Flour Milling Industry," pp. 231–246; V. N. Kasatkin (General Vasilii Nikolaevich Kasatkin, 1886–1963): Chap. XVI: "The Outline of the Evolution of Trade in North Manchuria," pp. 269–278; V. I. Surin (Viktor Il'ich Surin, 1875–1967) and I-li Chun, Chap. XVIII: "The Interior Trade," pp. 297–314; N. S. Zefiroff (Nikolai Stepanovich Zefirov, 1887–1953) and A. F. Yagolkovsky (Anton Floreanovich-Stanislavovich IAgolkovskii), Chap. XXII: "The Chinese Eastern Railway," pp. 397–454. Also: Map III: "Political Map of Manchuria," between pp. 32–33; Map XI: "Forest Concessions on the Eastern Line," between pp. 176–177; Map XIII: "Harbin and Suburbs," between pp. 304–305.

Chuma v Man'chzhurii v 1910–11 g.g. Kharbin: Fototip. Sherer, Nabgol'ts i Ko., 191?, [49 unnumbered plates].

Clausen, Soren and Stig Thøgersen, *The Making of a Chinese city: History and historiography in Harbin*. New York: M. E. Sharpe, 1995, xvi, 236 p., [8] p. plates, map.

Clyde, Paul Hibbert, *International rivalries in Manchuria 1689–1922*. 2d ed. rev. Columbus, OH: Ohio State University Press, 1928, xv, 323 p., fold. map.

Cotterell, Arthur, *China: A history*. London: Pimlico, 1988 (1990), xxiii, 355 p., illus., maps.

Delanty, James John, *John F. Stevens and his role in the struggle for the control of the Chinese Eastern Railway, 1917–1922*. M.A. thesis. California State College at Fullerton. 1970, v, 129 leaves, map.

Doudka, Williams, "D. L. Horvath's Daughter [Obit.]," *The Independence*, Daily Edition, August 3, 2005, p. 5.

Efimova, Miroslava Igorevna, *Harsh vineyard: A history of Catholic life in the Russian Far East*. Victoria, BC: Trafford Publishing, 2008, xvii, 280 p., illus., maps.

Fang, Edwin Lo-tien, *Manchuria: A second Korea? An outline of Japan's Manchuria policy from its inception to its climax*. Shanghai: Commercial Press, 1934, xi, 430 p., illus.

Felton, Mark, *The devil's doctors*. Barnsley, South Yorkshire, England: Pen and Sword Military, 2012, 198 p., [8] plates.

Fuchigami, Hakuyol, *Harubin no kaisoi*. rev. ed. Tokyo: Keigadol, 1966.

Furier, Andrzej, *Polskie slady na Dalekim Wschodzie: Polacy w Harbinie: materialy z konferencji naukowej zorganizowanej w Szczecinie w dniach 23-24 pazdziernika 2008 g*. Szczecin: Ksiaznica Pomorska im. Stanislawa Staszica w Szczecinie, 2008, 207 p., illus.

Gamsa, Mark, "The Many Faces of Hotel Moderne in Harbin," *East Asian History*, 2011, no. 7, pp. 27-38, illus.

Gentes, Andrew Armand, *The mass deportation of Poles to Siberia, 1863-1880*. Cham, Switzerland: Palgrave Macmillan, 2017, xix, 262 p., illus., maps.

Gold, Hal. *Unit 731: Testimony*. Tokyo: Yenbooks, 1996, 256 p., illus.

Golowanjuk, Jascha, *Min gyllne väg från Samarkand [My golden road from Samarkand]*. Stockholm: Wahlström & Widstrand, 1937, 244 p.

Gottschang, Thomas Richard, *Migration from North China to Manchuria: An economic history, 1891-1942*. PhD. University of Michigan, 1982, viii, 278 leaves., maps.

Grochowski, Kazimierz, *Polacy na Dalekim Wschodzie*. Harbin w Chinach: Harbin Daily News Press, 1928, x, 222 p., 53 tables, illus.

Gul'dman, V. K., *Pomiestnoe zemievladienie v Podol'skoi gubernii*. Kamenets-Podol'skii: Tip. Podol'skago gubernskago pravleniia, 1898. 362, 46, 26, 3 pp.

Gutman, Anatolii IAkovlevich. *The destruction of Nikolaevsk-on-Amure: An episode in the Russian Civil War in the Far East, 1920*; translated with an introduction by Ella Lury Wiswell; edited by Richard A. Pierce. Kingston, Ont.; Fairbanks, AK: Limestone Press, 1993, xxxiii, 395 p., [12] pages of plates, illus., maps. (Russia and Asia, no. 2).

Haerbin yin—xiang/Haerbin Shi cheng shi gui hua ju, Haerbin Shi cheng shi cheng shi gui hua xue hui Glance Back the Old City's Charm of Harbin. Urban Planning Bureau of Harbin Municipality: Urban Planning Society of Harbin Municipality. Beijing: Zhongguo jian zhu gong ye chu ban she, 2005-2006, 2 v., illus. (some in color), maps (some in color).

Harmsen, Peter, *Nanjing 1937: Battle for a doomed city*. Philadelphia; Oxford: Casemate, 2015, 336 p., maps.

Harmsen, Peter, "Russians in the Service of the Japanese Emperor," China in WW2...the 1931-45 Conflict and the Birth of Modern, posted September 27, 2016. http://www.chinaww2.com/2016/09/27/russians-in-the-service-of-the-japanese-emperor/

Hongo, Jun, "Earthquakes in Japan: Getting a Handle on Earthquakes," *Japan Times*, April 24, 2007, p. 2.

Hoyt, Edwin P., *Japan's war: The great Pacific conflict, 1853-1952*. New York: McGraw-Hill, 1986, xi, 514 p.

Hsieh, Chieh-shih, "Communication to Foreign Ministers of Various Powers Despatched by H. E. Mr. Hsieh Chieh-Shih, Foreign Minister, Manchoukuo, Mar. 12, 1932, p. 7-8" in *Proclamations, Statements and Communications of the Manchoukuo Government*. Hsinking, Manchuria: Dept. of Foreign Affairs, Manchoukuo Government, 1932, 22 p. (Series: Publications of the Department of Foreign Affairs, Manchoukuo Government, Series No. 1.)

Hunter, Janet, and Ogasawara, Kota, *Price shocks in disaster: The Great Kantō Earthquake in Japan, 1923*. London: London School of Economics and Political Science, Economic History Department, 2016. [Series: Economic History Working Papers, No. 253/2016], http:eprints.lse.ac.uk/68618/

Hutchins, Grace, *Japan's drive for conquest*. New York: International Publishers, 1935, 31 p., map. (International pamphlets, 47)

Jennings, John M., *The opium empire: Japanese imperialism and drug trafficking in Asia, 1895–1945*. Westport, CT: Praeger, 1997, x, 161 p.

Jowett, Philip S., *China and Japan at war 1937–1945: Rare photographs from wartime archives*. Barnsley, South Yorkshire: Pen and Sword Military, 2016, 260 p.

Kasatkin, V. N., **see above** under "Chinese Eastern Railway."

Khisamutdinov, Amir, "Predprinimatel' V. F. Koval'skii i ego rol' v razvitii Man'chzhurii," *Problemy Dal'nego Vostoka*, 2000, no. 5, pp. 149–153. [Translated into English for Julie Sormark by Valentina Yarovaya and Alex Bykov as "Entrepreneur Kowalsky and His Role in the Development of Manchuria."]

King, Greg, *The court of the last tsar: Pomp, power and pageantry in the reign of Nicholas II*. Hoboken, NJ: Wiley and Sons, 2006, xiii, 559 p., [24] pages of plates, illus., maps.

Kovalsky, V. F., "Timber Concessions of V F Kovalsky in North Manchuria: Their contemporary position and future prospects—June 11, 1923 on the occasion of the 25th anniversary of the Chinese Eastern Railway, published by V.F. Kovalsky owner of the concessions." [Translated by Wang, Yunqiu, in *Bei fang wen wu*, 1991, issue no. 3(27).]

Lensen, George Alexander, *The damned inheritance: The Soviet Union and the Manchurian crises 1924–1935*. Tallahassee, FL: The Diplomatic Press, 1974, xi, 533 p., illus.

Lensen, George Alexander, *The Russo-Chinese War*. Tallahassee, FL: The Diplomatic Press, 1967, 315 p., illus., maps.

Lesnye kontsessii V. F. Koval'skago v Severnoi Man'chzhurii: ikh sovremennoe polozhenie i blizhaishie perspektivy [Timber concessions of V. F. Kovalsky in North Manchuria: Their contemporary positions, and future prospects]. Kharbin: Tip. Graficheskoe iskusstvo, 1923. [Hoover Institution Library reports, 36 p. ; Bakich bibliography *Harbin Russian imprints* (2002), 78 reports, 66 p. (23 p. of Russian text; 24 p. of English text; 19 p. of Japanese text).]

Liang, Chia-Pin, "History of the Chinese Eastern Railway: A Chinese Version," *Pacific Affairs*, 1930, v. 3, no. 2 (Feb.), pp. 188–211.

Liu, Yiannan, "Japan Kondo Forestry Company and International Hotel, Harbin," *Harbin New Evening News*, 2009, 8 November. Translated by Mrs. Kang Yu. [Liu is vice chairman of the Harbin Historical and Cultural Research Institute.]

Majdowski, Andrzej, *Kościół katolicki w Cesarstwie rosyjskim: Syberia, Daleki Wschód, Azja Środkowa*. Warszawa: Wyd. Neriton, 2001, 339 p.

Massie, Suzanne. *Land of the firebird: The beauty of old Russia*. New York: Simon and Schuster, 1980, 493 p., [64] pages of plates, col. illus.

McCormack, Gavan, *Chang Tso-lin in Northeast China, 1911–1928: China, Japan, and the Manchurian idea*. Stanford, CA: Stanford University Press, 1977, vi, 334 p., illus.

Meyer, Kathryn, *Life and death in the garden: Sex, drugs, cops, and robbers in wartime China*. Lanham, MD: Rowman and Littlefield, 2014, x, 272 p., illus.

Mitter, Rana, *Forgotten ally: China's World War II, 1937–1945*. Boston: Mariner Books, 2014, xii, 450 p., [16] pages of plates, illus., maps.

Moseley, George, *China since 1911*. New York: Harper and Row Publishers, 1968, 192 p., maps.

Moseley, Leonard, *Hirohito, emperor of Japan*. Englewood Cliffs, NJ: Prentice-Hall, 1966, ix, 371 p., illus., ports.

Moustafine, Mara, "The Harbin Connection: Russians from China," in Shen, Yuanfang, and Edwards, Perry, eds. *Beyond China: Migrating identities* (pp. 75–89). Canberra: Centre for the Study of the Chinese Southern Diaspora, Australian National University, 2002, 108 p.

Moustafine, Mara, *Secrets and spies: The Harbin files*. Milsons Point, Australia: Random House Australia, 2002, xxviii, 468 p., illus. [Series: A Vintage Book.]

Neja, Jarosław, "Harbin jako przestrzen zycia i dziatalnosci Polonii mandzurskiej," in Furier, Andrzej, ed. *Polskie slady na Dalekim Wschodzie: Polacy w Harbine: materialy z konferencji naukowej zorganizowanej w Szczecinie w dniach 23-24 pazdziernika 2008* (pp. 58–65). Szczecin: Ksiaznica Pomorska im. Stanislawa Staszica w Szczecinie, 2008, 207 p., illus.

Neja, Jarosław, "Polski król Mandżurii," Wprost, 2003, no. 9 (2 marca), 2 p. https://www.wprost.pl/41007/Polski-krol-Mandzurii

Nilus, Evgenii Khrisanfovich, *Istoricheskii obzor Kitaiskoi Vostochonoi zheleznoi dorogi, 1896-1923 gg*. Kharbin: Tipografiia Kit. Vost. zhel. dor. i T-va "Ozo," 1923, Tom 1: xviii, [xix] unnumbered plates, 690 p., illus., maps.

O'Dwyer, Emer, "Japanese Empire in Manchuria," *Oxford Research Encyclopedia of Asian History*. Online Publication Date: November 2017. doi: 10.1093/acrefore/9780190277727.013.78 [Includes section: Periodizing Manchukuo, The Building Years, 1932–1936.]

Patrikeeff, Felix, *Russian politics in exile: The Northeast Asian balance of power, 1924–1931*. Houndmills, England; New York: Palgrave Macmillan in association with St. Antony's College, Oxford, 2002, xiv, 230 p., maps.

Peattie, Mark R., Edward J. Drea, and Hans J. Van de Ven, *The battle for China: Essays on the military history of the Sino-Japanese War of 1937–1945*. Stanford, CA: Stanford University Press, 2011, xxv, 614 p., illus., maps.

"Pol-milliona na sudie [Half-million in court]," *Rubezh*, 1928, no. 7, p. 5, illus.

Quested, Rosemary K. I., *"Matey" Imperialists? The Tsarist Russians in Manchuria 1895–1917*. Hong Kong: University of Hong Kong, 1982, iv, 430 p., map.

Rappaport, Helen, *The last days of the Romanovs: Tragedy at Ekaterinburg*. New York: St. Martin's Griffin, 2008, xvi, 254 p., [16] pages of plates, illus.

Royde-Smith, John Graham, and Dennis E. Showalter, "Word War I: 1914–1918," *Encyclopedia Britannica*, November 23, 2018. https://www.britannica.com/event/World-War-I

Shen, Mo. *Japan in Manchuria: An analytical study of treaties and documents*. Manila: Grace Trading Co., 1960, 463 p., illus., map.

Shepherdson-Scott, Kari Leanne, *Utopia/Dystopia: Japan's image and the Manchurian ideal*. PhD. Duke University, 2012, xvi, 431 p.

Skora, Wojciech, "Sytuacja materialna Polonii mandżurskiej w 1929 roku (w świetle raportu kosula RP Konstantego Symonolewicza)," *Przegląd Orientalistyczny*, 2010, nr. 3–4, pp. 125–140. [Text translated in English by J. Sormark, 20 pp. unpublished; references in footnotes refer to the translation.]

Sladkovskii, M. I., *History of economic relations between Russia and China*, New York: Taylor and Francis Group, 2008.

Spravochnik po Severnoi Man'chzhurii i KVzhd. Kharbin: Izd. Ekon. Biuro KVzhd, 1927. 607 p.

Stille, Mark, and Paul Wright, *The Imperial Japanese Navy of the Russo-Japanese War*. Oxford: NY: Osprey Publishing, 2016, 48 p., illus. [Series: New Vanguard, 232.]

Surin, V. I., **see above** under "Chinese Eastern Railway."

Surin, V. I. and I-li Chun, **see above** under "Chinese Eastern Railway."

Tarasova, Nina and others, *Nicholas + Alexandra: The last tsar and tsarina*. 2d ed. Aldershot, UK; Burlington, VT: Lund Humphries in association with the Hermitage Amsterdam, 2005, 127 p., col. illus.

Taube, Carl Gunnar, *Kriget som inte var något krig. Som krigskorrespondent i Manchuriet 18 September 1931–9 Mars 1932* [*The war which was not a war. By a war correspondent in Manchuria 18 Sept. 1931–9 March 1932*]. Stockholm: A. Bonniers Förlag, 1932, 131 p. [Includes the text of the Japanese press release.]

The Puppet State of "Manchukuo." Shanghai: China United Press 1935, viii, 278 p., 1 fold. map [China Today series, no. 4; edited by T'ang Leani-Li.]

Toland, John, *The rising sun: The decline and fall of the Japanese Empire, 1936–1945*. New York: Modern Library, 2003. [Paperback ed., xv, 954 p., maps. Series: Modern Library War.]

Tsao, Lien-En, *The Chinese Eastern Railway: An analytical study*. Shanghai: The Bureau of Industrial and Commercial Information, Ministry of Industry, Commerce and Labor, National Government of the Republic of China, 1930, ii, 198 p., fold. map.

Tuchman, Barbara W., *Stilwell and the American experience in China, 1911–45*. New York: Macmillan, 1970, xv, 621 p., illus., maps.

Turmov, G. P., and Yanling Zhang, *Bai nian qian you zheng ming xin pian shang de Zhongguo = Kitai na pochtovykh otkrytkakh sto let nazad*. Ha'erbin Shi: Ha'erbin gong ye da xue chu ban she, 2006, 318 p., chiefly illus., some color. [First published in Russian in 2006. Title translated into English: *China in postcards from 100 years ago*.]

Vargo, Lars, *Det Olyckliga århundradet: När Öst och Väst möttes*. Stockholm: Carlssons Bokforlag, 2016, 271 p.

Ves' Kharbin na 1923: adresnaia i spravochnaia kniga gor. Kharbina. Kharbin: Adres Redaktsii i Izdatel'stva. 48, 336, vii p. ; ...*na 1926 god adresnaîa i spravochnaîa kniga*. S. T. Ternavskiĭ, ed. Kharbin: Tip. KVzhd, 1926, x, 274, 534 p., illus.

Vespa, Amleto, *Secret agent of Japan*. Boston: Little, Brown and Company, 1938, xiv, [3]–301 p., illus.

"Vospominaniia A. V. Koval'skoi (Arizona, SShA), Sobranie A.A. Khisamutdinov" [Memories of A. V. Koval'skoi (Arizona, USA), Private collection of A. A. Khisamutdinov], cited in Khisamutdinov, Amir. "Predprinimatel' V. F. Koval'skii i ego rol' v razvitii Man'chzhurii," *Problemy Dal'nego Vostoka*, 2000, no. 5, pp. 149–153. [Translated into English by Valentina and Alex Yarovaya as "Entrepreneur Kowalsky and His Role in the Development of Manchuria."]

Wanter, Adam, *Three paths to one state: Polish national identity under Russian, Prussian and Austro-Hungarian occupation after 1863*. Research Thesis. Ohio State University. June 2012, ii, 56 l.

Wolff, David, *To the Harbin Station: The liberal alternative in Russian Manchuria, 1898–1914*. Stanford, CA: Stanford University Press, 1999, xiv, 255 p., [15] pages of plates, illus.

Wright, Tim, *The Manchurian economy and the 1930s world depression*. Paper prepared for the XIV International Economic History Congress, Helsinki, August 2006. 15 p. [Later published as an article in *Modern Asian Studies*, 2007, v. 41, no. 5, pp. 1073–1112.]

"Wystawa-Polacy-w Mandzurii 1897–1949," *Agencja Gazeta*. [From the private collection of Jerzy Czajewski.]

Xu, Zhixian, *Yin ji* [historical imprints]. Ha'erbin: Harbin Publishing House, 2013, 156 p., illus.

Yang, Daqing, *Technology of empire: Telecommunications and Japanese expansion of Asia, 1883–1945*. Cambridge, MA: Harvard University Asia Center, 2010, xvii, 446, [4] pages of plates, maps.

Yashnoff, E. E., **see above** under "Chinese Eastern Railway."

Yoshizawa Tatsuhiko, "The Manchurian Incident, the League of Nations and the Origin of the Pacific War. What the Geneva Archives Reveal." *Japan Focus: The Asia-Pacific Journal*, 2007, v. 5, no. 12. https://apjjf.org/-Yoshizawa-Tatsuhiko [Longer two-part article appeared in *International Herald Tribune/Asahi Shinbun*, no. 30, 2007.]

Young, Carl Walter, *The international relations of Manchuria: A digest and analysis of treaties, agreements, and negotiations concerning the Three Eastern Provinces of China, prepared for the 1929 Conference of the Institute of Pacific Relations in Kyoto, Japan*. Chicago: Published for the American Council Institute of Pacific Relations by the University of Chicago Press, 1929, xxx, 307 p., frontispiece map.

Young, Carl Walter, *Japan's jurisdiction and international legal position in Manchuria. Japanese Jurisdiction in the SMR Areas*, Volume 3. Baltimore: John Hopkins Press; London: Oxford University Press, 1931, xxxv, 332 p.

Young, Louise, *Japan's total empire: Manchuria and the culture of wartime imperialism*. Berkeley: University of California Press, 1998, xiii, 487 p., [1] page of plates, maps. [Series: Twentieth-century Japan, 8.]

Youtai ren zai Ha'erbin [*The Jews in Harbin*] in Wei, Qu, and Shuxiao, Li, eds. *Zeng ding ben, di 2 ban*, rev., 2d ed. Beijing Shi: She hui ke xue wen xiam chu ban she, 2006, 285 p., chiefly illus.

Zefiroff, N. S., and A. F. Yagolkovsky, **see above** under "Chinese Eastern Railway."

Endnotes

ACKNOWLEDGMENTS

1. http://manoa.hawaii.edu/library/research/collections/russia/russian-northeast-asia-collection. Click on *Catalogue* to get the entire range of material offered at the Russian Northeast Asian Collection. The Russian émigré collection about China is an important resource for scholars.

CHAPTER 1

1. Manchuria is a historic region of northeastern China, which today consists of Liaodong, Jilin, and Heilongjiang, often named the Three Eastern Provinces [Dongbei] by the Chinese.
2. Podol'skaia guberniĭa—a province along the southern section of the Kingdom of Poland. It is the province that is located the closest to the Black Sea.
3. Chinese Eastern Railway (CER) is the historic name of a railway across Manchuria built by Imperial Russia 1897 to 1903 and which linked Chita on the Chinese border to Russia with Vladivostok in the Russian Far East.

CHAPTER 2

1. Family registry from the Harbin Poles Memorial Museum in Szczecin, Poland. "Introduction to Podolia," http://www.geocities.ws/Podolia. For a history, see Gul'dman, *Pomiestnoe zemlevladenie*, p. 113.
2. Manuscript map of the pre-partition Poland (before 1772) with political subdivision and its linguistic areas at the end of World War I. Gubernia of Podolia is shown in the southeast. Library of Congress, G6521. F7 1914. P6 Vault (gift Woodrow Wilson papers). Map given to President of USA Woodrow Wilson by Ignacy Paderewski, famous Polish pianist and patriot in preparation of regaining Poland's independence in 1918. It shows the location of the Russian Kingdom of Poland as well as Polish governorates in NW and SW Russian Countries. Ruthenians and White Ruthenians are called nowadays Ukrainians and Belorussians. This is from a paper: Czajewski, Jerzy, "Roman Catholic Cemetery in Harbin (1903–1958)" (Szczecin), p. 5. Gubernia can be translated as "Govoron" or "Province" (District). Podolśkaia guberniĭa—Podolia is now in western Ukraine.
3. Interview with Vika Kowalska. These sentences were not written but were told to the family over her lifetime.

4. Most of the Ukraine land between the Dniestr and Dniepr Rivers belonged, from a historical aspect, to the big and mid-sized estates of the Polish aristocrats, as well as to small petty gentry holdings. Polish and Russian identity is significantly different. Poland is historically Roman Catholic and the Polish language is written using the Latin alphabet, while Russia is Orthodox Christian and uses the Cyrillic alphabet. Poland was part of the Russian Empire 1814–1918, but Poland has always been a separate nation. See research thesis by Adam Wanter (2012), l. 23.
5. Gentes, pp. 129–149; interview with Jerzy Czajewski; and "Weapons and Warfare: Polish Rebellion of 1863–1864," https://weaponsandwarfare.com/2009/05/09/polish-rebellion-of-1863. "After the Revolt was crushed, thousands of Poles were sent to Siberia, hundreds were executed and homes and villages throughout Poland were destroyed by the violence." The collapse of the uprising took thousands of Polish lives. According to Russian official information, 396 persons were executed and 18,672 were exiled to Siberia.
6. Interview with Jerzy Czajewski.
7. Khisamutdinov, "Predprinimatel'," p. 149.
8. Interview with Jerzy Czajewski about information on the Volunteer Fleet.
9. Ibid.
10. The Volunteer Fleet seemed to have been in service at a later date. He may have traveled on a different ship although there seems to be some indication that it was with this line.
11. The Dobrovol'nyi Flot [The Volunteer Fleet] was a product of the Russo-Turkish War of the late 1870s, which prompted some Russian merchants into funding the purchase of fast steamships that could be converted into commercial raiders in the event of war. They were usually commanded and crewed by naval seamen. The ship pictured is the *Vladimir* (postcard).
12. Borysiewicz, "Wladyslaw Kowalski," p. 94.
13. Wolff, p. 30.
14. Kasatkin, Chapter XVI, p. 273.

CHAPTER 3

1. Koval'skii, "Vladislav....o samom sebie," pp. 15–17.
2. The Trans-Siberian Railway construction had commenced from Vladivostok on May 31, 1891, when Tsar Alexander III had issued a decree to start the construction of the railway. Crown Prince Nicholas, who three years later would become tsar, inaugurated the construction of the Vladivostok-Khabarovsk Railway in Vladivostok.
3. Khisamutdinov, p. 149.
4. Ibid.
5. Horvath's Memoirs, foreword, W. Klemm, p. 1.
6. *Chuma v Man'chzhuriia,* plate 1.
7. Koval'skii, "Vladislav....o samom sebie," pp. 15–17.
8. Ibid., p. 15.
9. Courtesy of the Museum of Russian Culture in San Francisco.
10. Ibid.
11. Khisamutdinov, "Predprinimatel'," p. 150.

12. Ibid.
13. Wolff, p. 43.

CHAPTER 4

1. According to Horvath's Memoirs (Chapter XI, p. 2, footnote 188): The so-called Honghuzis operated often in considerable gangs and sometimes terrorized whole districts. They extended to all parts of China as a result of civil wars, famine, lack of work and income, and similar causes. The local authorities were powerless to cope with this evil, which could perhaps be stopped only by improving the economic conditions of the people or by general administrative order. The timber concessions of the railway and individual Russians were especially subject to such Honghuzi raids and being kidnapped, where they expected to receive considerable ransom.

    V. K. Arseniev writes in his book *Dersu the Trapper* (p. 181) about brigands (Honghuzis) and how "Dersu sorted out people into a kind of classification, there had to be rich and poor, idle and workers. Then when it came to honest and dishonest, the criminal class is sorted out, and form a kind of class by itself, which the Chinese call 'Honghuzis.'" Russian brigands according to Arseniev "work singly or in pairs and never form bands like the Chinese."

2. Loukashkin, Box 47, Folder 2.
3. Arseniev's *Dersu, the Trapper* is a true account that describes a similar impression as Vladislav's of the forests and surroundings in the Ussuri/Manchuria region (p. 57—second expedition). The Japanese film director, Kurosawa Akira, made the movie *Dersu Usala*, set in the forests of Eastern Siberia/Ussuri River Valley (Russia and China) at the turn of the century and built on Arseniev's appreciated book. Kurosawa's movie received first place for best foreign film at the Moscow Film Festival in 1975.
4. Interview with Vika Kowalska.
5. Koval'skii, "Vladislav....o samom sebie," p. 15–17.

CHAPTER 5

1. Emperor Kublai Khan was the grandson of Genghis Khan. He was the ruler of the Yuan Dynasty in China and Mongolia from 1260 until 1294.
2. Shepherdson-Scott, pp. 12–13.
3. Chang, Jung, p. 185.
4. Hoyt, p. 27.
5. Li Hongzhang (1823–1901) was a leading politician and diplomat in the Qing imperial court who lost popularity with the Chinese after their loss in the Sino-Japanese War. He was the leading Chinese official for the peace negotiations. He was best known for his pro-modern stance as a negotiator, and, in China, for his success against the Taiping Rebellion and his role in China's industrial and military modernization.
6. Wolff, pp. 1–13: "Introduction."
7. Nilus, p. 30A.
8. Bakich, "Origins...," p. 4.
9. Fang, p. 29.

10. Yashoff, Chapter IV, p. 35.
11. Fang, p. 27.
12. Clyde, p. 43.
13. Tsao, p. 2.
14. Clausen and Thørgersen, p. 24.
15. Bakich comment (email 11/20/2018): "the agreement on the construction of the CER involved several contentious issues, although Russian sources tended not to bring this up. The agreement was disputed later and there are arguments that the versions of the contract in French, Russian, and Chinese differed on a number of crucial points."
16. Turmov and Zhang, p. 317.
17. Koval'skii, "Vladislav....o samom sebie," pp. 15–17.

CHAPTER 6

1. Bakich comment (email 12/6/2018).
2. The statistics for the cost of the construction of the railway varies, but according to Tsao's analytical study (p. 11), the National Government of the Republic of China stated that the cost was US$223,332,502 across Manchuria. The cost for the South Manchurian Railway was US$40,507,732.
3. Bakich comment (email 12/6/2018).
4. Turmov and Zhang, p. 53.
5. CCTV [China Central] television documentary of the Chinese Eastern Railway from the 1980s.
6. Bakich comment (email 11/20/2018).
7. Postcard—private collection of Jerzy Czajewski.

CHAPTER 7

1. Tsao, p. 2.
2. Meyer Henri, from *Le Petit Journal*, January 16, 1898, from Bibliotheque Nationale de France.
3. Chang, Jung, p. 267.
4. Lensen, *The Russo-Chinese War*, pp. 142–143.
5. In the beginning, 750 railway guards were stationed along the rail line. At the end of 1899, this number rose to 4,500, and by July 1900 there were 11,000 guards along the railway line. According to Bakich, *Origins of the Russian Community on the CER*, page 9.
6. Wolff, pp. 67–71.
7. "Boxer Rebellion...," pp. 145–146.
8. Horvath, Chapter XI, p. 10; Tuchman, p. 40.
9. Tuchman, p. 40.
10. Tsao, p. 11.

Stolen Dreams

11. The Brynner family, related to Yul Brynner, had business interests along the border with Korea.
12. Brynner, p. 39.

CHAPTER 8

1. Map XIII: Harbin and Suburbs, between pp. 304–305; see "Chinese Eastern Railway" in the bibliography.
2. Bakich, "Russian City...," pp. 141–142.
3. Clausen and Thørgersen, p. 136.
4. Bakich, "Russian City...," pp. 141–142.
5. Zefiroff and Yagolkovsky, Chapter xxii, p. 397
6. Khisamutdinov, "Predprinimatel'," p. 150.
7. Interview with Jerzy Czajewski.
8. Surin, Chapter XIII, p. 243.
9. In 1985, Vika and Julie visited this property before it was demolished.

CHAPTER 9

1. Nilus, p. 44A.
2. Map III: Political Map of Manchuria, between pp. 32–33, **see** "Chinese Eastern Railway" in the Bibliography.
3. Koval'skii, "Vladislav...o samom sebie," pp. 15–17.
4. This picture was part of the family's collection, but I cannot find the original. Shown here is a postcard.
5. Zefiroff and Yagolkovsky, Chapter XVIII, p. 453.
6. Koval'skii, "Vladislav...o samom sebie," pp. 15–17.
7. Ibid.
8. Ibid.
9. Turmov and Zhang, p. 181.

CHAPTER 12

1. Tsao, p. 3.
2. Zefiroff and Yagolkovsky, Chapter XVIII, p. 436.
3. Bakich, "Origins," p. 9.
4. Tsao, p. 11.
5. Courtesy of the Museum of Russian Culture, San Francisco.
6. Zefiroff and Yagolkovsky, Chapter XVIII, p. 432.
7. Ibid., p. 431.
8. Ibid., p. 433.

9. Ibid., p. 433.
10. Tsao, p. 10.
11. Zefiroff and Yagolkovsky, p. 431.
12. Ibid., p. 432.
13. Ibid., p. 445.
14. Zefiroff and Yagolkovsky, pg. 445.

CHAPTER 13

1. Stille, p. 8.
2. Ibid., p. 10.
3. Horvath's Memoirs, Foreword, W. Klem, p. 3.
4. Bunting.
5. Clausen and Thøgersen, p. 32.
6. Ibid., p. 32.
7. Stille, pp. 14–15.
8. Young, Carl Walter, *Japan's jurisdiction*, p. 54.
9. It was on January 9, 1905, Father Georgy Gapon led a group to the Winter Palace in St. Petersburg to deliver the petition signed by 135,000 people. According to some accounts, as many as 150,000 peaceful marchers joined them, carrying pictures of the tsar, whom they still saw as their national father, and Russian flags. Several hundred protesters died when troops opened fire on them.
10. Rappaport, p. 52.
11. Ibid., pp. 52–53.
12. Ibid., pp. 51–53.

CHAPTER 15

1. Turmov and Zhang, p. 103.

CHAPTER 16

1. Bakich comment (email 6/13/2018).
2. Turmov and Zhang, p. 93.
3. Chiasson, p. 154.
4. Bakich, "Russian city," p. 140.
5. Wolff, pp. 90–91.
6. Ibid., p. 91.
7. Borysiewicz, "Wladyslav," p. 89.
8. Wolff, p. 106.
9. Engineer Stanislav Kierbedz, CEO of the CER Stock Company in St. Petersburg, constructed the bridge over the Sungari River, and engineer Ignacy Cytowicz designed the

Harbin Railroad Station. The Sungari Mills was built by Ludwik Czajkowski and the first European Brewery by Jan Wróblewski who designed the architectural plans for the city of Harbin. A further breakthrough concerns mining engineer Kazimierz Grochowski who pioneered the mines, which led to the discovery of oil, coal, and gold. Engineer Adam Szydlowski was the founder of the company European Harbin, and Adam Czajewski founded the first spirit distillery in Harbin. The Polish Lopato Karaites family built the first tobacco factory producing cigarettes, which remains today as a cultural heritage building.

10. Private collection of Jerzy Czajewski.
11. Chinese Eastern Railway, V. I. Surin, Chapter XIII, "The Flour Milling Industry," pp. 232–233.
12. Sladkovskii, p. 122.
13. *China, Diplomatic and Consular Reports for the Year 1911*, p. 9.
14. Postcard, April 1, 2012, https://commons.wikimedia.org/wiki/File:Churin_department_store_in_Harbin.jpg

CHAPTER 17

1. Vika Kowalska's recollection.
2. A bushy tailed, stocky type of squirrel.
3. Quested, p. 199.
4. Meiklejohn, http://www.disasterhistory.org/the-manchurian-plague-1910-11#more-584. The statistic in this article comes from footnote 15: "The Plague: Paotingfu," *North China Herald*, February 10, 1911, p. 297.
5. *Chuma v Man'chzhuriia,* plate 49.
6. Quested, p. 199. Dr. Wu Lien-teh led the professional medical team that finally quelled the plague. He was celebrated as a hero. The Manchurian outbreak was the worst such epidemic in recorded history.

CHAPTER 18

1. King, plate 16.
2. Massie, p. 282.

CHAPTER 19

1. British Consulate. Kowalski Timber Concession, p. 3 (228); Concession Contracts.
2. Symonolewicz, November 1929 (No. 2559/29), p. 13.
3. British Consulate. Kowalski Timber Concession, p. 3 (228); Concession Contracts.
4. Map XI: Forest Concessions on the Eastern Line, between pp. 176–177, see "Chinese Eastern Railway" in the bibliography.
5. British Consulate. Kowalski Timber Concession, p. 1 (226).
6. Kasatkin, Chapter X, p. 177.

7. Quested, p. 210.
8. Kasatkin, Chapter X, p. 181.
9. Interview with Dr. Genia Aksenoff, Tokyo, whose father was employed by Vladislav's company in Yablonia, where he and his family lived on the concession for many years and where Genia grew up and went to school.
10. Private collection of Jerzy Czajewski.

CHAPTER 21

1. Chang, Jung, pp. 269–270.
2. Ibid., p. 366.
3. Ibid., p. 370.
4. Ibid.
5. Clausen and Thøgersen, p. 38.
6. Bakich, "Russian City," pp. 142–143.
7. Quested, p. 214.
8. Tsao, p. 37.
9. Quested, p. 214.
10. Tsao, p. 38.
11. Quested, p. 214.
12. Bakich, "Russian City," p. 143.

CHAPTER 22

1. Chang, Jung, pp. xviii–xix.
2. Peattie, p. 52.
3. Moseley, p. 32.
4. Royde-Smith and Showalter.
5. Ibid. Statistics from US War Department, 1924.

CHAPTER 23

1. *100th (1917–2017) Anniversary of the Russian Revolution: October,* University of Hawaii, Hamilton Library, prepared by Patricia Polansky, Russian bibliographer.
2. Rasputin (1869–1916) was a self-proclaimed "religious healer" who was favored by the Russian imperial family. Tsar Nicholas and Tsarina Alexandra had enormous faith in his power to bring relief to their son, Tsarevich Aleksei, who was suffering from hemophilia.
3. Tarasova, p. 14.
4. Golowanjuk—various chapters.

CHAPTER 25

1. Hoyt, p. 42.
2. Xu, p. 26.
3. Ibid., p. 33.
4. Horvath's Memoirs, Chapter IX.
5. Hoyt, p. 52B.
6. Ibid., p. 52D.
7. Kasatkin, Chapter X, p. 173.
8. Grochowski, p. 188.
9. Ibid.
10. Kovalsky, "Timber Concessions," p. 1.
11. Ibid.
12. Photo from Museum of Russian Culture, San Francisco.

CHAPTER 26

1. Symonolewicz, November 1929 (No. 2559/29), p. 8 [English translation].
2. Ibid., p. 13.
3. Chiasson, p. 2.
4. Quested, p. 176.
5. Symonolewicz, November 1929 (No. 2559/29), p. 9 [English translation].
6. Bakich, "Émigré identity," p. 56.

CHAPTER 27

1. Tsao, pp. 35–36.
2. Ibid., p. 36.
3. Ibid.
4. Ibid.
5. Ibid.
6. Bakich, "Russian Education," p. 274.
7. Vika's seventh grade diploma.
8. Zefiroff and Yagolkovsky, Chapter XXII, p. 452.
9. Tsao, p. 36.
10. Meyer, p. 81. Further, Bakich comment (email 12/6/2018): Some sources dispute the figure of 200,000 and claim that there were 160,000 emigres from Russia.

CHAPTER 28

1. Kasatkin, Chapter X, p. 202.
2. Ibid., p. 185.
3. Aksenoff interview, Harbin, 2008.
4. Photo from Museum of Russian Culture, San Francisco.
5. Aksenoff interview.
6. Lesnye kontsessii, 1923.
7. Aksenoff.
8. Kasatkin, Chapter X, p. 193.
9. Ibid., p. 181
10. Mariusz Borysiewicz, *Polish Pioneer of Industrialization in the Far East*, p. 100.
11. Kasatkin, Chapter X, p. 181.
12. Grochowski, p. 186.

CHAPTER 29

1. Bakich comment (email 12/6/2018).
2. Doudka, p. 5.
3. Horvath's Memoirs, Chapter IX, p. 18.
4. Chiasson, p. 44.
5. Horvath's Memoirs, Chapter X, pp. 4–20.
6. Ibid., p. 21.
7. Ibid., p. 29.
8. Chiasson, p. 99.
9. Bakich comment (email 12/6/2018).
10. Delanty, pp. 62–63.
11. Ibid., p. 61.
12. Ibid., pp. 111–112.
13. Gutman, pp. xxiv–xxv.
14. Ibid., p. ix.
15. Ibid., p. 186.
16. Bakich comment (email 12/6/2018).

CHAPTER 30

1. Bakich comment (12/6/2018 email).
2. Bakich, "Émigré identity," p. 56.

Stolen Dreams

3. Pictures were given to Jerzy Czajewski by Joel Grossman who is a relative of the last owner of the refinery—Leo Zikman. They are in Czajewski's private collection.
4. Ibid.
5. Ibid.
6. Ibid.
7. Ibid.
8. Symonolewicz, November 1929 (No. 2559/29), p. 17 [English translation].
9. Ibid., pp. 17–18.
10. Ibid.
11. Ibid., pp. 18–19.
12. "Pol-milliona na sudie," recounts Kovalsky's court case against the Russo-Asian Bank. His lawyers were Vasilii Fedorovich Ivanov (1885–1944) and Mikhail Emmanuilovich Gil'cher (1874–?).
13. Symonolewicz, November 1929 (No. 2559/29), p. 19 [English translation].
14. Bakich comment (email 12/6/2018).

CHAPTER 31

1. Interview with Vika about the architect Aleksandr Aleksandrovich Bernardatstsi [Bernadazzi] (1871–1931), the son of a famous architect with the same name.
2. Picture provided by Jerzy Czajewski.

CHAPTER 32

1. Map XI: Forest Concessions on the Eastern Line, between pp. 176–177, see "Chinese Eastern Railway" in the bibliography.
2. Symonolewicz, November 1929 (No. 2559/29), p. 13 [English translation].
3. Khisamutdinov, "Predprinimatel'," p. 151.
4. Kovalsky ad: from *Spravochnik po Severnoi Man'chzhurii i Kvzhd* (1927).
5. "Wystawa-Polacy...", provide by Jerzy Czajewski.
6. Loukashkin Papers, Box 46, Folder 1.
7. Ibid.
8. Ibid.

CHAPTER 33

1. Vika Kowalska's recollections.
2. Ibid.

CHAPTER 34

1. Moustafine, "The Harbin Connection," p. 145.
2. Gamsa, p. 2.
3. *Youtai ren*, p. 94.
4. Postcard from Museum of Russian Culture, San Francisco. provided by Amir Khisamutdinov.
5. Quested, p. 263.
6. Ibid., p. 261.
7. Jennings, pp. 79–80.
8. Ibid., p. 53.
9. Clausen and Thøgersen, p. 104.
10. Khisamutdinov, "Predprinimatel'," p. 152.
11. Ibid.
12. Photo provided from the personal collection of Jerzy Czajewski.
13. Photo provided from the personal collection of Jerzy Czajewski. Numerous Polish organizations were formed such as the well-known H. Sienkiewicz Secondary School in 1915, sports clubs, and social organizations. There was a short-lived Alliance of Military Poles in Manchuria and the Polish National Committee for Siberia and Russia, 1918–1920. These organizations, in addition to their administrative duties, took care of the clerical and administrative matters regarding Polish citizens who were refugees from Russia. Vladislav sponsored the *Gospoda Polska* (Polish Inn) located on Glukhaya Ulitsa (Street), which is where the Polish Consulate later was located for many years. See *Ves' Kharbin na 1926*, pp. 108–110.
14. *Ves' Kharbina na 1923*, p. 112.
15. Borysiewicz, "Wladyslaw Kowalski," p. 89.
16. Borysiewicz, "Wladyslaw Kowalski," p. 92. The St. Jozaphatus Church was constructed with his contribution of timber. It cost 11,000 Mexican dollars (at the time, 1 Mexican dollar equated to ½ a US dollar) to build the church, and Vladislav contributed 4,000 worth of lumber and supplies. The Catholic bishop formed a local Polish society with Vladislav as honorary president.

Stolen Dreams

He was an active contributor to the Polish community, Polish schools, and Polish organizations.

17. Private collection of Jerzy Czajewski. The St. Jozaphatus Church was constructed with his contribution of timber. It cost 11,000 Mexican dollars (at the time, 1 Mexican dollar equated to ½ a US dollar) to build the church, and Vladislav contributed 4,000 worth of lumber and supplies. The Catholic bishop formed a local Polish society with Vladislav as honorary president. He was an active contributor to the Polish community, Polish schools, and Polish organizations.

18. Confucian Temple Building, Harbin. Pictures: www.ConfucianTemple. Displayed is a placard with the name of Vladislav as well as other major donors. Confucian Temple Building, Harbin, visited by Kang Yu, Vika, and Julie. Interview with Mrs. Kang Yu during Vika's visit to Harbin and to the temple in 1985.

19. Private collection of Jerzy Czajewski.

20. Ibid. Also, interview with Jerzy Czajewski.

21. Photo provided from the personal collection of Jerzy Czajewski.

CHAPTER 35

1. Bakich comment (email 12/6/2018).
2. British Consulate. Kowalski Timber Concession, p. 2 (227).
3. Ibid., pp. 2–3 (227–228).
4. Ibid., p. 2 (228).
5. Ibid., p. 4 (229).
6. Ibid., p. 2–3 (227–228).
7. Ibid., p. 4 (229).
8. Ibid., pp. 5–6 (229–230).
9. Ibid., pp. 4–5 (228–230).
10. Ibid., p. 5 (230).
11. General Chu Tsin-tan is the name as spelled in the resourced documents.
12. Ibid., p. 6 (231).
13. Ibid.
14. McCormack, pp. 9–10.
15. Young, Louise, pp. 36–37.
16. British Consulate. Kowalski Timber Concession, p. 2 (227), pp. 5–6 (230–231).
17. Sherlaimoff interview.

CHAPTER 36

1. Vika Kowalska's recollections.
2. Ibid.
3. Ibid.
4. Ibid.

CHAPTER 37

1. Quested, p. 263.

CHAPTER 38

1. Toland, p. 5.
2. Hongo, p. 2.
3. Hunter and Ogasawara, p. 10.
4. Kasatkin, Chapter X, p. 206.
5. Hoyt, pp. 71–72.
6. Symonolewicz, November 1929 (No. 2559/29), pp. 15–16 [English translation].
7. Ibid., p. 16.
8. Ibid.
9. Ibid.
10. McCormack, cover.
11. Zhang Zoulin train wreck, https://www.google.com/search?q=zhang+zuolin+wrecked+train&tbm=isch&source=iu&ictx=1&fir= M
12. Symonolewicz, November 1929 (No. 2559/29), pp. 16–17 [English translation].
13. Ibid.

CHAPTER 39

1. Hotel Negresco: https://en.wikipedia.org/wiki/Hotel_Negresco Visit was described by Vika to her daughter Julie.
2. Nikolai Andreevich Orlov born in Russia, was a famous concert pianist for years in Moscow. He settled in Paris in 1922 and traveled the world performing.

Stolen Dreams

3. Rahman, Tania, "Fascinating History of Old Palace," [1 p.], http://croydonheritagefestival.co.uk/the-fascinating-history-of-old-palace/
4. Poznan Fair, http://www.poznanfair.pl, p. 1, Poznan Fair 1928, Fakty Liczby.

CHAPTER 40

1. Poznan travel—international travel for everyone, 1928, the goal was to promote the achievements that Poland and Poznan had made in the past ten years of liberty and freedom.
2. From the private collection of Jerzy Czajewski.
3. Interview with Jerzy Czajewski.
4. Translation: The award of the Order of Polonia Restituta by Jerzy Czajewski. Also, see https://en.wikipedia.org/wiki/Order_of_Polonia_Restituta
5. From the private collection of Jerzy Czajewski.
6. Koval'skii, "Vladislav....o samom sebie," pp. 15–17.
7. Bakich comment (email 12/6/2018).
8. Ibid.
9. Symonolewicz, November 1929 (No. 2559/29), p. 7 [English translation].

CHAPTER 41

1. Article provided by Jerzy Czajewski. Translation by Olga Bakich.
2. Ibid.
3. Taube, pp. 7–39.
4. Although this is referred to as an *incident*, it was the start of a well-planned and executed invasion of Manchuria. To avoid being accused of peace violations of international law and war-renouncing treaties, it had become a Japanese military strategy to refer to their military operations as *incidents* and not as a *war*.
5. Ibid., pp. 12–14.
6. Ibid.
7. Lytton Report, League of Nations, Appeal by the Chinese Government, Report of the Commission of Enquiry, Official Nr. C663, M 320, 1932 VII, Geneva October 1, 1932, p. 9.
8. Peattie, p. 66.
9. Tuchman, p. 168.

10. Ibid., p. 171.
11. Ibid., p. 173.

CHAPTER 42

1. Tuchman, p. 166.
2. Ibid., p. 174.
3. Lytton Report, League of Nations, Appeal by the Chinese Government, Report of the Commission of Enquiry, Official Nr. C663, M 320, 1932 VII, Geneva, October 1, 1932, p. 9.
4. Tuchman, p. 174.
5. Vespa, p. 27.
6. Ibid., p. 32.
7. Harmsen, "Introduction."
8. Vespa, p. 29.
9. Ibid., p. 36.
10. Hsieh, p. 7.
11. Ibid., p. 8.
12. Vespa, pp. 57–59.
13. Bing.com/images: Lord Lytton—Manchuria.
14. Xu, p. 156.
15. Tuchman, pp. 172–174.
16. Vika Kowalska's recollections.
17. The old grandfather clock still stands in the house today.

CHAPTER 43

1. Stille, pp. 4–6.
2. Young, Louise, p. 33.
3. Hoyt, p. 138.
4. In 1935, ¥1 = US$0.28 to US$0.29 (Hutchins, p. 13). In 1935, US$1 = ¥3.48 (currency converter).
5. Hutchins, p. 13.
6. Ibid.

7. Ibid., p. 10.
8. Ibid., pp. 10–11.
9. Patrikeeff, p. 115 and Yang, p. 98.
10. Hutchins, p. 17.
11. Vespa, pp. 32–33.
12. Ibid., p. 33.
13. Personal family documents.
14. Jerzy Czajewski interview.
15. Vika Kowalska's recollection.
16. Ibid.
17. Liu.
18. Ibid.
19. Ibid.
20. Vika Kowalska's recollection
21. Neja, p. 1.
22. Newspaper article summaries from Olga Bakich: "Za dolgi zaderzhan V. F. Koval'ski," *Russkoe slovo*, 1934, 13 ianv.; "Zaderzhanie V. F. Koval'skogo," *Zaria*, 1934, 13 ianv.
23. Newspaper article summary from Olga Bakich: "Koval'skii v tiur'me", *Zaria* 1934, 2 fev.
24. Testimonial by Ada Kowalska.
25. Vespa, pp. 148–149.
26. Ibid.
27. Testimonial by Ada Kowalska.
28. Ibid.
29. Liu, article 11/8/2009.
30. Bakich comment (email 12/6/2018).

CHAPTER 45

1. Hoyt, p. 111.
2. Ibid.
3. Ibid., p. 114.

4. Ibid.
5. Ibid., p. 115.
6. Ibid., p. 112.
7. Ibid., p. 117.
8. Ibid.
9. This organization is known as *Biuro podelam rossiiskikh emigrantov v Man'chzhurii* according to Olga Bakich.
10. Bakich comment (email 12/6/2018).
11. Ibid.
12. Ibid.
13. Felton, pp. 17 and 20.
14. Ibid.
15. Ibid., between pages 88–89.
16. Gold, pp. 23–24.
17. Ibid., pp. 25–26.
18. Ibid., pp. 49 and 54.
19. Felton, p. 30.
20. Ibid., pp. 4–7.
21. Gold, pp. 47–48.
22. Felton, p. 3.
23. Ibid., p. 36.
24. Gold, p. 44.
25. Felton, pp. 1–8.
26. Chang, Iris, pp. 216–217.
27. Felton, p. 39.

CHAPTER 46

1. Email from Olga Bakich, February 25, 2019, as cited in *Nash put'*, June 27, 1937.
2. Xu, pp. 149–157.
3. Ibid.

Stolen Dreams

4. Prime Minister Konoe Fumimaro was Emperor Hirohito's cousin and had the emperor's full support. He committed suicide the evening before he was to appear in front of the Tokyo War Criminal Court in December 1945. Per L. Mosley's book, "He killed himself rather than face trial as a war criminal."
5. Xu, pp. 149–157.
6. Vargo, p. 180.
7. The Marco Polo Bridge Incident of 1937: http://www.chinastudyabroad.org/indepthchina/1040-the-marco-polo-bridge-incident-of-1937, p. 1.
8. Ibid., pp. 1–2.
9. Tuchman, p. 225.
10. Chang, Iris, p. 6.
11. Ibid.
12. Ibid.
13. Tuchman, p. 225.
14. Jowett, p. 27.
15. Vespa, p. 210.
16. Bakich comment (12/6/2018 email).
17. Breuillard, pp. 1–6, 23–24.
18. Vespa, p. 230.

CHAPTER 47

1. Hoyt, p. 59.
2. Vespa, p. 128.
3. Bickers, p. 104.
4. Vespa, p. 152.
5. Beck, see "Japan's Growing Military, 1894–1903" in the Bibliography.
6. Ibid., "The Building Years."
7. Neja, p. 2.
8. Concession Contracts.
9. League of Nations/Lytton Report, p. 105. A statement was written in the Lytton Report, that "The Manchukuo Government has stated that it will respect private property and all concessions awarded by either the Central Government of China or by the former government of Manchuria, provided the concessions

were legally granted in accordance with the laws and regulations previously enforced. It has also promised to pay the lawful debts and obligations of the former administration and has appointed a Commission to pass upon claims of indebtedness." This declaration was, however, ignored.

10. Testimonial by Ada Kowalska.
11. Ibid.
12. Ibid.
13. Document provided by Elena and Ada Kowalska.
14. Ibid.
15. Interview with Dr. Genia Aksenoff.
16. Ibid.

CHAPTER 48

1. Vespa, pp. 231–232.
2. http://www.newworldencyclopedia.org/entry/Manchukuo
3. Portrait of Jerzy Bogumił Litewski (1891–1980; Polish consul in Harbin, 1938–1945). This portrait is from Książnica Pomorska w Szczecinie (Pomeranian Library in Szczecin).
4. Occupation of Poland (1939–1945), https://en.wikipedia.org/wiki/Occupation_of_Poland_(1939%E2%80%931945)
5. Six million Poles, about 21 percent of its population, were killed between 1939 and 1945, half of the victims being Jewish—Soviet Repressions of Polish Citizens (1939–1946), https://en.wikipedia.org/wiki/Soviet_repressions_of_Polish_citizens_(1939%E2%80%931946)

CHAPTER 49

1. Jerzy Czajewski, *Roman Catholic Cemetery in Harbin*, p. 13.
2. Fuchigami, p. 39.
3. From Mikhail Scamony-Shapshinsky collection copyright Ksiaznica Pomorska w Szczecinie. Provided by Jerzy Czajewski.
4. Neja, "Polski król Mandżurii."

EPILOGUE

1. Account about Kondo was provided by Olga Bakich.